ASPECTS OF AMERICAN HISTORY

Aspects of American History presents a fresh and succinct analysis of a selection of major events, individuals and ideas in the history of the United States. The essays are linked by a broad framework of central themes – race, citizenship and American identity – giving the reader access to a new interpretation of US history. In each essay Simon Henderson:

- introduces fresh angles to traditional topics
- consolidates and analyses recent research and debate
- provides succinct analysis to complex issues.

Arranged chronologically – from the birth of the nation to the 'war on terror' – each chapter in *Aspects* works as a stand-alone, topic-focused stimulus for further debate, while the central themes that run through the book enable readers to make comparisons and trace major developments across American history. This is an invaluable resource for anyone looking for an engaging general survey of US history.

Simon Henderson is a secondary school history teacher and part-time PhD student whose major research interests are American race relations.

ASPECTS OF
AMERICAN HISTORY

Simon Henderson

Routledge
Taylor & Francis Group

LONDON AND NEW YORK

First published 2009
by Routledge
2 Park Square, Milton Park, Abingdon, Oxon OX14 4RN

Simultaneously published in the USA and Canada
by Routledge
270 Madison Ave, New York, NY 10016

Routledge is an imprint of the Taylor & Francis Group, an informa business

© 2009 Simon Henderson

Typeset in Garamond by Taylor & Francis Books
Printed and bound in Great Britain by
CPI Antony Rowe, Chippenham, Wiltshire

British Library Cataloguing in Publication Data
A catalogue record for this book is available from the British Library.

Library of Congress Cataloging in Publication Data
Henderson, Simon, 1979–
Aspects of American history / Simon Henderson.
p. cm.
Includes bibliographical references.
1. United States–History. I. Title.
E178.6.H46 2009
973–dc22
2008037952

ISBN10: 0-415-42341-4 (hbk)
ISBN10: 0-415-42342-2 (pbk)
ISBN10: 0-203-88129-X (ebk)

ISBN13: 978-0-415-42341-0 (hbk)
ISBN13: 978-0-415-42342-7 (pbk)
ISBN13: 978-0-203-88129-3 (ebk)

FOR MY PARENTS –
THE BEST TEACHERS

CONTENTS

CONTENTS

ACKNOWLEDGEMENTS

During the writing of this book I have been very fortunate to benefit from the expertise of several outstanding scholars in various aspects of the American past. Without ever having met me personally, the following have kindly read and commented on drafts of the essays in this volume: Edward Ayers, Philip Morgan, Michael Holt, Eric Foner, Heather Cox Richardson, William Freehling, Frederick Hoxie, Richard Carwardine, James Cone, Margaret Walsh, Lloyd Ambrosius, Michal Rozbicki and Michael Hunt. I thank them sincerely for their time and suggestions.

Susan-Mary Grant has provided me with help, support and expert teaching over many years. Her encouragement and advice during this project are much appreciated. Thanks also to Keith Brewster for his support and understanding as the manuscript increasingly took time away from my ongoing PhD thesis. I am also grateful to Emma Langley, Eve Setch and Alison Yates at Routledge for their help in the development of this book.

Thanks to all my friends, colleagues and students at Teesdale School, especially Cassie, Clare and Ken. Kate, Debbie and Paul have been a great source of encouragement and support. I could not ask for more loving sisters than Rachel and Emma, who have read various essays included in this volume. Finally, this book is dedicated to my parents whose love and support is constant and priceless.

INTRODUCTION

At the conclusion of a trip to Washington DC in the summer of 2007 I was driven to the airport by an Ethiopian taxi driver. He was a US resident who hoped to apply for citizenship in the future. When I asked him why he had moved to America, leaving family behind in his homeland, he spoke of the promise of a better life. The United States, he asserted, gave him the chance to earn money and live his life in safety and freedom. He was not naive or overly idealistic, he talked about the difficulties of his daily existence, problems of healthcare and racial prejudice, but maintained that America was a better place.

The concept of America as a better place is central to the foundation myth of the nation. From the beginning it has consciously struggled to realise exceptionalism. This American promise and the effort to extend it to all peoples in the United States are at the core of my fascination with the history of the nation and provide a central focus for this volume.

Readers who wish to explore a narrative of American history will not be satisfied by the pages that follow. *Aspects of American History* – as the title suggests – focuses on specific features of American history. The central themes tying these different aspects together are race, citizenship and American national identity. Although it is true that the development of an 'Americanness' has been constructed through a cultural exchange between various ethnic groups, it is also clear that American national identity has, at various times in the nation's past, not embraced racial diversity. The Declaration of Independence to a large extent commits America to a 'civic nationalism', a shared set of principles and beliefs promoting democracy and freedom bound together by the ideal that all men share equality and liberty. A 'racial nationalism' which saw American identity in terms of ethnic difference has, however, at various times, competed with this civic nationalism. The Constitution, for example, enshrined one facet of racial nationalism by

1

endorsing and protecting slavery.[1] The extent to which citizenship, and consequently full inclusion in the American nation, has been denied to varying racial groups is a major focus of many of the chapters that follow. The struggle over the parameters of that citizenship impacted significantly on the development of an American identity.

American nationalism was also constructed by internal political conflicts about how best to pursue the self-governing experiment. This nationalism did not emerge complete once the shackles of British imperialism had been thrown off. Instead it developed slowly as the nation grew. Influenced by an extremely self-conscious American exceptionalism, the United States was shaped by competing interpretations of the legacy of the American Revolution and how to protect it. These interpretations included rival opinions on the place of ethnic minorities in America and where the boundaries of citizenship should be drawn. In the early twenty-first century the US still contends with the consequences of this important aspect of its past. It is in this context that the themes of race, citizenship and national identity provide the threads which weave the essays in this book together.

This book does not provide an exhaustive survey of all areas of the American past that can be connected to these themes; there are obvious omissions. Furthermore, I am aware that the important place played by class and gender in the emergence of a national identity are not covered in the pages that follow. The reader is reminded, however, that this volume focuses only on certain *aspects* of the American past. The principal intention is to introduce students and the general reader to the main interpretations of these different aspects in relation to the central themes of the book. Whilst the work is set out chronologically and can certainly be read in this fashion, each essay also stands alone. Students are encouraged to use these essays as assistance when preparing to write a paper or participate in a seminar discussion. The references and bibliography provide ample pointers towards more in-depth discussion of the issues being explored.

Chapters 1 and 2 focus on the shaping of the United States from the colonial period through to the American Revolution. Discussion centres on the extent to which the concept of an *American* people was forged out of the cultural and ethnic diversity of colonial America. The question of why the colonies decided to break from British control is also considered. The values and hopes of those who supported independence help us to understand how the United States conceived of itself in its formative years. Chapter 3 analyses the process which led to the ratification of the Constitution and contends that it was this document that played a crucial role in the development of American nationalism. Furthermore, the Constitution and its interpretation in relation to race and citizenship are recurring themes throughout this volume.

One of the glaring contradictions in the American founding is the presence of slavery. The revolt against the British was framed as a struggle for liberty against tyranny; the Americans were not prepared to be shackled by their imperial slave-masters. As men who were created equal they believed in their right to life, liberty and the pursuit of happiness. Yet many of the leaders who spoke so eloquently in favour of independence were themselves slave-holders. Chapter 4 explores the relationship between slavery and two of the nation's founding giants, George Washington and Thomas Jefferson. Discussion focuses on their attitude to the tensions between human bondage and the American ideal and how historians have represented their records in this area.

Chapter 5 provides an examination of the role of political parties in the early republic. The essay explores how these parties provided a rallying point for different interest groups and how political participation and campaign ceremony helped forge a national political identity. The main focus of this chapter, as the title indicates, is the extent to which party-spirit was dangerous for the American nation. The extent to which political groups could contain the issue of slavery provides a link to Chapter 6, which investigates the causes of the American Civil War. This chapter seeks to explain the extent to which slavery was the primary cause of America's seminal military experience. Links can be made between this essay and Chapter 7, which looks at Southern and Confederate nationalism. As well as exploring a further element of Civil War causation, this chapter seeks to discover the extent to which American nationalism was fractured in the antebellum period. With slavery as a major influence, many southern leaders argued that their region represented a separate nation before, during and after the Civil War.

Chapters 8 through 10 focus on the impact of the Civil War on concepts of liberty, racial equality and national identity. Through an examination of Lincoln's ideas and policies during the Civil War, Chapter 8 seeks to explore the extent to which he effected a change in the meaning of the nation. The 'new birth of freedom' he spoke of during the Gettysburg address and his moral reading of the Constitution indicated a changing interpretation of that document. Chapter 9 focuses on the extent to which such a change impacted on the lives of African-Americans in the postbellum period. Reconstruction saw significant advances for black southerners and an expanding concept of citizenship. The Fourteenth and Fifteenth Amendments were eventually eroded as Reconstruction stalled; however, a more liberal interpretation of their meaning in the 1950s and 1960s breathed life into the civil rights movement. Chapter 10 looks at the way the memory of the Civil War has been contested in American memory and the impact this has had on national identity.

Chapter 11 focuses on the emergence of legally codified racial segregation in the American South. It shows the way in which the promises of Reconstruction were turned back and how the nation retreated from a racially inclusive memory of the Civil War. The essay has obvious connections with Chapters 9 and 10 but it also lays the historical context for discussions of black protest and the civil rights movement which appear later in the volume. As Jim Crow segregation descended over the South, in the West the last Native Americans were being moved onto reservations. Chapter 12 highlights the mixture of paternalism and prejudice in policies towards the Indians either side of the turn of the twentieth century. Both chapters explore the limits of citizenship in relation to racial identity. Chapter 13 moves from the discussion of Native American experience in the previous essay to focus on the way the West has been represented in popular imagination and historical interpretation. The chapter provides a historiographical survey of the place of the West in American national identity.

A crucial element of this identity has been forged in the immigrant heritage of the nation. America's foundation myth is built on the belief that the country is chosen; it is exceptional and offers a haven from the corruptions of the Old World. The inscription on the Statue of Liberty welcomes the 'huddled masses, yearning to breathe free'. Chapter 14 explores American attitudes towards immigration and assimilation and what this tells us about the parameters of citizenship. The chapter closes with a brief discussion of contemporary immigration patterns and the challenge for the American future.

Chapter 15 focuses on the struggle by women to gain the vote from the period of Reconstruction through to the early twentieth century. Their citizenship was not as comprehensive as that of their male counterparts. It is incorrect, however, to frame the struggle for the vote in traditional feminist terms. Racial identity played a crucial role in women's political struggles in this period and the chapter examines the interplay between both race and gender in the campaign for the vote and the ways in which the boundaries of citizenship were drawn.

Chapters 16, 17 and 18 focus on the struggle by African-Americans to achieve equality of opportunity in the United States. The experience of black people runs throughout this volume. Chapter 16 explores the ways in which the foundations were laid for the civil rights movements of the 1960s and argues that such a movement should not be conceived of in limited chronological terms. Chapter 17 looks at the policies of John F. Kennedy and Lyndon B. Johnson and their contribution to the passage of the landmark civil rights legislation of the 1960s. The most influential black leaders of this 'Second Reconstruction' and beyond were Martin Luther King and Malcolm X. Chapter 18 explores their legacies and relevance within the context of the contemporary problems of black America.

Chapters 19 and 20 briefly discuss the role of American foreign policy in the formation of national identity. The American foundation myth makes a clear distinction between the United States and the rest of the world and an examination of America's role in global conflicts reveals much about the nation's sense of itself. Chapter 19 discusses how America approached involvement in the First and Second World Wars and the conflict in Vietnam and what this reveals about America's sense of mission. Chapter 20 explores similar themes in relation to the events of 9/11 and the subsequent 'war on terror' which led the nation into the war in Iraq. This chapter also looks at the way in which those conflicts have promoted an increasingly prescriptive patriotism and citizenship.

1

NATION IN EMBRYO

The development of colonial America

The North American colonies were home to men and women from a myriad of different cultures and backgrounds that faced considerable environmental challenges to their continued existence. Looking back from the twenty-first century, amidst the rampant advance of globalisation, it is difficult to comprehend the unique situation of cultural exchange that was experienced by the colonists. Stirring a cocktail of different races, language, custom and religions, 'the New World produced a kaleidoscope of human encounters'.[1] The rich human tapestry of the colonists' ambitions and motivations provided for significant diversity in the British colonies which would eventually become the United States of America. This chapter provides a survey of these colonies, their racially varied inhabitants, and the patterns of development they followed – patterns which had profound consequences for the future of America. Despite the obvious differences between the societies of the eastern seaboard, there was a tentative sense of collective separateness from Britain which eventually led to independence from the mother country. Pointers towards how this impulse emerged from the great diversity of the colonial experience will also be considered.

It is important to recognise that study of the colonies has wrestled with the issue of regionalism. How to divide up the thirteen colonies into distinct geographical areas has provoked debate. As Michael Zuckerman has argued, 'if men of the eighteenth century could not concur on the regional alignments that characterised the country, historians and geographers who have the help of hindsight have done no better'.[2] Scholarly quarrels over how many regions to subdivide the colonies into have abounded with some choosing four, some preferring five and some settling for a simple division of North and South. By focussing on the regional centres of New England, the mid-Atlantic, Chesapeake Bay and the lower South my intention is to show important differences in the shape of colonial society which had an impact on the development of an embryonic nation.

Perhaps no colonial region has been studied more closely than New England. Historians for some time focussed their attention on the Puritan town believing it to be the prototypical American community; however, it would appear that in many ways it was in fact atypical of the American experience.[3] The Puritan leaders who established the Massachusetts Bay Colony believed their society was to be a 'city upon a hill', looked to as an example by the rest of the world. As Daniel Boorstin explains, 'the Puritan beacon for misguided mankind was to be neither a book nor a theory. It was to be the community itself'.[4] The society built in New England was closer to the pattern of rural England than any other of the colonies. The homogeneity of the region led Crevecoeur to describe New Englanders as 'the unmixed descendants of Englishmen'.[5]

Unfavourable physical environment and the cultural heritage of Puritanism meant that the New England colonies did not develop a market economy in the way that other areas of British North America did. Social development remained closer to the founding patterns in New England than in any other of the colonies.[6] The relatively homogeneous society of New England led to the development of the most egalitarian community in the colonies. There was not an extreme distinction between different social classes or between the propertied and the landless. Compact settlement and the propensity of small landholding enterprises meant that, even in the eastern Massachusetts counties, the number of landless men did not usually exceed 20 per cent. There was not, of course, absolute equality – an absence of social or economic distinctions – but there was a common minimum standard of living and there was less inequality than in rural Scotland or Ireland, for example. In eighteenth-century New England the vast majority of work was performed by native-born whites and there was little receptiveness to slave or indentured labour.[7]

It is important, however, not to overemphasise the homogeneous and static nature of New England society. Firstly, New England is a regional term that covers separate colonies which did have distinct differences. Secondly, there were subtle changes occurring in the eighteenth century which affected the colonies of the north-east. Crevecoeur may have suggested that the population was made up of Englishmen and their descendants, but, by 1760, three in ten New Englanders originated outside of England. New England was more homogeneous than the rest of North America but there were 5,000 Africans and 4,000 Scots, Scots-Irish and Irish who constituted a significant minority.[8] Rapid population increase from the early eighteenth century to the eve of the Revolution put pressure on land supplies and led to a rise in land speculation. The impulse towards greater geographical mobility was felt in New England as in other areas of America. As Richard Hofstadter argued, 'the urge to exploit the land was changing the old order, the Yankee entrepreneur was replacing the Puritan villager'.[9] We must be careful, however, not to overemphasise the significance of this change. More recent scholarship has challenged the traditional declension approach of those like Hofstadter and shown continuity in the internal economic development of the Massachusetts Bay region. Market forces were at work from the early seventeenth century and did not emerge suddenly to smash Puritan idealism in the eighteenth century.[10]

In the cities of New England, most notably Boston, there was a growing poverty problem and the development of a depressed labouring poor in the years after 1700.[11] In fact studies of the region have uncovered evidence to show that eighteenth-century New England had a greater distribution of poverty than areas of the South.[12] It is clear that the idealised image of an egalitarian society fails to recognise the complex realities of significant socio-economic stratification in New England. Nevertheless, it remained different in relative terms to the other colonies. Its sense of mission, essentially slave-free society and strong commitment to common laws and rights, was profoundly important for the development of America.

In the mid-Atlantic colonies there was much greater diversity than in New England. Indentured servitude, slave and wage labour were all used in colonies that had a more developed ethos of self-interest than anywhere else in colonial America.[13] Landholding in the middle colonies was much more diverse than in New England. In New York landlords favoured renting over selling and tried to hold up land prices. In this environment hired labourers, indentured servants and slaves formed a substantial and relatively poor population. South of New York, in the agrarian heartland of Pennsylvania, Delaware and New Jersey, land was not so expensive and property was more equitably distributed. In 1742 the governor of New Jersey described the people of his province as 'the most easy and happy people of any colony in North America'.[14] In urban areas of the middle colonies such as Philadelphia, however, there was a growing restlessness among working people from the 1740s onwards. The lower classes of the city began to voice frustration, just as they did in Boston. The political mobilisation of the working classes was crucial in the changing political culture of the colonies in the eighteenth century.[15]

Between 1710 and 1770 approximately 85,000 Germans arrived in the North American colonies with almost three-quarters settling in

Pennsylvania. Like the English who arrived in New England, the majority of Germans came in family groups and sometimes in large neighbourhood or community groups. Many of them made use of the redemption system through which they borrowed money from shippers to gain passage to the New World and then entered into a labour contract with employers who redeemed their loans from the shippers. The Germans brought with them a wide variety of religious groupings and formed a strong community identity. Unlike the Scots or French Huguenots of the middle colonies they did suffer from discrimination and experienced a xenophobia directed towards them from Anglo-Americans.[16]

In Pennsylvania, as in New England, religion was an important factor in the development of social and political institutions. The Quakers of Pennsylvania shared a sense of mission and search for utopia with their Puritan counterparts.[17] By 1756 Quaker involvement in the government of Pennsylvania had come to an end as their representatives in the colonial Assembly withdrew. Whereas the Puritans of New England had tempered their utopian vision in the face of the practical realities of the situation in America, the Quakers clung to their principles with an impressive rigidity. Their failure to make accommodations to the changing colonial situation, however, rendered their continued rule in Pennsylvania untenable. Strict adherence to their principles caused them to become more inward looking and left the Quakers unequipped to take any part in the social forces stirring revolution in the years preceding 1776.[18]

The colonies of the Chesapeake Bay region, Virginia and Maryland, were not influenced by the sort of religious utopianism which impacted on Pennsylvania and New England. Indeed, the Chesapeake and the colonies of the Carolinas and Georgia developed in such contrast to New England and the mid-Atlantic that, as one historian has argued, 'they may be designated hinterlands of exploitation rather than settlement'.[19] Those who had to suffer this exploitation were increasingly black. Even in the late seventeenth century there were few Africans in the North American colonies and there were only a small number of slaves in the Chesapeake region. Indeed, slavery as an economic system took many decades to emerge in the Chesapeake. By 1760, however, there were 284,000 blacks in the southern colonies and 60 per cent of them lived in Virginia and Maryland.[20] Why this increase and why the emergence of large-scale slavery? Part of the reason lies in the social and economic makeup of the southern colonies. Here, unlike the mid-Atlantic and New England, the majority of the population were males who came to the New World without a family. Many of these young men were indentured servants who laboured on the land. At the turn of the eighteenth century, when demands for labour were increasing, there was a slowdown in supply from Britain and Europe as men were less willing to make the journey across the Atlantic. Black labourers, and specifically slave labourers, offered an opportunity to fill the labour shortfall. Slavery offered lifetime service whereas indentured labour had a finite life span. Furthermore, perceptions of African culture made Europeans less likely to ask moral and legal questions about human bondage.[21]

In his seminal study of Virginia, Edmund Morgan argued that the story of American freedom and American slavery were intimately connected. Virginia was dominated by rich and powerful landed gentry who dominated the politics of the colony. They reaped the financial rewards of the labours of thousands of indentured servants. When these men had served their contracts, however, they were free to make their own way. Without the capital to buy land they increasingly formed a restless poor who posed a threat to Virginia's elite – a threat which became real in Bacon's Rebellion of 1676. Black slavery allowed Virginia's planters to purchase labourers for life who would not be set free to roam the countryside. Slavery also allowed the white poor to join with their betters in a racial compact wherein whiteness guaranteed freedom.[22] Morgan argued that the self-confidence the Virginia planters gained from the static society they presided over made them less fearful of the mob than those in other colonial regions and so more forceful in leading the push for independence. His arguments remain attractive although critics are right to probe why a similar situation did not emerge in other slaveholding colonies.[23] It should also be noted that planters who wished to increase the profits to be made from tobacco had shown a desire for slave labour long before the turn of the eighteenth century. The problem was that the supplies from Africa were not readily available.

Of these other colonies it was South Carolina, heavily influenced by the Caribbean experience of slavery, which had the largest concentration of slaves. In Virginia and Maryland slaves were able to lay the foundations for a secure African-American society and were involved in a more paternalistic day-to-day contact with masters. In the Carolinas and Georgia they worked on large plantations in brutal and isolated conditions.[24] 'South Carolina, as it fattened on its slaves and staples, developed the most lordly and most leisured ruling class in America.'[25] We see in South Carolina a key shift from a slave-owning society to a slave society with a closed system of race relations.[26]

North Carolina, however, followed a different pattern and relied less on slave labour as it eventually came to be characterised by a large rural middle class. The colony was originally inhabited by colonists pushing south from Virginia and north from South Carolina. The North Carolina piedmont was not occupied until the 1750s, at which time it was a frontier region. It slowly became dominated by corn, wheat and livestock agriculture worked by English, Scots-Irish and German farmers.[27] These distinct differences inherent in the southern colonies laid the foundations for an internal tension in what would become the South, a tension which contradicted those who championed southern nationalism in the immediate antebellum years.

The colony of Georgia was founded by philanthropists in the early eighteenth century as a buffer between South Carolina and the Floridas and as a place for the working class, petty criminals and vagabonds of London and other English cities to prove their worth. The project prohibited slavery and rum in a society of small and earnest landholders. A different type of utopia than that envisioned by the Puritans of New England or the Quakers of Pennsylvania, Georgia nevertheless was confronted by American realities just as they were. At the root of the problem was the unrealistic vision of the London philanthropists who founded the colony. They 'were trying to make Georgia fulfil a European dream. They were less interested in what was possible in America than what had been impossible in Europe.'[28] Increasingly frustrated colonists toiled on unfertile land which they were not permitted to sell. Furthermore, the silkworms in Savannah died, proving that the climate was unsuited to the Georgia trustees' preferred crop. These trustees finally admitted defeat in 1752 and handed their charter back to the Crown. After this point the colony increasingly imported slave labour and rapidly became a planter society closer to the model of South Carolina. By the eve of the Revolution, Georgia was sparsely populated and the poor relation of the other American colonies.[29]

What has been sketched above is a picture of the main regions of the colonial period and how they differed from one another. Michael Zuckerman, though, has decried the focus on the regional dissimilarity in the colonial experience, arguing that differences have been overemphasised at the expense of commonality. He asserts, 'historians of the colonies have turned to regional orderings of provincial experience because they cannot find any overarching meanings in that experience and will not impose any overarching meanings on it'.[30] On the contrary, regional diversity enriches the story of colonial America. Recognising the different shape of the regions that made up the early America makes the process by which people formed a country all the more dynamic and historically appealing. Attempts to reach for commonality of experience that was not present overstate the extent of an American identity in the colonies. Something new was developing, but to speak of a common sense of Americanness in the colonial period is an exaggeration.

Within the different regions of colonial America there existed a diverse array of racial identities. These identities were not static and were not clearly formed in the way a modern conception of racial identity would suggest. The colonial period provided only the beginning of a process by which these identities were developed. Almost all people in the colonies encountered Native Americans at some time. The arrival of the Europeans on the North American continent brought diseases which wiped out thousands of Indians. The fact that several Indian groups adapted and survived, however, meant that in most of the colonies Indians and Europeans lived side by side. In the Carolinas more than a dozen separate peoples formed the 'Catawaba' nation. Adapting to the process of European colonisation, the Catawaba traded with the English, accommodated changing economic circumstances and survived.[31] So contact with Europeans was not simply a case of destruction for the Indians: there was a place for negotiation, a middle ground between the settlers and the Native Americans. Adaptation and accommodation were crucial elements in relationships between colonists and settlers which were in constant flux.

Nevertheless, the lines of separation between the colonists and the 'Indians' were increasingly clearly drawn as key differences emerged. These differences were most clearly present in contrary patterns of gender relations, concepts of kinship versus the idea of the nation-state, and dissonance over the notion of land ownership.[32] Euro-Americans' sense of collective identity was reinforced by comparison with the Indians. The British plan of 1764 to regulate relations with the Indian nations failed not only because of unwieldy bureaucracy but also because the colonists rejected its inherent racial fairness. The suggestion that Native Americans were also subjects of the Crown and had rights that should be protected was threatening to the Euro-American concept of their future.[33]

Among Euro-Americans, however, there were numerous ethnic groups which provoked cultural tensions among white peoples. Benjamin Franklin gave voice to the xenophobia of many Englishmen in Pennsylvania when he referred to 'Palatine boors ... who swarm into our settlements, and by herding together, establish their language and manners, to the exclusion of ours'.[34] It is too simplistic to see a tripartite separation of the peoples of the colonies into the racial categories of white, red and black. The Palatine Germans, for example, forged a self-conscious, collective identity, casting themselves as poor refugees in need of help. Their effort to achieve self-determination in the mid-Atlantic region revealed tensions among the different ethnic groups which made up the white peoples of the colonies.[35] The longevity of ethnic distinctions also varied. French Huguenots, for example, quickly disappeared as a cohesive group. Their high rates of inter-marriage with other Europeans meant they became 'American' in the way that Crevecoeur's description suggested was archetypal.[36] Englishmen who moved to the colonies, however, did not suddenly become Anglo-Americans overnight. They first joined subcultures in different colonial regions where they became Anglo-Virginians or Anglo-New Englanders.[37]

Just as the white people of the colonies were sub-divided into a number of different distinct ethnic groups, so the black immigrants were not homogeneous. Africans arriving as slaves in America, for example, spoke many different languages and were drawn from a vast geographical area of Africa. Even the journey from capture to the waiting slave ships of the coast could take months. In this time iden-tities could be reshaped even before the crossing of the Atlantic.[38] When they did arrive in the New World their identity was largely shaped by the experience of slavery. Whilst Europeans did look down on other races as inferior they did not treat blacks or Indians the same across all of the colonies.[39] The experience of slavery played a crucial role in constructing racial identities. In Virginia, for example, the attempt to legally distinguish slaves from other labourers shaped the racism which came to dominate white–black relationships in the colony.[40] The dominance of slavery in the experience of African-Americans in the colonies means we have little evidence of their reaction to European culture, only a response to the situation of human bondage. For blacks in the colonies their identity was divided between the old and the new worlds, the memories of Africa and the realities of America.[41]

Given the great racial and ethnic diversity of the colonies the most obvious question which emerges is: How did this heterogeneous people become Americans? The answer is not simple; indeed the racial multiplicity of American society remains a feature of the United States to this day. Furthermore, racial identities were in such flux during the constant cultural exchange of the colonial period that modern con-ceptions of racial difference are largely inadequate. A significant part of the answer, however, lies in the relationship between the colonies and the mother country. The different races of people that made up the colonial population differed from one another in a myriad of ways. Importantly, however, they all had to contend with the fact that their lives were to a large extent shaped by political powers very far away.[42]

Increasingly it was pressures from England which shaped a collective colonial experience.

In the first half of the eighteenth century changes in the colonies led to increasing Anglicisation. A common English law system, religious revival which broke down cultural boundaries and a consumer revolution all brought a shared Anglo-American identity closer.[43] English consumer goods flooded into the colonies and rich Americans mimicked the tastes and purchases of English gentlemen, just as the lower classes copied their social betters.[44] Non-English European colonists adopted the tastes and cultures of this new consumer society and as a consequence they were increasingly assimilated. Relations with the mother country also helped shape a separate colonial identity in other ways. The Seven Years War required inhabitants of the New World to take sides in an imperial conflict. The Palatines' decisions to support the British war effort, for example, played a large part in their integration into the mainstream colonial society and helped shape their political identity.[45]

In a paradox of exclusion colonists who regarded themselves as Englishmen increasingly felt that they were not being treated in the same way as men and women who lived in England.[46] This fostered a spirit of separateness which flowered further in the revolutionary struggle. A sense of being American was fostered by a belief that what was being created in the New World was different from European society. As the colonists sought recognition of their Britishness they challenged the contempt shown towards them by the metropolitan elite. As a consequence the colonial identity that emerged was both rooted in British culture whilst also consciously trying to affect change and adapt Britishness to an American experience.[47] The story of how decisions made in London impacted on the colonists' move towards independence will be explored in Chapter 2. It should be noted, however, that to speak of a truly American nationalism in the colonial period and even during the revolutionary struggle is misleading, even hugely anachronistic. Sources of separateness were heavily provided by an adaptation of British traditions and ideals.

Power in the colonies and in the new nation that emerged after the Revolution was, therefore, Anglicised and dominated by white Americans. The great racial and ethnic diversity which characterised the colonies continues to be a feature of American society today. Then, as now, however, racial identity provided a major factor in the distribution of wealth and power. It is important that we recognise that the eventual Anglicisation of the colonies emerged from a myriad of different cultural exchanges across a large and diversified colonial landscape. It was not predestined that the colonial world would become dominated by the interaction between London and men of America who believed they were protecting the rights of the British Constitution. At no point was the path from colonies to nation straight and clear. Nevertheless, the more the colonial elite conceived of themselves as freeborn Englishmen with important rights and privileges the more they came into conflict with imperial authorities. This conflict started a process which led to the creation of an American nation. How and why this story unfolded is the subject of Chapter 2.

2

REASONS FOR REVOLT

The birth of the United States

When the thirteen American colonies declared their independence on 4 July 1776 they argued that 'all men are created equal' and have 'certain unalienable rights, that among these are life, liberty and the pursuit of happiness'. The colonists argued that the 'laws of nature' entitled them to spell out to the British why they wanted to break from the empire. Chief among these natural laws were their rights as free men, which had been restricted by King George III's government. The Americans claimed they were being made slaves by a tyrannous British establishment. The words of the Declaration of Independence and the high ideals they express echo down through history. Edmund Morgan asserts that on the road to independence the colonists discovered, 'nothing more or less than the principle of human equality'.[1] This principle did not, however, encompass the one in five Americans who were black slaves. Furthermore, in their founding document the Americans also accused King George of 'cutting off our trade with all parts of the world' and 'imposing taxes on us without our consent'. The elucidation of economic grievances, the contradictions of freedom and slavery, and the close connection between ideals and economics have led some to assert that the real driving force behind the birth of the United States was economic self-interest.

This essay seeks to briefly explore how historians have interpreted the reasons behind the Americans' decision to declare their independence from the British Empire. How genuine were the expressions of ideals by revolutionary leaders and where did these ideals originate? How important were trade and tax in the movement for independence? What changes were there in colonial society which stimulated the fissure with the mother country? When men spoke of liberty were they expressing the same ideal? How could such diverse colonies form a new nation? Before addressing these questions, let us first turn to a succinct narrative of the crucial events leading to independence in the period from 1763 to 1776.

Following the conclusion of the Seven Years War with France, the British faced the problem of paying for their victory and the cost of defending the colonies. Policy makers in London were understandably worried about passing the burden of these expenses onto the British people in the form of taxation. The colonists, however, could be taxed in order to help service the war debts. Importantly, from 1764 the administration of American colonial policy shifted from the Board of Trade to Parliament, a body less easily influenced by American lobbyists. The Chancellor of the Exchequer, George Grenville, saw the need to fund the protection of a vast new territory gained following victory over the French. In 1764 the Sugar Act was passed and the Stamp Act was announced which was to go into effect the following year.[2] The colonists feared the Sugar Act would harm the northern rum industry and have further economic consequences which might threaten the colonies' ability to maintain British imports. The Stamp Act meant that almost anything which was written or printed would have to be on specially stamped paper from London, which carried a tax.

The Americans were shocked by Parliament's decision to enforce taxation on them without consultation with their elected representatives, who traditionally decided internal taxation. Protest was expressed in newspapers and pamphlets across America. Representatives from the colonies met in New York at a Stamp Act Congress which denied the ability of Parliament to tax the colonies. One New Yorker argued that the British government had 'invited despotism to cross the ocean, and fix her abode in this once happy land'.[3] The Americans, to varying degrees, argued that Parliament could not tax them because they were not represented in that body. The Glorious Revolution of 1688 had shown Britons that Parliament had supremacy over the Crown. If this was the case, if Parliament had supremacy, then surely it could tax the colonies. At the time of the Stamp Act crisis the colonies had not gone so far down the road of political revolution to deny parliamentary authority entirely. Pamphlet writers instead made a distinction between 'internal' taxes and 'external' taxes. 'In practice, if not in theory, the British were offered a deal. If they gave up the power to tax, the colonies were willing to permit them to keep the power to regulate trade and commerce.'[4]

The lines between internal and external taxes were, however, very fine. Many in Britain thought they were ridiculous. The Stamp Act was repealed in 1766 but the Townshend duties of the following year were designed to replace it. Duties were to be collected by customs officials in America on items imported from Britain. John Dickinson, who had been a member of the Stamp Act Congress, expressed the views of many in the colonies when he objected to the Townshend duties. These were still an example of unacceptable taxes because they were not designed to regulate trade but were being collected in America so as to raise revenue.[5] Boston led the way in resisting the Townshend duties with a non-importation campaign and mob violence directed at customs officials. Edmund Burke told Parliament that the Americans believed 'we mean to oppress them ... they intend to raise a rebellion against us'.[6]

To suppress this rebellion the British sent troops to Boston in 1768. The inhabitants of the city were appalled at this expression of British power. A standing army was traditionally viewed as a warning of tyranny and Sam Adams referred to the troops as 'the terror of the enemies of liberty'.[7] Bostonians sneered at the troops and insulted them; children showered the red coats with snowballs. Eventually the soldiers were provoked. When shots were fired in March 1770 three Bostonians lay dead and eight were wounded. One historian has called the Boston Massacre a 'street brawl'.[8] It was not a cold and calculated slaughter of innocents as the term massacre evokes. The recourse to violence to maintain control in Boston was, however, 'the ultimate symptom of the ineffectiveness of the British government's authority'.[9] Parliament responded to the anger in the colonies following events in Boston with a repeal of all the Townshend duties except that on tea. As the colonial economy experienced an upturn, opposition to the British lessened and non-importation schemes were abandoned. A peace, or, more aptly, a truce settled over events.[10]

This truce was, though, short-lived. Bostonians published a document which listed all of the abuses of American rights by the British and by 1773 independence was being discussed in the colonies. All that was needed to touch off renewed hostilities was a new parliamentary initiative. This came in the shape of the Tea Act which gave the East India Company an exclusive right to sell tea in America. Such a move would hurt many merchants and several ports stopped the tea from being delivered. In Boston in 1773 the now famous Tea Party took place as rebels disguised as Indians dumped £10,000 of tea into Boston Harbour.[11] This provoked outrage from the British who responded in 1774 with a series of Coercive Acts. Town meetings were banned, troops were quartered in Boston and General Gage, commander of the British forces in America, was made governor of Massachusetts. The lesson being delivered to Boston was also for the benefit of the rest of the colonies, colonies who sent representatives to meet in the first Continental Congress in 1774. That meeting produced a firm declaration that Parliament could not legislate in regard to America.[12] Gone were the previous distinctions between internal and external taxes and between taxation and legislation: the Americans were on the brink of reaching for independence, though the time had not yet come for this. George Washington argued that, whilst there was no consensus on independence, neither would the colonists consent to their privileges being abused. He could not decide 'where the line between Great Britain and the Colonies should be drawn'.[13]

The British were determined to draw that line with a clear stroke which maintained their authority. Parliament passed a bill to close the whole trade of New England. This was a step too far for many Americans and the first shots of the revolutionary war were fired on the road from Concord to Boston in April 1775. As the colonists violently denied the authority of Parliament they reached out to the King to intervene on their side against Parliament and ensure the colonies did not leave the Empire. George III responded by declaring America in rebellion.[14] In the winter of 1775 the Americans had arrived at the crucial moment and were faced with the final decision of whether to break their ties to the mother country and strike for independence. A decisive moment came in January 1776 when Thomas Paine's *Common Sense* was published. The pamphlet was widely read in the colonies and the style of writing appealed to the common man as it fuelled the calls for independence. Paine's prose had a particular impact on Pennsylvania, whose delegates to the Continental Congress were delaying the final move to break from Britain. America was ripe for Paine's words and on 4 July 1776 the United States was born and the world changed forever.

Let us now turn to how this famous story has been interpreted and probe the meanings, motives and metamorphoses that lay beneath the string of events. Neo-Whig historians have taken seriously the words of the colonists when expressing their grievances with the British. Bernard Bailyn argued that the American Revolution was driven by an ideology which believed that the colonies were victims of a conspiracy to enslave them. The colonists saw 'overwhelming evidence ... that they were faced with conspirators against liberty determined at all costs to gain ends which their words dissembled'. It was this passionate belief that 'in the end propelled them into Revolution'.[15] Gordon Wood has referred to the 'vitality of the Americans' ideas' in the move towards independence.[16] Those who wrote pamphlets and spoke out against the British legislation from the Stamp Act through to the Coercive Acts did so because they were motivated by the ideals of rights and liberties which they believed were under grave threat.

The origins of these ideas themselves have also received considerable scholarly attention and led some to argue that the break from Britain was stimulated by a desire to preserve an existing model of liberty rather than create a radically new one. The colonists therefore 'revolted not against the English constitution but on behalf of it'.[17] Theirs was an attempt to stop the erosion of liberty which would, it was believed, eventually lead to the destruction of the English constitution itself.[18] The language of disaffected British Whigs was utilised by the colonists to express their own increasingly heightened fears that liberty was being attacked. Looking at revolutionary thought as pre-modern, neo-Whigs have, therefore, located the ideological origins of the American Revolution in classical republican thought. Wood argued that 'the principles of republicanism permeated much of what the colonists read and found attractive'.[19]

Historians, who wrote with the intention of locating the genesis of the movement for independence in ideals, were refuting the work of a Progressive school of thought which saw economic determinism as crucial to the coming of the Revolution. For these scholars the idealism of revolutionary pamphlets was a smokescreen for class minorities who promoted their own self-interest.[20] Those who doubt the sincerity of the colonists' expression of idealism can point to the truce between 1770 and 1773 as a period where commercial prosperity provided the conditions for a quietening of rhetoric and protest about the loss of liberty.[21] It could be argued that the Americans simply did not like paying taxes, especially when their economic fortunes were at a low ebb – as they had been after the Seven Years War. Economic self-interest undoubtedly played a part in the coming of independence. No lesser American colonist than George Washington was continually troubled by his often disadvantageous economic ties to Britain. Washington let others make legal and constitutional arguments about the Stamp Act; his attentions were more focussed on the prospect of economic independence.[22]

Certainly it is true that internal economic changes in the colonies impacted on the coming of independence. It is also no coincidence that the centres of most passionate revolt were also the centres of the most vigorous trade. Economic inequality was a crucial concern in the revolutionary movement but not only that perceived between the mother country and her colonies. The iniquitous distribution of wealth in the colonies themselves received attention from those who saw a break from Britain as an opportunity to transform society in America also.[23] A one-dimensional Progressive view of the manipulation of events by a class minority pursuing their own economic self-interest fails to recognise the role of diverse interests in shaping the conditions in which independence emerged. It is crucial to acknowledge, though, that these competing interests were not always locked in struggle, that there was also reciprocity and negotiation at work.[24] Reducing the story of the Revolution to class struggle and economic determinism misleadingly diminishes the real complexity of the past.

We need to recognise that the impulse to separate from Britain was rooted in changes in the nature of colonial society and that symbiotically these very changes were influenced by strains with the mother country. These transformations and tensions were political, ideological and economic, and intrinsically linked to one another; it is ineffectual to try and simplistically rank them in terms of historical importance. Furthermore, attempting to study the colonists' actions on a straight and clear line of development is futile and by so doing we 'attribute to the men of previous ages an extraordinary simple-mindedness'.[25] Economics, power, sovereignty, conceptions of tyranny and liberty, self-interest and idealism were all important but they did not drive the colonists in isolation. They were inter-connected and represented manifestations of changes in the fabric of colonial America from which independence grew. The move for independence was part of a complex power struggle between the colonies and the mother country but was also driven by a contest over where power should rest in the colonies themselves.

The rhetoric that the colonists expressed in the lead-up to 1776 reveals the existence of social strain in the colonies. 'The grandiose and feverish language of the Americans was indeed the natural, even the inevitable, expression of a people caught up in a revolutionary situation.'[26] Joyce Appleby argues that a modern liberalism was at the heart of the colonists' ideas and existed alongside the classical republican ideology that the neo-Whig school identified. This liberalism emerged from the socio-economic changes that were occurring within America. The development of a free market economy had a key impact upon this new liberal theory which prompted the colonists to question their ties with Britain. Americans drew heavily on the work of liberal writers, most notably John Locke, and developed an ideology for a new society. 'Liberalism in America became more than an ideological gloss on market economics; it was a description of a modern utopia which could garner the loyalties of a broad range of Americans.'[27]

Americans increasingly conceived of their natural rights, which they believed it was the government's responsibility to protect. The colonists invoked the ideas of writers like Locke and Harrington, and even when they were not directly cited they had a key influence on American thinking. The crucial reason why these ideas were so influential is that they carried more clarity in America.[28] Thomas Paine's *Common Sense* spoke to an increasingly millennial vision in the colonies and he saw the future in America. As well as arguing that to create this new future Americans had to break from the British, Paine also expressed a vision of freedom and equality which worried conservative elements in American society. Although he supported independence, John Adams referred to *Common Sense* as 'poor, ignorant, malicious, short-sighted'.[29] The egalitarianism of Paine's vision threatened wider social transformations. Crucial to the changes in colonial society which birthed independence were the pressures from ordinary men and women to have a stake in the social order and enjoy fully the natural rights and economic freedom which the liberal vision embraced.

Changes in urban politics in the colonies in the first half of the eighteenth century were crucial to a rising political participation. The role of the mob became important in the political struggles of colonial cities and the numbers of those actively involved in political debate and dispute rose. 'The barometric pressure of political culture was on the rise during the half-century preceding the Stamp Act Crisis.'[30] In these years the colonies developed 'autonomous provincial political environments' in America.[31] These political developments provided the pre-conditions for the fight against British policies in the period after 1763 as a more politically literate people responded to the policy made in London. After 1763 new and more radical men assumed leadership of the struggle against the British. Rising demands for change came from almost every level of society before it was voiced by those at the very top as the spirit of liberty spread throughout the social order.[32] This social order was also shaken by the religious revivals which swept America throughout the first half of the eighteenth century and provided a great democratising force. The Baptist religious revolution of the 1760s, for example, 'challenged gentry values and their social order more sharply and reached even lower into the social order for its recruits'.[33] More so than ever before ordinary men and women expressed their desires for the future and spoke to power in new and more direct ways.

Americans increasingly talked of liberty, although the word meant different things to those who used it. The gentry class in the colonies believed it was their natural place to represent the rest of society and liberty was something that they should have the privilege of enjoying. As Michal Jan Rozbicki explains, 'the right to the fullest enjoyment of liberty became the heart of colonial gentry's self-definition'.[34] When they spoke of liberty they did not understand it to be a concept which promised to bring egalitarianism to the American colonies. Liberty represented a set of privileges which was afforded by elevated social status. The assertions of the colonial gentry that Britain was denying their liberty were part of an argument for more equality between colonial and metropolitan elites.[35] This liberty was something different to the conception of the word as understood by the Boston mob or backwoods planter who used it to express an anti-elitist sentiment. When colonial gentry framed their language in an egalitarian manner they often did so in order to win the support of the public.

Faced with British military power, most obvious to the colonists in the Boston Massacre, Americans developed a sense of separateness from Britain. To argue that they crafted a fully fledged American nationalism at this point is, however, misguided. Americans saw themselves as members of the British Empire and their ideals emanated from a British political tradition. Yes, there was a sense of something new developing in the colonies but this remained very much in the context of a relationship with the mother country. Indeed the presence of significant loyalist feeling during the War of Independence shows how strongly some wanted to stay members of the Empire.

Nevertheless, Americans were increasingly aware that they were being treated differently from men and women who lived in England. Denied their English rights as Americans, the colonists looked to natural rights ideology, the same natural rights ideals to which those in Ireland had turned when interpreting their relationship with England.[36] Calls to enjoy natural rights appealed to the ordinary people of the colonies and it was they who increasingly adopted, and adapted, the language of liberty which had traditionally been used by the colonial elite. They wanted greater equality and justice in relationships with Britain but they also wanted their local experiences to realise a more egalitarian state of affairs. Calls from the political class of the colonies to protect liberty filtered down to the lower ranks of society who themselves began to speak of autonomy and the desire to transform their own place in the colonial world, a development which concerned the elite in America.[37] Social strains of this sort in Virginia led many planters to feel that a break from Britain would allow them to establish a new government which would alleviate the threats they faced from a rising tide of ordinary farmers who desired a more egalitarian society.[38] Social protests and popular disturbances were a central element in the move towards independence. Artisans and farmers grasped the political ideology of equality and colonial elites responded in their use of language.[39] Importantly, however, when talking of liberty, colonists at different levels of the social strata did not always mean the same thing. The Revolution, therefore, was not only about breaking British control over America but also about which Americans should control their new nation. Differing interpretations of the meaning of liberty were part of the struggle for power in the colonies.

The desire to resolve this struggle was given impetus by the changes in colonial society which brought a developing sense of American identity. The colonies were increasingly drawn closer together. A consumer revolution occurred in the mid-eighteenth century which saw a larger number of colonists purchasing British goods. This shared experience as consumers brought the different colonists closer to one another. Indeed inter-colonial trading connections provided a foundation for anti-British protests and coordinated revolutionary action.[40] This consumer revolution played its part in the development of the move for independence. Imported goods provided the colonists with new questions about their relationship with the mother country. 'British manufactures came to symbolise dependence and oppression.'[41] During the controversy over the Tea Act the colonists drew on a legacy of protest in the consumer marketplace. Drinking tea was equated with accepting slavery at the hands of the British. Refusing to take tea showed a separation from the mother country. 'Within this mental framework, tea sustained an inchoate spirit of nationalism.'[42] This was though a very tentative sense of nationalism. The emerging nation lacked a fully formed identity. A clear American national identity only emerged in the years after the Revolutionary War.

On the eve of this conflict 'government was coming unhinged throughout the colonies as usually law-abiding people took matters into their own hands'.[43] This dislocation posed not only questions about the relationship between the colonies and Britain but also represented a challenge to traditional structures of authority within colonial society. In America something new was developing and the increasingly aggressive British policy after 1763 helped to speed up its evolution. The numbers of those who demanded the enjoyment of liberty and equality grew as pressure from below acted to propel change through 'the revolutionary politics of pursuing happiness',[44] a happiness that the colonists increasingly believed lay outside of the British Empire. Americans were ever more conscious that they were not enjoying the rights and privileges of Englishmen and a separate identity grew from this.[45]

This sense of separateness did not translate into a fully formed national identity. Only with the construction of the Constitution did Americans build the concrete foundations of nationalism. Reflecting the struggle of the Revolutionary period concerning who should rule at home, this Constitution did not extend life, liberty and the pursuit of happiness to all of the peoples of the new nation. The colonial gentry cemented their position of power in the new republic. Furthermore, race provided an inescapable determinant when framing the parameters of citizenship in the new nation and this has had a profound impact on the development of American national identity.

3

THE CONSTITUTION
Makings and meanings

After declaring themselves independent from the mother country, Americans had to construct a system of government to fulfil their dreams for a new nation and ensure longevity for the United States. The problems which were encountered during the period of the Articles of Confederation led many to believe that a different model of government was needed. The federal Constitution which emerged from this impulse for change was crucial to the survival of the fledgling republic. As John Murrin has argued, 'people knew that without the Constitution there would be no America'.[1] The document that emerged from the Philadelphia Convention for ratification by the states is still the framework which governs America today. The story of the making of the Constitution and the meanings the founders invested in it are therefore crucial to an understanding of American national identity. In many respects it created a framework for nationhood which ran ahead of an embryonic sense of nationalism. This chapter seeks to briefly explain why the Constitution was adopted and to probe what its supporters believed it would achieve. In its preamble, the text refers to 'we the people'. The story of the American people was and is intimately connected to the development of the Constitution.

One year after the Declaration of Independence, the Continental Congress presented a document which created a union of the different states of the new American nation. Not until 1781 did all of these states accept and ratify the plans and therefore establish the Articles of Confederation. The new system of government had no executive at its head but Congress was granted the power to control diplomatic relations and requisition soldiers – vital during the continuing struggle with the British. Fear of central power concentrated in the hands of the few was writ large in the structure of the Articles, however. The states retained their own sovereignty and freedom and they continued the crucial realms of commercial rights and taxation. The Articles could only be amended by a unanimous decision and any major decisions still required the approval of nine of the thirteen states. As Gordon Wood has summarised, 'the Confederation resembled more an alliance among closely cooperating sovereign states than a single government – something not all that different from the present-day European Union'.[2] The Articles of Confederation were inadequate as a device to build a nation and bind the states together under the aegis of an effective central government. The Articles conceded too much to individual state sovereignty.

We must be careful, however, not to dismiss the Articles of Confederation as an attempt to construct a government for America that was always doomed to failure. The system was able to tie the states together with sufficient strength to defeat the British and ensure that the fledgling nation survived its infancy. Furthermore, it was under the Articles that the Northwest Ordinance was passed in 1784 which provided the future model for the admission of new territory and then states into the Union. With the benefit of considerable historical hindsight we can see considerable signs of health in the new nation and this should not be ignored. Nevertheless, progress in the organisation and settlement of the West is particularly significant because it was the only area of policy in which the national government could claim any real success. It was only in this area that Congress had power to act independently of the state governments.[3] The Articles did not provide strong enough central governmental direction for the nation. There was an increasing feeling among many American leaders that the Articles of Confederation were inadequate and that government needed to be restructured if America was to prosper. By the middle of the 1780s oratory and writings were full of allusions to a critical period for America, of unease concerning impending crisis and turbulence. The war with Britain had been won but the American Revolution was about much more than breaking the yoke of colonial control. The Revolution brought with it an expectation that American society would be transformed. The difficulties of the 1780s were all the more troubling because these hopes were confronted by problems and fears.[4]

In 1781 Congress proposed an amendment to the Articles which would allow the collection of a 5 per cent impost on imported goods. Rhode Island would not ratify the amendment. As a consequence, in 1782 a new system which sought some more powers for the national government was proposed by Robert Morris, Superintendent of Finance. He wanted to balance the national budget, fund national debt and establish a national bank. His proposals were met with significant opposition and he turned to the army to help make his case. In late 1782 a group of officers petitioned Congress for action, warning that a mutiny may ensue if they continued to hesitate. George Washington faced down those who had threatened mutiny and James Madison sought to work out a compromise in 1783. The revenue plan which was passed in April of that year agreed an impost lasting for twenty-five years and, importantly for the future, worked out a system of apportioning national expenses among the states which counted slaves as three-fifths of the free population. The new plans did, however, fall well short of the Morris proposals.[5]

In the period 1784 to 1786 Congress continued to struggle with the task of effectively running the country. There were tensions over the relationship between the states and the national authority and the dominant political issues were how to fund debt and regulate commerce. Virginia and Maryland, for example, both claimed authority over navigation on the Potomac, which made customs evasion an easy task. At the Mount Vernon Conference of 1785 the two states agreed a number of important initiatives to help unify the regulation of trade and commerce. Madison then invited representatives of the other states to meet at Annapolis in 1786 to discuss similar issues on a national level. Attendance at the meeting was poor.[6] Attempts to strengthen the Articles of Confederation from 1781 through 1786 had met with little success as any significant amendments were unable to clear the hurdle of unanimous ratification. As the national government struggled to exert its authority, so the state governments grew in their power and willingness to flout Congress. It was becoming increasingly clear to the nation's leaders that something more than piecemeal change was needed.

This impulse for change was provided with a further catalyst by events in Massachusetts. Farmers in that state were bearing the strain of low agricultural prices and high taxes and rose in rebellion in the autumn of 1786 under the leadership of Daniel Shays. The mob defied the state government and stopped the collection of debts. Historians have subscribed to a consensus that sees the rebellion as a significant force in the strengthening of the cause of the federalists. If Massachusetts, a state with one of the most balanced and well-constructed constitutions, could fall prey to the destruction of property and threats to liberty, then a crisis surely was impending. Proponents of a stronger national government urged that action needed to be taken to stave off anarchy. It is worth noting, however, that the brutal repression of the rebellion also raised fears about centralised power. Reaction to Shays' rebellion mirrored the struggle over how much authority Americans were prepared to invest in a national government.[7]

That debate started in earnest at the Philadelphia Convention of 1787. It was at this meeting that James Madison unveiled his plans for a new system of government for the United States. It was at this meeting that the fundamental foundations of the American nation were laid. As one historian has observed, 'No narrative is more important for the subsequent course of American history than the drafting and ratification of the federal Constitution and the successful inauguration of the new national government.'[8] Limits of space here preclude a detailed analysis of all aspects of the Constitutional Convention. We will focus on two important and inter-connected decisions which were crucial in the construction of the Constitution – the issues of representation and the place of slavery.

The Virginia Plan, written by Madison with assistance from others in the Virginia delegation, proposed a totally new form of government. A national legislature was to have two houses: the lower was to be elected by the people and would then elect the upper house. This legislature would have the power to negate any state laws which contravened the articles of union and could use force to gain the compliance of the states. There was to be a national judiciary and an executive who would be elected by the legislature and would be ineligible for re-election. Crucially, in the Virginia Plan, membership of the two houses of the legislature was to be based on the proportion of taxes or size of free population in each state. For the next two weeks the Virginia Plan was not significantly challenged but then the smaller states signalled that they would never accept a proportional representation system in both houses of the legislature. The New Jersey Plan – jointly prepared by members of that state as well as Connecticut, New York, and Maryland – proposed a unicameral legislature in which each state had one vote. The smaller states wanted a stronger national government than that facilitated by the Articles of Confederation but they were afraid their interests would become subservient to the demands of the larger states. The New Jersey Plan was rejected. Debate over the issue of representation dragged on for the next month. In early July the deadlock was broken when a committee proposed by Roger Sherman of Connecticut decided by a split vote to accept an upper house based on one state one vote and a lower house based on proportional representation.[9]

This decision on the shape of the future Congress of the United States has often been referred to as the Connecticut or Great Compromise. In reality there was no such compromise. The arguments of the smaller states were to some extent based on a different conception of federalism and republicanism than that elucidated by Madison. His explanation of his position in the Federalist, however, was part of the debate on ratification which took place after the Constitutional Convention. There was broad agreement among federalists and anti-federalists on the principles of separation of powers, checks and balances and the rule of law. There was not extensive political theorising and philosophical debate during the convention itself. The key decision made during the meeting in Philadelphia came from hard-headed practical bargaining based around interests.[10] This was certainly the case in the decision over representation in the legislature. Madison believed that the extension of a large republic would protect the interests of all against majority factions. He contended that there was little that would unite the diverse interests of the larger states as a force against their smaller counterparts. Proponents of proportional representation and their opponents did not spend over a month searching for common ground; rather they attempted to convince the other side of their position. Madison and his allies failed; they did not see a compromise but a defeat. In Sherman's committee the larger states were outvoted five to four. The small states carried their position in the vote.[11]

Without resolution of the issue of representation there would not have been meaningful progress towards a Constitutional document. Interconnected with this issue was the place of slavery in the federal republic. Balancing the interests of slave holders with free labour advocates was essential if agreement was to be reached on the Constitution. In accordance with the revenue plan of 1783 it was decided that slaves would count for three-fifths of a free person when apportioning both taxes and representation. As Madison would go on to explain in *Federalist no. 54*, application of this measurement for both representation and taxation was fair because two different systems of measurement would allow exaggeration of numbers when considering representation and a downplaying of numbers for taxation apportionment.[12] The original debate over representation and slavery at the convention had been between those who wanted to count slaves and those who did not. George Pinckney led those who fought to protect the rights of slave holders and the three-fifths clause can be seen as a victory for their cause. The clause gave the South significant political leverage in the new political system.[13] The extent to which this was a victory for slave-holding interests is highlighted by the contradiction inherent in the 'compromises' over representation and slavery. The decision over representation was consistent with the principle of equality because representation in the lower house was based on population alone. The decision on the three-fifths clause, however, 'belied the principle by a provision that gave white southerners an extra share in the government'.[14]

Another crucial decision faced by the delegates was that concerning the foreign slave trade. Northern delegates worried that the three-fifths clause would encourage increased importation of slaves and that this would also weaken one part of the Union that the others were obliged to protect. One delegate asserted that the trade was simply inconsistent with the American character and supported a prohibition of slave importation. A hard-headed bargain was struck which would not allow Congress to stop slave imports until 1808 but did allow duties on this importation.[15] The word slavery was never mentioned in the Constitution but its presence permeated the final version of the document. Southerners had gained significant protection for their peculiar institution during the course of the convention.[16] Representatives of the slave interest made by far the most vociferous demands that their concerns be addressed and the rest of the delegates had to acquiesce to a significant extent. 'The Constitution neither strengthened nor undermined slavery; faced with a fundamental moral problem the delegates chose ultimately to avert their gaze.'[17]

Once the convention had finalised the text of the new Constitution it was sent to the states for ratification. When nine out of the thirteen states ratified, the new system of government would be inaugurated. It is in the ratification debates that we can move our discussion from the makings of the Constitution and focus on its meanings. Slavery was a significant topic during the ratification debates. It was discussed at some length in Massachusetts, Pennsylvania, Virginia and South Carolina. In Rhode Island ratification was held up in 1789 and 1790 by an anti-slavery faction. These discussions were not dominated by moral considerations – though they were in evidence – but rather focussed on the political and economic ramifications of the persistence of the peculiar institution. Americans were unsure about the extent to which slaves were to be counted as property or persons and the three-fifths clause did not solve this conundrum. Importantly, when constructing the parameters of American nationhood and citizenship the founders affirmed the association between white freedom and black subjugation. 'The ratification process, in that sense, was a pivotal point in the retreat from the revolutionary ideals of 1776.'[18]

For those who took part in the debates over the ratification of the Constitution this legacy of 1776 was important. Federalists and anti-federalists debated the extent to which the Constitution was the correct model to protect the revolutionary heritage. The opposing sides had a different understanding of the nature of republican government. Anti-federalists believed in the small republic and asserted that elections at a local level provided a substantial representation of the middling men of society. Stretching the elective principle over the whole nation would, however, see the dominance of the elite in an aristocratic legislative body.[19] Madison provided the most famous elucidation of the contrary view in *Federalist no. 10*. He argued that a republican government which stretched over a large country could protect all interests more successfully than a republican system in a small territory. For Madison a large republic made it more 'difficult for unworthy candidates to practice with success the vicious arts by which elections are too often carried'.[20] Madison believed that republican government would protect the people from the dangers of faction. The anti-federalists, however, saw in their opponents' plan the prospect of aristocratic rule by the elite. Their successful calls for a Bill of Rights to guarantee certain individual liberties grew out of their understanding of republican government.[21] As Gordon Wood has argued, 'the Anti-Federalists' lack of faith was ... in the organisations and institutions that presumed to speak for the people ... they were localists, fearful of distant governmental, even representational, authority'.[22]

Where the anti-federalists saw the dangers of a distant and elite central governmental power, federalists were motivated in their support for the Constitution by a fear of excessive democracy. A further chapter in the struggle of the Revolutionary period over who should rule at home, the ratification debates saw federalists attempt to safeguard the position of elites. Madison and many of his federalist allies had become increasingly concerned by the excesses of the state legislatures during the 1780s. Too much democracy had led to men of questionable virtue pursuing narrow and factional interests rather than exercising enlightened leadership. Too much popular influence could lead to great turbulence for state and national polities. Madison had faith in the people to elect to office wise and distinguished men. His was an elitist conception which believed the people had the right to vote in elections but should leave office-holding to men of sufficient virtue.[23] The federalists believed that disinterested men were needed to preside over a society riddled by different private interests. This, they believed, undermined America's capacity for republican government. The Constitution was therefore designed to save American republicanism. In this respect the federalist founders were a conservative force rather than intentional harbingers of a vibrant new political structure.[24]

This discussion of the motives of the founders and meanings of the Constitution requires a brief survey of the historiographical debate surrounding such issues. Charles Beard's progressive interpretation of the Constitution as an economically inspired document designed to protect property and social status was influential well into the middle of the twentieth century, when focus shifted beyond simplistic economic conceptions of interests and engaged fully with political ideology.[25] Wood argued that the founders had much more fundamental concerns in mind than their own personal credit in 1787. They saw themselves as men committed to the good of the nation; protectors of the republican experiment.[26] It was Gordon Wood who further developed the progressive interpretation of the Constitution in his seminal work *The Creation of the American Republic*. He rejected economic motive but still saw the emergence of the Constitution as a social conflict. 'The Federalists meant to restore and to prolong the traditional kind of elitist influence in politics that social developments, especially since the Revolution, were undermining.'[27]

For Wood the ratification debate represented a clear shift from classical republican to a more modern politics in America. During the debates the federalists were forced to justify the merits of the Constitutional document and in so doing they marked a transition to modern political theory. The federalists used 'popular and democratic rhetoric' to justify their system of government and 'thereby contributed to the creation of that encompassing liberal tradition which has mitigated and often obscured the real social antagonisms of American politics'.[28] Some critics of this belief in a shift from classical to liberal republicanism at the time of the ratification have argued that liberal thought challenged the classical tradition at the time of the Revolution. Joyce Appleby argues that this liberalism emerged from socio-economic changes occurring in the colonies leading up to 1776.[29]

The historiographical consensus is now that there was no sharp distinction between classical and liberal republicanism. This leaves a problem, though, when trying to ascertain the different motives and meanings of the federalists and anti-federalists during the ratification debate. 'If there was no apparent conflict between liberalism and classical republicanism ... these terms cannot serve as a meaningful way of distinguishing between the ideological differences that the Federalists and Anti-Federalists expressed.'[30] Indeed there were differences among anti-federalists themselves that further complicates neat characterisations and ideological categorisations. There was a 'plebeian populism' which provided opposition to the Constitution and the concept of a natural aristocracy made up of men of republican virtue. This provided a different type of opposition to the Constitution than that expressed by elitist anti-federalists.[31] In fact many of the most prominent anti-federalist leaders were 'socially indistinguishable from the Federalist spokesman and often were as fearful of the excesses of democracy in the state legislatures as the Federalists'.[32] There was a clear rift over the conception of republican and democratic government which separated grass-roots and elitist anti-federalism.[33]

If we recognise a conception of liberty which was rooted in an elitist tradition which pre-dated the American Revolution then we can see that classical and liberal notions of liberty both derived from the same core ideals. Many of the men on either side of the federalist and anti-federalist debate were from the same social elite but had differing views on the shape of government.[34] The concepts of classical and liberal republicanism cannot be used to adequately explain the differences between federalists and anti-federalists, argues Max Edling. He believes that the debate over the Constitution was one concerning the formation of a nation-state. The anti-federalists' fundamental objection was to the creation of a strong central government which they feared would become too powerful. 'The best way to make sense of the ideological differences expressed in the debate over ratification is therefore to regard it neither as a debate about democracy nor liberalism, but as a debate about state formation.'[35] Anti-federalists saw a standing army and central collection of taxes as a threat to individual rights, freedom and property. Federalists argued, however, that without a strong national government Americans trusted these things to luck. The Constitution was to provide a national government strong enough to protect these rights and freedoms.[36]

This conception of the fundamental difference between federalists and their opponents during the ratification also brings into focus the important role of the anti-federalists in the American founding. Despite losing the argument to such distinguished patriots as Madison, Washington and Hamilton, the anti-federalists continued to exert influence over American political thought. Anti-federalism was a way of viewing the world and it was suspicious of too much central power which evolved into a strict interpretation of the Constitution.[37] This strict construction of federal power played a key role in opposition to the Alien and Sedition Acts and a national bank. It was also prevalent in Calhoun's nullification argument and in secessionist ideology before the Civil War.[38] The anti-federalist belief in the small republic and a more direct form of representation which opened up the political arena to a wider number of constituents made them forward looking. 'In 1787–88 it was not the Federalists but the Anti-Federalists who were the real pluralists and the real prophets of the future of American politics.'[39]

This future would be shaped at every turn by the Constitution. The Constitution became the touchstone of American nationalism. When the actions of the Washington administration seemed to confirm the anti-federalists' fears about federal power they did not denounce or reject the Constitution. In fact they viewed it as an inscrutable standard which was used to call their opponents to account. Amidst a clearly delicate sense of nationalism in the early republic, the Constitution became the focal point for national identity. An identity that was particularly fragile in the late eighteenth century. Americans built a constitutional roof before they erected the national walls beneath it.[40] The Constitution has developed as a living document. It provides the fundamental adhesive of American nationhood. As the United States expanded and developed so the Constitution adapted to these changes. To continue the metaphor used above, as the walls of nationalism developed, alterations were made to the constitutional roof. Central to these alterations were contested notions of who was to be included in the statement 'we the people of the United States'. Struggles to realise a truly universal interpretation of the first seven words of the Constitution provide the central theme for many of the essays in this volume.

4

FLAWED HEROES

Washington, Jefferson and slavery

George Washington and Thomas Jefferson are America's most celebrated founding fathers. Monuments to their legend adorn the nation's
capital, the site for which was chosen by and then named after the first
president. In 1963 Martin Luther King stood in the sight of the
Washington monument and implored America to live up to the true
meaning of its creed, quoting Thomas Jefferson's words that all men
are created equal. Jefferson and Washington, however, were slave
holders. Their lives, like those of so many other Americans in the
eighteenth century, were inextricably linked to slavery; an institution
which clearly drew the parameters of American citizenship. Joseph
Ellis has described the issue of slavery as 'the proverbial ghost at the
banquet'.[1] Washington led the fledgling American nation as it threw
off the shackles of British imperialism. However, in 1796, when his
slave Oney Judge fled in order to quench a 'thirst for complete freedom', Washington denied her attempts to achieve liberty.[2] Jefferson
contradicted his famous 1776 statement of equality for all men when
five years later he wrote, in *Notes on the State of Virginia*, that blacks
were 'inferior to the whites in the endowments both of body and
mind'.[3] Jefferson strongly opposed any mixing of the black and white
races and yet he fathered children with his slave mistress, Sally
Hemings.

Jefferson's place as an American icon is such that it is difficult to
scrutinise his career and person 'without appearing to assault the very
core of American society'.[4] Indeed Washington and Jefferson's duality,
as national heroes and as slave holders, raises questions about their
role as symbols of the nation. Does their status as slave masters provide
an irremovable stain on their record as American icons or does such
a condemnation reflect an unhelpful presentism? It is wrong to apply
twenty-first-century standards to men of the eighteenth century.
Instead we must view their ideas concerning slavery against one

another and in the context of men of their generation. To find fault with the founders is not to diminish their place in American heritage but it helps illuminate further the nation's struggle to frame and live up to its chosen creed.

Unlike Jefferson, who wrote about the issue of slavery and struggled to justify its existence in a land dedicated to liberty, Washington made few public statements on the issue. A man with the highest public profile in Revolutionary America, Washington knew that it was 'imprudent for him to speak about slavery openly'.[5] As Commander-in-Chief of the Continental Army, chairman of the Constitutional Convention and then president of the United States, he was present at some of the most important discussions about slavery but he remained largely silent on the issue. Perhaps because of this hesitance to speak publicly about the issue, historians have long disagreed on the evolution of Washington's views on slavery. What is certain, however, is that there was a change in his thinking as his life progressed. The final expression of his views on slavery came in his will. Washington wrote that he wished for all of his slaves to be freed upon the death of his wife. He not only willed that his slaves should go free but he maintained that this should happen after the death of his wife. This was, in part, to ensure the survival of families formed because of marriage between his slaves and those of his wife but also to protect her from the distress of having to deal with the separation of families during her lifetime.[6] In this consideration he showed more concern for his slaves than Jefferson who freed only five slaves in his will and left some 200 others to be auctioned. Jefferson also had no compunction when splitting up his own slaves from their families.[7] Indeed, writing about the black race Jefferson observed, 'love seems with them to be more an eager desire, than a tender delicate mixture of sentiment and sensation. Their griefs are transient.'[8] It would be easy to criticise Jefferson in comparison to Washington on this matter. It is worth noting, however, that the former had much greater debts than the latter and that Jefferson lived longer than Washington and had children who would inherit his estate. Economically, it was much easier for Washington to use his will to ensure eventual freedom for his slaves.

Washington's views were consistent with other planters of his generation. By the time he was a young man the slave system was well established in Virginia and Washington's life became inextricably linked with slavery. By the age of sixteen he already personally owned 24 slaves and by 1799 the figure was 164. The slaves who worked his land were treated as beasts of burden and he exhibited a largely detached attitude towards them.[9] Given that he freed his slaves while others of his generation, most notably Jefferson, did not, the question then is, when his mind was made up, when was he compelled to untangle himself from the slave system? It is here that historians have disagreed and admirers of the first president may be disappointed. Given his status as the pre-eminent founding father it would be gratifying for Americans if their first great leader had experienced an epiphany, if the moral contradiction of slavery in the land of liberty had irresistibly prodded his conscience. The majority of Americans in the late eighteenth century did not, however, see slavery as an anomaly, a system out of place in a 'democratic' America. Slavery was imbedded in the Constitution and an accepted part of US life. Furthermore, Washington was not a natural idealist; his primary concern was the day-to-day reality of power. As Joseph Ellis has noted, Washington was a man of 'rock-ribbed realism'.[10]

Henry Wiencek points to an event at Williamsburg in 1769 which he believes provides the turning point in Washington's thinking on slavery. It was there that he took part in a raffle, some of the prizes for which were slave children. Wiencek argues that, with this raffle, 'Washington reached a moral nadir, and from that depth began a long moral transfiguration that concluded in the writing of his will'.[11] This would indeed provide a neat explanation for his change of heart and one which would be recognised and appreciated by twenty-first-century observers. Nevertheless, Washington lived in the eighteenth century and he continued to buy and sell slaves regularly for many years after the incident at Williamsburg.[12] It was realism and self-interest which best explains Washington's reactions to the slave system; he had an 'obsessive concern with his own economic interests'.[13]

As early as the 1760s Washington realised that he had too many slaves and that, after reducing the size of his tobacco crop, he required less labour. Nevertheless, his concern with economics also made him an assiduous pursuer of runaway slaves. He took slave flight very seriously indeed and made great efforts to recover runaways after they had fled.[14] As mentioned above, Washington was keen to ensure that slave families were not split up when they were either bought or sold. This moral position was, however, also influenced by economic considerations. When he articulated arguments for not buying slaves he kept his options open by suggesting an acceptable price in case his situation changed. He also worried about selling his slaves during the Revolutionary War because he feared that depreciating currency in Virginia would affect the price he received.[15]

Washington's realism and his economic self-interest can be seen in his response to slavery during the Revolutionary War. In the early stages of the conflict he had objected to plans to enlist slaves in the Continental Army. However, when the British offered freedom to the slaves of patriot masters who fought with them, Washington reversed his position. The inclusion of slave soldiers in his forces saw Washington consider a wider role for blacks out of the 'exigencies of war'.[16] As the conflict continued he supported a plan to enlist slaves with a promise of freedom when peace was concluded. Though, when that peace came, he was adamant that blacks should not escape with the retreating British. Indeed, Washington wanted some of his own slaves returned. Sir Guy Carleton, British Commander-in-Chief, refused to return runaways. Although annoyed by the British position, Washington was a realist and understood that pressing the issue would simply result in further hostilities. The British position prevailed at the peace negotiations.[17]

Washington remained silent publicly on the issue of slavery despite its increasing pertinence following the defeat of the British. But in his private correspondence of 1783 and thereafter we see the beginnings of a commitment by Washington to emancipation and abolition. His good friend the Marquis de Lafayette suggested that they jointly buy an estate where they would employ only free blacks and Washington spoke with Lafayette of his desire to get rid of his Negroes. In 1785 Washington agreed with two leading Methodists that slavery should be abolished although he did not sign their petition for slave emancipation. In 1786 Washington wrote to Virginia Quaker Robert Pleasants that he wished to see an end to slavery. Although the letter was advising Quakers not to interfere with slaves who were happy with their masters and to leave the matter up to legislative authority, Washington did endorse an end to slavery.[18]

Kenneth Morgan therefore sees 1783 as the key turning point in Washington's thinking on slavery. After this point he grappled with inner tensions concerning the slavery issue, though he kept his thoughts to himself; public pronouncements on the evils of slavery were not expressed.[19] It was as if Washington preferred to ignore slavery; that he would have supported its extinction not least because it would remove, for him, a persistent tension. Dorothy Twohig has highlighted the difficulty of deciding whether Washington's 'disgust with slavery rested on moral grounds or primarily on the grounds of the institution's economic inefficiencies'.[20] It is also conceivable that Washington disliked slavery because of the way it permeated his existence as planter, leader and President; he could not emancipate himself from the slave problem.

Washington fully understood the politically explosive nature of the slavery issue and he remained silent during the debates in the

Constitutional Convention. Later, as President, he realised that any moves to interfere with slavery would threaten the permanence of the Union. Undoubtedly sensitive to the reality that he, as the Executive, owned slaves, he hired white servants to do the publicly visible work at his residence.[21] Washington wanted to avoid any act or utterance which would ignite the slavery issue on the national stage. He believed he had no constitutional power to move against slavery even had he been willing to do so and he realised that as President even a private act would have significant public repercussions.[22] For Washington, 'when the fate of the new Republic was balanced against his own essentially conservative opposition to slavery, there was really no contest'.[23]

Washington used his will to get free in death from the slave system he could not escape in life. He had no 'Road-to-Damascus-like conversion concerning slavery'.[24] For moral – though not necessarily principally – political and economic reasons, he came to be increasingly aware of the tension created by slavery and his position as a slave holder and leader in America. Freeing his slaves in his will allowed Washington to make a clear statement to posterity that he knew slavery was wrong. Death allowed him to touch a little of the idealism that pragmatism and realism had never allowed to flourish during his life.

Idealism was not something Thomas Jefferson shied away from. The author of the Declaration of Independence, the champion of the separation of church and state, and one of the great intellectuals of his generation, Jefferson was a man of high ideals. He is an American icon and he was a slave holder. On the issue of slavery he spoke publicly with candour and certainly in more depth than Washington. It was Jefferson's idealism that has ensured both his veneration and, more recently, criticism. He has further to fall than Washington because his deeds have to be measured against such eloquent words and admirable ideals. The image of Jefferson as a slave owner is well known; less familiar and more troubling is the reality of his racist thinking.

Several eminent biographers of Jefferson have venerated his image at the expense of a true exposition of his relationship with the institution of slavery and his views on race. Virginian historians Dumas Malone and Merrill Peterson both defended Jefferson's record and pointed to evidence that he wanted to end slavery, referring to his early plans for emancipation in Virginia and to his opposition to the institution during the Revolutionary period.[25] More recently, Joseph Ellis tried to defend Jefferson against the claims that he fathered children by his slave mistress, Sally Hemings.[26] Ellis later conceded, when presented with DNA evidence, that the sexual liaison had occurred, but he was certainly loath to accept it before this point. Deference to an iconic image of Jefferson prevented a more critical exposition of his behaviour by the majority of scholars.[27] We need to move beyond unhelpful attempts to defend Jefferson, whilst also avoiding a presentist approach, and simply analyse Jefferson's deeds and beliefs.

During his time serving in the Virginia Legislature in 1776–79 Jefferson proposed a complete overhaul of the new state's laws. As chairman of the revision committee he proposed that any slave emancipated had to leave the state within a year and free blacks coming in to Virginia were to be outlawed. His law would also have banished any white woman who had a child by a black or mulatto man. This opposition to free blacks in the state after the Revolution contrasted with his advocacy of manumission in 1769 because then the free blacks would have had no political role in society under British rule. After 1776 free blacks would either have had to be given citizenship and the franchise or they would provide a danger as a large non-voting population.[28] This position reveals much of the Negrophobia which will be discussed below. The extent of Jefferson's opposition to slavery should not be exaggerated. His attack upon the slave trade in his draft of the Declaration of Independence – Congress removed the section during the editing process – blamed the British for forcing slavery on the colonies.[29] This rhetoric emerged from Jefferson's beliefs concerning nation and race. Just as the British and Americans engaged in hostilities so a free black nation would necessarily pose a violent danger to their white former masters.[30]

In 1778 Virginia outlawed the slave trade, though there is no evidence that Jefferson participated in any direct way in securing this law. In his *Notes on the State of Virginia* (1781) Jefferson asserted that he had offered an amendment to the revised legislation which would have emancipated all slaves born after the act was passed. The children of slaves would have been educated at public expense until they were eighteen and then colonised outside the state. But no copy of this amendment has survived. When a law allowing for masters to manumit their slaves was passed in 1782, Jefferson did not free any of his own.[31] Jefferson sent a draft for a new Virginia Constitution to Madison in 1783 but asked him not to share it with his colleagues. The plan for emancipation included in the draft would not go into effect until 1800 and was somewhat ambivalent. Jefferson did not publicly advocate abolition when discussing a new Constitution for Virginia.[32] Jefferson did attempt to ban slavery in the new territories of the West during his time in Congress in 1784. The Ordinance of 1784 would have banned slavery in the western lands after 1800. Although, had slavery got a foothold there, it is possible the slavery prohibition could have been repealed. The Ordinance failed to pass by one vote and has been cited as 'Jefferson's last public attempt to limit or end slavery'.[33]

The anti-slavery provision in the 1784 Ordinance, however, was not Jefferson's. It belonged to Timothy Pickering. The 1787 Northwest Ordinance, which was passed and provided for the immediate freedom from slavery of that area, was not Jefferson's work.[34] In 1819 when Congress debated the controversy surrounding the admission of the Missouri territory, Jefferson argued against prohibiting slavery in the West because of the national turmoil it would cause. Important here is the impact of the three-fifths clause of the Constitution on Jefferson's actions. In 1784 and 1787, under the Articles of Confederation, there was no such clause. During the debates on Missouri, however, Jefferson was reluctant to support a plan to stop slavery expansion as this would have had a significant impact on the slave-holding voice in the House of Representatives.[35] At several points in his life as a public servant Jefferson had the opportunity to strike against the institution of slavery but he did not. We must now turn to the reason why.

Like Washington, Jefferson feared that freeing the slaves would have grave consequence for the perpetuity of the Union. Unlike Washington, however, his intellectual engagement with the slavery issue led him into 'a deeply troubling, unsure and apologetic racism'.[36] Put simply, Jefferson did not believe that all men were created equal because he thought blacks were inferior to whites, indeed inferior to Native Americans. Jefferson believed the African-American to be dull in imagination, without taste and anomalous. He commented that he had never found a 'black that uttered a thought above the level of plain narration'. The Negro was 'inferior to the whites in the endowments both of body and mind'.[37] Jefferson did believe that the slaves should be declared a 'free and independent people'. He did not believe, however, that free blacks and whites could co-exist.[38] In large part this stemmed from his conception of race and nation. He believed that the presence of two peoples in one country and their tendency to mix had a negative impact on both. Jefferson shared the concerns of his contemporaries about slave rebellions and he felt a large free black population would lead to violence.[39] He was also repulsed by the idea of race mixing and believed that freed blacks had to be removed from America. Jefferson wrote of the slave that 'when freed he is to be removed beyond the reach of mixture'.[40] Washington and Lincoln, for that matter, supported colonisation schemes, and Jefferson believed that the ill-feeling promoted by the experience of slavery meant that white and black could not live side by side. Nevertheless, neither Washington nor Lincoln had the same Negrophobia as Jefferson, whose definition of American patriotism provided the foundations for racial constructions of national identity in the nineteenth century.[41]

Given this explanation of Jefferson's racial ideas it is easy to understand that historians were reluctant to accept a rumour that originated in Jefferson's lifetime that he had a slave mistress – except that those who defended him were also those who chose not to focus on his Negrophobia. Many of Jefferson's biographers simply could not bring themselves to believe that the American icon had fathered mulatto children and then kept them in bondage. The man who wrote the Declaration of Independence enslaving his own children? Surely not. In 1998, however, DNA evidence proved convincingly that Jefferson had had a sexual relationship with Sally Hemings.[42] Indeed, Joseph Ellis, who had long defended Jefferson against the claim, was forced to concede that 'Jefferson began his sexual liaison with Sally Hemings in Paris around 1788 and was the father of all her children.'[43] During their relationship Jefferson continued to argue that mixed-race children damaged the fabric of the Republic. Sexual relationships between slave master and slaves were common in Virginia at this time, but what is revealing about the Hemings affair is the mind of Jefferson, which suggests 'an interior agility at negotiating inconvenient realities'.[44] Put another way, Jefferson seemed to be in denial. He believed miscegenation to be abhorrent but he fathered Sally's children.

Jefferson scholars have attempted to mediate between eighteenth-century attitudes and the glaring hypocrisy of his actions when viewed from the vantage point of the twenty-first century. Andrew Burstein explains that Jefferson could rationalise his relationship with Hemings without feeling guilt because of the reasoning afforded him by the culture of sensibility.[45] Peter Onuf asserts that Jefferson's views on race and nation led him to believe that colonisation was the only solution to the racial problem. Inherent in this view was the belief that miscegenation was irresistible and the only solution was to remove blacks from society. Because effective control over personal and home life could not be exercised, blacks had to be colonised in order to end miscegenation.[46] Nevertheless, it is difficult not to conclude, as did his contemporary, Edward Coles, that Jefferson's colonisation scheme was a 'delusion'. He failed to meet the challenge of the slavery issue with a positive programme, one which brought freedom and equality to all men as opposed to removing the racial problem with a physical separation of whites and blacks.[47] Jefferson knew slavery to be wrong but he justified it with spurious pseudo-scientific racism. He had the opportunity to strike against the institution he hated and feared but he did not.

So where does this leave Jefferson and Washington in the pantheon of American heroes? Even accepting the fact that the economic situation made it easier for Washington, Jefferson, the great thinker and champion of liberty, could not match the first President's emancipation gesture. This does not detract from Jefferson's other considerable achievements: his visionary approach to the West; his influence on the separation of church and state; his role in creating the Democratic Party; and his many other accomplishments.[48] In his time Jefferson had the reputation of a dangerous social radical. Alongside Washington, however, he was not a leader on the slavery issue. In this area they failed the test which was met by some of their less celebrated contemporaries. Jefferson's mentor, George Wythe, gave his slaves their freedom. Jefferson's young neighbour, Edward Coles, migrated to Illinois in 1819 and gave each of his slave families their freedom and 160 acres of land. He was later elected as governor of the state on an anti-slavery platform and protected the state's laws from pro-slavery forces.[49]

Timothy Pickering, Alexander Hamilton, St George Tucker: the list of those who were more vocal in opposition to slavery and more active in striking against it than Jefferson or Washington could go on.[50] Certainly we must not exaggerate anti-slavery feeling and it is true that many were motivated by a desire to neutralise the problems of slavery or simply get rid of blacks from their lives. It is not, however, an effort in anachronism to criticise the two great founders for their approach to the institution of slavery. As American icons we must judge them by the highest standards and that at least includes a comparison with others of their generation who did more to stand against slavery. The fact that popular and academic historians sought to resist history for so long, by defending the records of Washington and Jefferson on slavery, revealed much about the nation that the two men helped to found. Ellis argues that discussions of Jefferson's legacy 'end up being less about him than about us'.[51] Jefferson embodies the reality of the America black people have come to know, 'a place where high-minded ideals clash with the reality of racial ambivalence'.[52] Both he and Washington force Americans to consider their problematic and contested racial past. Both are American heroes and icons but their flaws reflect the problems inherent in the past, present and future of the nation that venerates them.

5

IGNORING WASHINGTON'S WARNING

Antebellum party systems

In his farewell address before he retired to Mount Vernon, George Washington warned the nation against the dangerous spirit of party.[1] Washington saw political parties as 'parasitic, divisive and destructive'.[2] Republican principles in the young America regarded factions as a threat to the stability of the nation. Anti-party feeling stretched well into the 1830s and beyond. Whig President, William Henry Harrison, criticised parties in his inaugural address as 'harsh, vindictive, intolerant, and totally reckless'; parties were in direct opposition to liberty.[3] Yet by the mid-1840s America had an extremely sophisticated and well-organised party system, the second of such political structures in the first sixty years of the republic.

Aware of the divisive issue of slavery, however, Washington warned that sectional party affiliations could destroy the fabric of the nation. Ultimately the first President was correct, though party spirit could also function to diffuse sectional tensions. As influential as any man in the development of the second party system, Martin Van Buren believed that interparty conflict was 'the optimal way to avoid naked sectional division in the country'.[4] The first parties were crucial agencies in the development of the Constitution and the construction of what it was to be an American, as they competed to protect the republic from danger. In this sense parties helped to develop a sense of national spirit, drawing on the signs and symbols of the Revolution and vowing to protect and guide the self-governing experiment. Partisan competition, though, required substantive issues to nourish it and party spirit was unable to resist sectional strife. Washington was right to warn his nation about the dangers of the spirit of party, though the first two party systems were not universally threatening.

Traditional revolutionary republicanism believed that the republic's safety necessarily required limitations of the power of government. Republicanism also emphasised the importance of community consensus and the common good. In this sense partisan politics which split the community were dangerous to the health of the new republic.[5] In states like Virginia, which had a settled social structure, deference politics militated against the emergence of a vibrant two-party system in the 1790s.[6] Jeffersonians embraced a settled social structure where land ownership gave men the independence that would restrain a destructive self-interest. The ideal of Jefferson's republic of farmers was closely linked to fears about partisan politics. The growth of artificial wealth, of credit and speculation, would promote factions.[7] Parties indicated a breakdown of the commonwealth and of social harmony and in this sense 'implied a failure of the Founding Father ideals, an unnatural and unnecessary growth of the socio-political order'.[8]

Ironically, however, it was the very ideals of republicanism which inspired the development of the first two-party system. Jefferson was faced with a tension between his fear of parties and his opposition to the policies of federalists like Hamilton. Debates over the role of the federal government, the founding of a national bank and attitudes towards the press and the French Revolution provoked 'superheated' political passions.[9] Jefferson used republican fears about faction to stir opposition to Hamilton, whom he painted as the head of a powerful clique and in so doing engaged in partisan politics himself. It was this fact that sat uneasily with the Virginian. After the 1792 New York gubernatorial election saw Jefferson's choice, George Clinton, defeat the Hamilton-backed John Jay, Jefferson wrote to Monroe of his discomfort concerning the nullification of some of Jay's votes. He argued that for Clinton 'to retain the office when it is probable the majority was against him is dishonourable'.[10] As the 1790s progressed and party conflict crystallised between the Federalists and the Republicans, Jefferson found himself, inconsistent with his professed hatred of faction, playing the role of a party leader.[11] Jefferson helped to institute a culture in which citizens bound together through party affiliation competed to protect the republic. The first two-party system emerged, therefore, from political disagreements over the future direction of the nation. Parties offered men the opportunity to shape that future.

So what of the fears of Washington, Jefferson and others that parties would promote disunity in the new nation? Certainly the first political system had a moderately sectional shape. Federalists were strongest in the north-east and Republicans found their most loyal support in Virginia. This provided an obvious threat to national unity. After 1800, defeated New England Federalists developed a conscious regional identity exemplified most dramatically by the secessionist impulse of the Hartford Convention of 1814. Indeed, by 1814 the first two-party system was failing to achieve national integration.[12] The desire to achieve victory on the national political stage, however, had previously led the parties to expand their appeal beyond narrow sectional interest. The Republican party broadened its support by reaching out from Virginia to constituencies in the northern states like New York and Pennsylvania, and Federalist Party leaders saw in this example the need to forge cross-sectional alliances. Furthermore, the parties reached out to different socio-economic groups. Federalist policies which focused on stronger central economic regulation tended to gain support from the more wealthy, with Republicans regarded as the party of the common man. Whether a citizen voted Federalist or Republican depended on his views concerning national authority. Federalists sought to uphold the status quo established by the Constitution and were suspicious of challenges from lower down the social structure.

The focus of partisan politics was on the presidential election, and Republican victory in 1800 showed that the opposition could prevail and government could be changed peacefully. To triumph in this electoral contest parties needed to be more than sectional blocs. In this way party political competition benefited the Union by affirming the structure of the Constitution and bringing different geographical interests together.[13] Indeed, before the Federalist and Republican parties emerged Congress regularly divided into sectional blocs. Once a two-party system emerged in the 1790s this sectionalism was reduced and when the Federalist Party slowly faded away after 1800 so sectional tension rose again.[14] The first two-party system began to wane as sectional tensions arose; the party system did not create those tensions.

Partisan politics did not hinder the development of a distinct national character and shared heritage; in fact in many respects they helped to stimulate and reinforce them. The party system was sensitive to the diverse demands of different elements of the republic and it provided a way for these disparate groups to influence the decision-making process. In this respect the first two-party system helped bring together the 'heterogeneous elements of the Union'.[15] The first generation of Americans inherited the task of working out the future shape of their democracy and nationhood.[16] Federalists and Republicans brought together diverse groups from different regions of the nation as they sought to protect their ideal for the republic's development.

Even though they promoted competing visions of the nation's future, political parties drew heavily on the symbols and rituals of the same revolutionary heritage. As Jean Baker argues, 'nearly every partisan representation from the naming of parties and the location of events to the raising of liberty poles, the appropriation of George

Washington, and the language of electioneering originated with the American Revolution'.[17] As the second two-party system formed both Whigs and Democrats saw their parties as originating from Jeffersonian ideology.[18] The shared symbolism and ideological inspiration of competing political groups helped to reinforce a shared national heritage. Electioneering, party meetings, parades and ratification conventions were all part of the ceremonies of politics which 'taught Americans how to be just that – Americans'.[19] Beginning with Jefferson and his supporters and continuing into the nineteenth century, most notably during the Jacksonian era, America was increasingly democratised and the concerns of ordinary citizens were addressed.[20] This engaged citizenry, connected by bonds of party affiliation, were committed to the safety of the republic and this strengthened the Union despite partisan conflict.

The leaders of the revolutionary generation remained, however, wary of party spirit and did not regard themselves as professional politicians. The first political parties were much weaker coalitions than those that came after and this was largely because the founders' generation did not actively promote party organisations. Indeed, men like Jefferson and Hamilton were suspicious of what they saw as unscrupulous career politicians like DeWitt Clinton and Aaron Burr.[21] Antiparty feeling was a long-term dynamic which was expressed consistently throughout the antebellum period and into the Civil War.[22] The ambivalence towards parties, the national political consensus ushered in by the Republican dominance of the early nineteenth century, and their acceptance of a more diversified economy and a national bank saw the demise of the first party system. In some states like Tennessee the first party system had not taken hold at all.[23] It is worth noting that these conceptions of first and second party systems are constructs adopted by historians and political scientists and were not familiar to men and women of the nineteenth century. Nevertheless, as Federalists ceased to provide an effective opposition and presidential elections were dominated by Republicans, so they faded into obscurity.

It was this waning of inter-party competition which helps explain the dangerous sectional split over slavery extension that developed in 1819 when Missouri applied for statehood. In the absence of cross-sectional political alliances Congress was divided along largely sectional lines. Observing the menace that this threatened, men like Martin Van Buren called for a new party system to counteract sectionalism.[24] In this respect there was recognition that party systems were artificial, part of a conscious effort to bind the federal polity together.[25] The second party system was important in helping to protect the Union against the sectional tension inspired by the issue of slavery, though that very issue was increasingly used to promote partisan conflict until it could no longer be contained. Richard McCormick and Eric Foner are chief among those who see the two-party system as 'artificial' because it could exist only in the absence of real conflict over the slavery issue. Michael Holt disputes this thesis, arguing instead that the slavery issue could be contained by and used to stimulate the two-party system.[26]

Weighing of these two interpretations will follow, but first we must address the historical explanation for the formation of the second party system of Democrats and Whigs. Several different factors emerge as influential in the process and they will be briefly surveyed below. What is particularly interesting, however, when testing the threat of partisan politics to the stability of the republic is the sectional influence on the construction of non-sectional parties. In 1828 only the middle states were evenly divided as northerners overwhelmingly supported Quincy Adams whilst the South voted for Jackson. When southerner Henry Clay faced Jackson four years later, there was no sectional divide and therefore parties in the North were balanced. In 1836 southern Whigs attempted to outflank southern Democrats on the slavery issue by questioning the safety of the institution in the hands of a Yankee-dominated Van Buren administration. So we see that sectional approaches to a series of presidential elections contributed significantly to the formation of bi-sectional national party affiliations.[27]

In many respects it was these presidential election contests which provided the major stimulus for the emergence of the second party system. The dominance of Republican candidates from Virginia from 1800 through to 1824 diluted the focus of partisan conflict over the presidency. The Republicans were unable to maintain the discipline to offer a single candidate to succeed Monroe. Four men emerged to contest the occupancy of the White House and the fall out from this election stimulated political divisions. Jackson became the main opponent of Quincy Adams and politicians began to plot their course within the context of presidential elections. By 1836 there were two parties contesting elections in every one of the states.[28] A growing lack of meaningful political combat in presidential elections as the Republicans reached ascendance and the Federalists faded had seen the waning of the first two-party system. The election of 1824 reinvigorated a political conflict which could tangibly affect the course of the republic. The second party system did not emerge suddenly but developed in a series of stages between 1824 and 1840.[29]

The role of Jackson in this process is significant. The nation's seventh president was a truly polarising figure. His unprecedented use of the veto, support for strict state rights doctrine whilst also standing firm against the nullifiers, and his war on the Bank of the United States divided opinion. The Whig party emerged as a coalition primarily united by their opposition to 'King Andrew I'. They were at first a negative affiliation in the sense that they were tied together by their disagreements with the policies of the President rather than possessing a coherent programme of their own. Democrats too were shaped by the personality and policy of Jackson. A Mississippi party member recalled, 'I found myself a democrat without being able to explain why I was of that party ... I began as a follower of Jackson.'[30] When Jackson left office both parties faced a dilemma as the personality that had helped shape the differences between them was no longer relevant. There had to be more to the Whig and Democrat parties than a simple approval of or opposition to Andrew Jackson.

Undoubtedly the major Jacksonian policy that provoked a political response was the bank issue. Federalists and Republicans had defined their differences in the 1790s when debating Hamilton's financial programme and the chartering of the first national bank; similarly, Whigs and Democrats clashed over the bank issue in the 1830s. Nevertheless, the bank issue was not the only economic concern which stimulated the growth of the second party system. Whig economic policies articulated during the financial crisis of the late 1830s were largely responsible for the surge in the party's support and eventual electoral triumph in 1840. Similarly, their failure to enact these policies following Harrison's death and the elevation of Vice-President Tyler played a large role in the election victory of the Democrats in 1844.[31] The Whigs believed that the national government should be used to promote economic growth and development, and campaigned against the Democrats' negative response to such initiatives. Nevertheless, the bank and related economic issues themselves did not create party differences. Wars over the bank simply helped to crystallise differing ideas of party and brought different political and cultural beliefs to the surface. Whigs articulated the ideal of power which was held in check by a balanced and fair constitutional system. They contrasted their beliefs with those who put their faith in potentially dangerous executives who exercised too much power. Whigs portrayed themselves as the representatives of a minority who only used party organisation to fight the power of a Democrat machine. If the interests of the moderates and the minority were to be protected, and the republic safeguarded, then they had to use party to achieve their goals.[32]

We return here to a potentially Union-strengthening element of the two-party system. Just as Republicans and Federalists had promised voters that they offered a vehicle through which to protect the heritage of the founding fathers, so the second party system provided constituents with a chance to meaningfully affect the future course of the nation. In this way the second two-party system absorbed and then adapted traditional revolutionary notions of republicanism. The idea of consensus as the prerequisite for the common good and the survival of the republic were replaced with a party system which was fuelled by partisan disagreement. Political conflict, however, often promoted common ground on matters of citizenship, political economy and, briefly, the extension of slavery. Essential republican ideals remained because parties offered the electorate a struggle over the future of the republic.[33] The basic tactic of partisan politics was 'identifying an antirepublican dragon, associating it with the opposition party, and crusading to slay it. ... Contest between the Whigs and Democrats had been explicitly portrayed as battles to save self-government, liberty and equality from power, privilege and despotism'.[34]

When these parties were bi-sectional, when they attracted a heterogeneous support from across various different regions of the nation, they helped to bind the Union together and to reinforce essential national ideals. The second two-party system saw one of the developments Washington had warned against help defend the republic from another of the threats he identified in his farewell address. The Democrats and Whigs competed as national parties with strong support in both sections of the nation. They helped to counteract the danger of sectional alignment and the incendiary issue of slavery. This reveals a paradox which was alluded to above. The second party system did not reflect the most blatant divide in the nation in the 1840s, that between North and South. Conversely, one of the factors that helps explain the emergence of this system was the largely sectional responses to presidential campaigns between 1824 and 1836.[35] The strength of these sectional issues ensured that each party had distinct northern and southern wings. Increasingly these wings ran 'janus-faced' election campaigns which articulated a party message closely tailored to its regional audience. Northern Whigs competed against northern Democrats on platforms which differed to those which characterised political conflict between southern Whigs and southern Democrats.[36]

Analysis of the eventual failure of politics to restrain the sectional forces is crucial when explaining Civil War causation and will be addressed in this context in Chapter 6. But a brief exploration is necessary, however, as a final assessment of the first American party systems. We have seen how political parties offered voters a chance to meaningfully affect the future of the republic; they gave citizens the opportunity to engage in political conflicts over how best to run the nation. This conflict, which was seen as threatening by traditional republican ideology, could sustain the health of the national polity. The passion with which politicians engaged in such struggles, however, meant that if parties developed a sectional shape the Union would face great peril. Politicians of the age were aware of this reality as well as historians writing centuries after. Despite this, even Van Buren, the principal champion of national parties being used to blunt sectional antagonism, was unable to resist the polarising power of the slavery issue. Having broken with the Democrat Party he had done so much to help create, Van Buren was nominated as the Free-Soil presidential candidate in 1848.[37] The questions over slavery extension, which were raised by the annexation of new land following the Mexican War, severely weakened the bonds that united northern and southern Whigs and in the 1852 election they represented a party who could not win on the national stage.[38]

Here we return to the debate over the ability of the second party system to deal with the slavery issue, an analysis of how 'artificial' and fragile that system was. The temperature of the sectional tension undoubtedly increased following the Mexican cession. Foner argues that the national political system that acted as a 'major bond of unity' was from the 1840s onwards increasingly disrupted by pressures resulting from questions over slavery.[39] McCormick asserts that the two-party system appeared to be in good health until about 1850, after which point 'under the strain of sectional issues confronting the nation, it began to crumble'.[40] Many have pointed to the passage of the Kansas–Nebraska Act in 1854 as the final blow to the second two-party system. This Act opened up the possibility of slavery moving into territory north of a line drawn by the Missouri Compromise (1820), which was designed to stop just such a move. The Whigs split along sectional lines as southerners supported the bill and northerners voted against a measure which opened the theoretical door for further slavery expansion. The Democrats were able to muster greater party unity with a significant number of northerners, led by Stephen Douglas, supporting their southern allies in passing the bill.[41] Indeed, Douglas's trumpeting of the popular sovereignty issue was an attempt to solve the political conflict over slavery and was consistent with his role as a Union politician who tried to diffuse the slavery issue.[42] The demise of the Whigs and the growth of the consciously sectional Republican Party saw the ultimate destruction of a party system which could not contain the slavery issue. In this reading of the collapse of the second party system we see the convergence of

Washington's worst fears; the divisive slavery question smashed the prevailing party system only for a new and more dangerous sectional party spirit to emerge and threaten the Union even further.

The reality was not that simple. If it was slavery alone that destroyed the party system why did it not destroy it before 1854? Remember sectional interests had helped to shape the emergence of that system. Furthermore, why was it that the Whigs collapsed but the Democrats did not?[43] The demise of the two-party system was more complex than a straightforward intrusion of sectional issues onto the political scene. Slavery played its part but it was not the only actor. Political parties had to offer voters a chance to defend republicanism and to shape the future course of the nation. Between 1850 and 1854 the Whigs increasingly struggled to do this. Initially, and mostly in the South, sectional problems were important. The Compromise of 1850 was accepted only conditionally in states like Georgia and Mississippi. The Whigs could not compete with Democrat promises to protect slavery after a Whig president, Taylor, had championed the admission of free states from the Mexican Cession. In other areas of the nation, however, it was political consensus that weakened the two-party system.

Holt argues that the two-party system could contain the slavery issue; it was not 'swept under the rug'.[44] Between 1850 and 1854 no new slavery-related issue dominated political discussions but it was in this period that the Whig party began to crumble. The parties concentrated on the type of economic policies that helped shape both the first and second party systems. Now competing to promote the economic boom of the early 1850s both Whigs and Democrats chartered railroads and banks. The parties came together on several important issues. This lack of choice was seen as a threat to republicanism because voters could not exercise influence over the future direction of the republic, it appeared government was being removed from the people.[45] In this context Douglas's Kansas–Nebraska Act can be seen as an attempt to reinvigorate party conflict over the issue of western expansion.[46] The Whigs could then unite behind opposition to a Democratic bill. Why couldn't northern Whigs convince voters that they could provide effective opposition to the Democrats? The answer is that the northern Whigs had been weakened by the emergence of the Know-Nothing anti-immigrant party, which attracted a significant following in the early 1850s and drained Whig support.[47] This erosion of the solidity of the two-party system before 1854 meant that the Kansas–Nebraska Act provided the final nail in that system's coffin. Anti-partyism was always strongest among the Whigs whose rhetoric placed themselves above party squabbles and depicted parties as a necessary evil to help safeguard the republic.[48] When they could not offer a viable alternative to the Democrats they faded. In this scenario it was the dynamic of party spirit itself which helped unravel the second party system.

With only the Democrats offering a workable national party by the end of 1854, voters sought an alternative, a way to protect the republican experiment. Skilful politicians provided northern voters who had drifted from the Whigs and Democrats with a new party. Identifying a dangerous 'slave power' with a healthy appetite for the expansion of slavery which threatened the nation, the Republican Party provided voters with the opportunity to tackle this menace. What emerged in the mid-1850s was the realisation of Washington's ultimate fears: a rampant party spirit increasingly divided along sectional lines. So was the first president right all along? The answer is both yes and no. The spirit of party was potentially threatening in a fledgling republic with a heterogeneous population. Traditional republican values saw the danger of the disruption of the common good. Nevertheless, this is not to say that the first two-party systems were an unqualified threat to the nation. It is too easy to look back with hindsight and see America hurtling towards Civil War. The second party system was capable, in its most robust form, of coping with the slavery issue, and it helped forge a national political identity and shared heritage. The rationale of party formation and survival, however, saw a party spirit which was increasingly drawn to the irresistible allure of sectional differences, differences which provided untold fare to nourish partisan appetites. Nonetheless, that party spirit and the sectional parties that brought Civil War closer shared Washington's motivation, namely a desire to protect the self-governing experiment.

6

SLAVERY AND THE CAUSES
OF THE AMERICAN CIVIL WAR

Abraham Lincoln wrote to future Confederate Vice President Alexander Stephens in December 1860, 'You think slavery is right and ought to be extended; while we think it is wrong and ought to be restricted. That I suppose is the rub.'[1] Historian William Gienapp has written that 'without slavery it is impossible to imagine a war between the North and the South'.[2] Undoubtedly, slavery was a key factor in the growing sectionalism of nineteenth-century America which eventually led to war. An understanding of the conflict, however, requires something more than a fundamentalist elucidation. Simple reductionist explanations of the Civil War which cite monocausal factors for the conflict still dominate popular perceptions of the origins of the conflict. These factors range from tariffs to modernisation to abolitionists to states' rights ideology. None of these explanations are wrong but overly simplistic interpretations of the conflict can lead to views of the past which cement a collective usable identity rather than to a history based on reality. 'Honest history answers our questions only by asking something of us in return.'[3] This chapter aims to answer the question of why the Civil War came. I ask the reader to consider how traditional and revisionist explanations can be synthesised to paint a comprehensive picture of Civil War causation.

The historiography of the causes of the conflict evolved during the twentieth century to eventually produce two broad schools of interpretation. In the 1920s Charles and Mary Beard produced an analysis of the sectional struggle driven by the economic difference between the North and the South. This approach was essentially restated in different terms in the 1970s with the concept of modernisation and the impact this process had on sectional tensions.[4] In 1940 James Randall moved away from the Beards' economic approach and argued that a 'blundering generation' of politicians allowed a conflict to emerge because of their short-sighted policies and party struggle, without which the war could have been avoided.[5] Randall provides an example of the school of historians that Kenneth Stampp argues see the conflict as essentially 'repressible'.[6] This interpretation of events minimises the central differences between the North and the South.

From the 1960s onwards there has been an increasing trend towards seeing slavery at the heart of the causes of the war. The Civil Rights Movement encouraged historians to re-examine the role of the peculiar institution and place black servitude in a prominent position as the key to sectional conflict.[7] Indeed Stampp's own reading of events places slavery front and centre. For him, 'the interplay of these proslavery and anti-slavery forces' was the key to the coming of the war rather than political blunders and economic differences.[8] Nevertheless, led by Joel Silbey, 'new political historians' have questioned an approach to the causes of the Civil War which relies on looking at the growing sectional divide solely from the view of the slavery issue and places over-emphasis on the extent of sectionalism. This school of thought focuses on political changes and the importance of non-slavery issues like nativism.[9] We can perhaps summarise the current situation by referring to 'revisionists' and 'fundamentalists'. The former school of thought points to political developments, the consequences of elections and the failed compromises of the 1850s when explaining the causes of the conflict, whilst the latter argues that the war emerged from a struggle between slavery and freedom.[10] The exploration of causation below attempts to bring these two strands of explanation together.

The issue of slavery asked searching questions of the American polity from the moment the nation was born in 1776. The famous words of the Declaration of Independence that 'all men are created equal' stood in direct contradiction to the reality of slavery. When delegates met at the Constitutional Convention in 1787 a number of compromises were required to reconcile northern and southern concerns about the issue of slavery. Constitutional provisions dealing with taxation and representation of slave-holding states, fugitive slave legislation and decisions on the slave trade were all necessary to ease the fears of southern states. The extent to which the Constitution explicitly and implicitly protected slavery was reflected in abolitionist William Garrison's famous condemnation of the document as a 'covenant with death'. In the late eighteenth century three Massachusetts anti-federalists, whilst not able to prophesy the extent to which slavery would test the rigidity of the Union, did know that 'this lust for slavery [was] portentous of much evil in America'.[11] Washington urged his countrymen to subordinate regional differences to the national cause and recognised the potential of slavery to exacerbate those regional differences.[12] His fellow founding father James Madison believed that if the slave population was diffused across an expanding western frontier then it would more speedily decline. He feared that restriction of slavery to a concentrated geographical region would entail the possible rupture of the Union.[13]

It is difficult to believe that the founding fathers would have disagreed with Lincoln when he stated that the nation could not 'endure permanently half-slave and half-free'. It became increasingly apparent, however, that the southern planters were not going to gradually emancipate their bondsmen. The 1793 invention of the cotton gin greatly increased the efficiency and profitability of harvesting the cotton crop and made slavery more profitable. By 1860 the southern slave population had reached approximately four million alongside eight million whites. Cotton exports in 1860 represented 5 per cent of America's GNP and more than half of the nation's exports.[14] It was a long-held southern belief that for this profitability to continue then new lands had to be utilised. A sectional rift concerning slavery had therefore emerged as the United States expanded its frontiers into the western territories.

When Missouri applied for statehood in 1819, northern federalists tried to impose a provision that slavery could not exist in the new state. Southerners reacted furiously to the proposal and the 'Missouri Compromise' had to be brokered which drew a line at 36 degrees and 30 minutes across the country. Below the line slavery would be legal; above, it would not. Jefferson worried that such a line would 'never be obliterated; and every new irritation will mark it deeper and deeper'.[15] As the Union acquired land from Mexico in the 1840s the debates over slavery extension did provoke irritation and a deeper sectional conflict. The three-fifths clause of the Constitution intensified this increasing sectionalism as southerners sought to safeguard not only their economic future but also their political voice by extending slavery into the territories.[16] As Eric Foner has argued, 'differences of opinion over slavery constituted an important obstacle to the formation of a national community'.[17] Indeed the very geographical expansion which helped shape national identity exposed the limits of that identity because of sectional struggles over slavery.

As many in the North came to realise that slavery was not going to die out naturally they became increasingly critical of the South. It was slavery that northern critics of their southern brothers focused on most clearly. Increasingly, northern spokesmen identified the southern slave system as a possible threat to their section and produced a critique of that system. Southerners were irreparably stained by slavery and were portrayed as 'helpless, lazy and unproductive'.[18] The dominant northern criticism of the South was elaborated to include social, economic and political vices, all of which were touched in some way by slavery. Horace Mann of Massachusetts was particularly worried by the lack of education in the South which could, he believed, undermine the foundations of republican government.[19] The emergence of the Republican Party in the 1850s intensified criticisms of the South. The ideals of free labour were contrasted with a slave society which damaged slaveholders and non-slaveholders alike. 'The Republican critique of southern society thus focussed upon the degradation of labour – the slave's ignorance and lack of incentive, and the labouring white's poverty, degradation and lack of social mobility.'[20]

Although it would be wrong to overemphasise radical anti-slavery feeling in the North, Garrisonian abolitionism had a larger impact on northern politicians than has been previously assumed. Garrisonians had sophisticated political aims and remained unfettered by ties of any one party; they encouraged sectional politicians of all affiliations to further the cause of anti-slavery.[21] Crucial in the northern critique of the South was the perception that a 'slave power' was dominating the national arena and perverting the republican experiment. This power threatened to control the federal government, and its potency increased as the 1850s progressed.[22] The feeling among some in the North that the South used the slave system to secure unfair political advantage can be traced back as far as the election of Jefferson, whom contemporary anti-slavery men called the 'Negro President' because of the way the three-fifths clause helped him secure the presidency.[23] Most dangerous to the safety of the Union was the fact that this critique of the South played a crucial role in the emergence of a northern nationalism. This nationalism identified the South as the enemy of freedom and was inextricably linked to anti-slavery feeling.[24]

The southern response to this intensifying attack upon their way of life was a more vocal defence of the slave system. After 1830 slavery increasingly provided the key issue which unified the heterogeneous elements of southern society and differentiated that society from the North.[25] Southerners accepted the morality of slavery and the evangelical conception of God. Indeed the evangelical South argued that God blessed the region and defended slavery. As the North and the South came to see each other from both sides of a divide over slavery they engaged in a debate over morality which provided 'the language of economic and political status'.[26] This status was fearlessly defended by an increasingly self-conscious and threatened South. The more the North criticised the South the greater the ferocity of the southern defence of their way of life. George Fitzhugh of Virginia was the prominent author of a growing body of literature in the 1850s which showed the benevolent and benign nature of the slave system when compared with the cold and ruthless northern free labour system.[27] Southerners believed it was they who protected the ideals and civilised society of the founding generation.

The development of a fractured American nationalism in the mid-nineteenth century was inextricably tied to increasing disagreements over the institution of slavery. It is a misconception, however, to view a modernising North moving inexorably into war with a pre-modern and feudal South dominated by slave labour. Both North and South shared in the modernising process created by the growth of print media and popular politics. Modernisation was a catalyst for change in both the North and the South and provided the conditions for a prolonged military conflict.[28] It is also dangerous to unduly emphasise the fragility of the Union and highlight the differences between North and South at the expense of their considerable shared heritage. The Union survived for as long as it did because of the mutual bonds of affection for it in the hearts of northerners and southerners alike.[29] A fundamentalist explanation of the coming of war which focuses on the relentless rush of a slavery-driven juggernaut fails to appreciate the subtle shifts in the polity of the 1850s which brought conflict closer.

Structural weaknesses in the American political system made it susceptible to the type of political crisis that emerged as the 1850s progressed. The perpetuity or otherwise of the Union provided a fundamental question that had been asked since the federalist and anti-federalist debate. To some extent the ambiguity of this issue allowed pro-slavery men in the South to contemplate safety outside of the Union. The debate over the legality of secession was viewed with pessimism by John Quincy Adams, who wrote in 1831, 'it is the odious nature of the question that it can be settled only at the cannon's mouth'.[30] As well as this ultimate question mark over the continuance of the Union, the political system erected by the Constitution left the American polity vulnerable to sectional strains. The provision for constitutional amendment raised the possibility of a significant change to the governing document which could adversely affect a section of the nation. In particular the South feared an attack on slavery. Furthermore, the creation of the Electoral College and the decision to award all of a state's electoral votes to the majority candidate promoted intense partisan contests. Only the 1852 presidential election, of those held between 1844 and 1860, saw the winning candidate poll a majority of the popular vote.[31] Ultimately it was the election of a minority and sectional candidate in Lincoln that provoked the lower South to secede. The faster growth of the free-state populations, combined with the Electoral College system, provided for a slow-boiling confrontation, especially when bi-sectional political parties broke down.

These political vulnerabilities, however, did not mean that the nation was doomed to an inevitable rupture. Nor does it mean that the second party system was unable to cope with sectional strains and slavery in particular. Michael Holt, foremost among the new political historians, has argued that that system actually thrived on such strains and tensions. Even when the controversy over slavery extension reached fever pitch following the Mexican Cession and debates concerning the Wilmot Proviso the party system held firm. By running 'janus-faced' campaigns that appealed to different sectional wings of the same party both Democrats and Whigs could effectively offer voters an alternative.[32] Holt asserts that it was the demise of this political alternative and not the slavery issue that was crucial to the collapse of the two-party system. Already weakened in the South following Taylor's policies in the lead-up to the Compromise of 1850, Whigs in the North lost out to the Know-Nothing Party.[33] Whilst capitalising on the issues of nativism, the Know-Nothings also provided a new party which offered an attractive alternative to men who felt traditional parties were increasingly unresponsive.[34]

Others argue that the demise of the two-party system was essentially because of the inability of that system to restrain the slavery issue. Foner asserts, 'the coming of the Civil War is the story of the intrusion of sectional ideology into the political system'.[35] Sean Wilentz refers to a 'chasm in the American political soul', which widened in direct correlation to the rise of the Republican Party and its anti-slavery agenda.[36] Elements of both arguments help to explain the political crisis of the 1850s. Issues other than black servitude did weaken the two-party system so that the Whigs were unable to deal effectively with the Kansas–Nebraska Act. Their problems became fatal when the slavery issue drove a sectional wedge into an already weakened national Whig Party. The slavery extension issue finished off the Whigs but it did not provide the root cause of their weakness before 1854. Crucially important was the emergence of the Republican Party in its place in the North. The consciously sectional agenda of the Republicans shows the danger of party spirit and sectional ideology working in tandem. The establishment and growing success of the Republicans started the end game which would force a sectional confrontation.

The Republicans ruthlessly politicised the caning of Senator Charles Sumner and the struggles between slave and free soil forces in Kansas. These issues provided examples of the dangers of the slave power and the brutality of the southern system, where violence and anti-republicanism reigned supreme.[37] Republicans preached that the slavocracy had a stranglehold on the federal government and the Dred Scott case and the LeCompton controversy were cited as evidence of this reality. In the South they looked with fear towards the growing power of the 'Black Republicans' and cited the John Brown raid and the election of Lincoln as grave dangers to the future of the southern way of life. These apprehensions and perceived terrors were played out in the press which 'nurtured anticipation and grievance. The "North" and the "South" took shape in words before they were unified by armies and shared sacrifice.'[38] This did not, however, make war inevitable in 1861. Had the pro-Union forces in the South marshalled their supporters more successfully then the nation may have averted conflict.

Nevertheless, just as the North increasingly developed an identity by comparing itself favourably with the South, so the South drew closer together when threatened from above the Mason–Dixon Line. After Lincoln's election and before his inauguration seven lower southern states seceded. Passionately defending the decision against his sister's – in the North – accusation that South Carolina had wilfully destroyed the Union, Louis Grimball wrote, 'you speak as if we are the aggressors ... when the fact is that we are oppressed and are contending for all we hold dear – our property – our institutions – our honour – aye and our very lives!'[39] What motivated such passions and the momentous decision to leave the Union? It would be simple to point clearly to the issue of slavery. Southern slave holders who feared that the peculiar institution could no longer be protected inside the Union frantically called for secession to safeguard slavery outside of the Union. In his 29 April 1861 message to the Confederate Congress, Jefferson Davis argued that slavery was indispensable to the South and northern attempts to imperil the institution drove the region 'to the adoption of some course of action to avert the danger with which they were openly menaced'.[40] Slavery was the crucial factor in the decision of the Deep South to secede and this was detailed in the campaigns of southern secession commissioners.[41] Fearful southerners saw the election of Lincoln as an expression by the northern people of their desire to destroy slavery. In an atmosphere of fear, 'secession was the product of logical reasoning within a framework of irrational perception'.[42]

It should be noted, however, that the relationship between slavery and the secessionist impulse was not straightforward. It is too simple to argue that the Deep South had a higher percentage of slaves and as a consequence they seceded first. In terms of sheer numbers of bondsmen Virginia had the most slaves and yet she did not secede until after the firing on Fort Sumter. Slave-holders called for Unionism to protect the institution of slavery as well as secession.[43] It is wrong to think of one South which acted with one mind concerning the slavery issue. The Upper South's decision to stay in the Union and wait to see what Lincoln did was based on a consideration of how best to protect slavery. It felt no compunction to secede before Lincoln's inauguration and the Fort Sumter crisis. Those in the Upper South still saw vibrant party competition in their states and could conceive of a repudiation of the Republican platform in the next presidential election.[44] Many in the Upper and border South also saw the potential dangers of secession and criticised lower southern fire-eaters. Western North Carolinian Unionists, for example, referred disparagingly to the Deep South as the 'cotton states' and argued that submitting to their 'arrogant oligarchies' would be humiliating.[45] A southern-wide referendum on secession after the election of Lincoln would have seen those in favour of leaving the Union at about 25 per cent. Therefore a pro-secession minority had to convince their fellow southerners that theirs was the best course for the South. The secessionists' plan was to turn the debate into a state-by-state decision on whether a state had the right to secede. With South Carolina voting for secession in December 1860 other lower South states had to decide if they could deny this right, and as several large slave-holding states seceded the Confederacy became more attractive.[46]

This is not to say that white non-slave-holders were duped; they understood the importance of slavery in the southern system and were extremely suspicious of the Republicans.[47] Rather there was something more than just a desire to protect slavery driving secession and war. There was a growing feeling among men that the United States needed to be purged of corruption and there was an increasing sense of impatience that the final act in the slow-boiling crisis of the 1850s should come.[48] Men acted within a framework of perception which saw war as a short-lived and cleansing process. Americans' experience of war in 1812 and then against Mexico in 1846 had been of brief military encounters. Frontier violence and the conflict in Kansas contributed to a belief that war would not be intensely violent.[49] The spirit of carnival that was witnessed in many northern cities as soldiers set off for war is further evidence of the romanticism and nonchalance with which many Americans conceived of military conflict. One journalist wrote of the coming conflict, 'let's go it while we're young. We never had a civil war before, you know ... and now we've got one we're just going to show the world that we can beat it at that as well as everything else'.[50]

Lincoln said in 1854, 'I hate it [slavery] because it deprives our republican experiment of its just influence in the world.'[51] Americans, North and South, were self-consciously aware that they were part of an exceptional experiment in republican government. Their responses to each other took place within this framework. Therefore it is undeniable that slavery and its expansion was the crucial issue in this sectional relationship. It was important to decide if the nation was to be slave or free, and increasingly, for many in the North, this duality needed to be rectified. The institution of slavery and the right to maintain it was relentlessly defended by the South. Northern self-perception was shaped by slavery and a distinct southern identity was dominated by slavery. Fundamental disagreements over black servitude provide the root causes of the Civil War. Conflict would be barely imaginable without this clear sectional divide.

There was, however, a twisting and uneven road to conflict, a road which was never leading with absolute certainty to one clearly defined destination. The fracturing of the party system in the 1850s led men to make portentous decisions which brought sectional confrontation closer without making descent into bloody civil war unavoidable. The emergence and expansion of a distinctly northern Republican Party committed to an anti-slavery agenda provoked an intensification of sectional tension. Still, war itself was not an unavoidable outcome of the sectional confrontation made likely by the growth of the Republicans. Further calculations and events combined to pull the nation closer to military conflict, none of which were predestined. Only a synthesis of traditional and revisionist interpretations of the coming of the Civil War can tell a truly comprehensive story of causation. Slavery was a perpetual catalyst but never an uncomplicated or isolated one.

7

SOUTHERN AND CONFEDERATE NATIONALISM

Northern victory in the Civil War gave legitimacy to the northern interpretation of American nationalism, and the defeat of the Confederacy discredited those who claimed a separate nationhood for the South. It is far too simplistic to plainly assert that the South was not a nation because it was not successful. When Lincoln moved to suppress the southern insurrection after Fort Sumter the majority of the citizens of Virginia, North Carolina, Tennessee and Arkansas rushed to the defence of their fellow southerners. A North Carolinian newspaper editor argued 'blood is thicker than water', as his state seceded from the Union.[1] The South endured a bloody civil war for four years and hundreds of thousands of southerners died for their 'nation'. One southern woman lost three sons in battle and yet she was still prepared to allow her fourth and only remaining son to serve the Confederate cause.[2] For the historian to ignore this human sacrifice and to abruptly write off southern nationalism as ephemeral and superficial is to minimise the complexity of the past.

As Drew Gilpin Faust has reminded us, when considering the idea of a southern nation, 'historians have fallen into the trap of using nationalism as a valuative rather than a descriptive concept'.[3] We must seek an objective assessment of southern nationalism, one which moves beyond the military and institutional failure of the Confederacy and the uncomfortable pro-slavery connotations that accepting its legitimacy presents. Gary Gallagher has written that it 'defies modern understanding', that a society with a majority of non-slave-holding yeomen would fight with such energy for a cause 'tainted by the institution of slavery. Yet the Confederate people did so.'[4] Presented below are an evaluation of claims for a distinctly southern nation both before and during the Civil War and a brief discussion of the impact this had on the South and the US as a whole. It is to be argued that whilst the antebellum South represented a strong sectional identity it was through the trials of war that this sectionalism grew into a Confederate nationalism. This nationalism, however, remained ultimately incomplete, not only because of the military defeat of the South but also because of its failure to effectively deal with the internal tensions of the region.

There are two dominant definitions of nationalism in the modern world. Ethnic nationalism, the like of which broke up Yugoslavia and the old Soviet Union, sees people define themselves by factors such as biological similarities, language, religion and culture. Civic nationalism, however, is based on a belief in common citizenship and allegiance to the institutions of government from which that citizenship emanates.[5] For much of its existence the United States has embraced civic nationalism, although this was constructed around an ethnic core. Indeed, the lack of distinctiveness in terms of eighteenth-century Americans' culture and language compared with their colonial masters in England is highlighted by Benedict Anderson when he refers to America as a 'creole state ... formed and led by people who shared a common language and common descent with those against whom they fought'.[6] The American colonists shared a cultural heritage and language with their mother country and fought to preserve the rights of liberty which had their ideological roots in the European Enlightenment. Yet even during the colonial period some southern leaders spoke of a cultural difference between the North and the South.

Certainly there is evidence of a strong myth that the antebellum South had a significantly different cultural and racial identity from the North. This myth indulged in a romanticism which viewed upper-class southerners as English cavaliers who maintained the ideals of honour and dignity whilst glorifying the southern belle.[7] A white ethnic nationalism was crafted from the belief that the southern elite were descended from the Norman conquerors while the northern Yankee traced his lineage back to the conquered Anglo-Saxons. Southern writers like William Simms and Nathaniel Tucker looked back to the revolutionary era as a time when deference, respect and hierarchy reigned. They too associated with the ideal of the southern Cavalier and looked with scorn towards the northern Yankee.[8] Southern nationalists, like *Review* editor, James De Bow, emphasised the cultural distinctiveness of the South but also, somewhat self-consciously, called for the region to grow and develop in competition with the North.[9] Indeed this comparison with the North is important as it was northerners who also contributed to the myth of a distinctly separate South. A growing northern identity was shaped in large part by a critique of the South. Representations of that region were not always critical, however. Charles Willis viewed the southern planter elite as a 'chivalrous blend of Old world charm and honour'. Many northern travellers conveyed an uncertainty about the materialism of the North and some saw the South as the region that more closely represented true American values.[10]

Although Americans clearly felt these distinctive regional differences in the antebellum period, we cannot deny significant similarities between North and South or the fact that southern society did not evolve in complete isolation to the rest of the nation. 'Southerners, of every sort, from the eighteenth century to the present, lived at the intersection of many lines of influence.'[11] There is very little evidence of a distinctly separate southern culture. In fact claims of a southern cultural distinctiveness sprang from the leaders of a region that felt threatened by an increasingly assertive northern section. White southerners were on the defensive and their response was to use elements of existing Anglo-American culture to paint a picture of themselves as a separate and unique people with their own civilisation.[12] Southerners' imaginings of themselves as unique and separate were real, however, and southern leaders played on this. As an astute observer of the South wrote, 'the politician universally succeeds in the measure in which he is able to embody, in deeds or in words, the essence, not of what his clients are strictly, but of their dream of themselves'.[13]

The principal cause of southern defensiveness and the driving force behind their perceptions of a distinct civilisation was slavery. At every turn the southern nationalist impulse was linked to the peculiar institution. Nationhood represents, in many respects, an 'imagined community'. Members of that community do not meet all other members; they are widely geographically dispersed and yet they still identify with one another.[14] The four million African-Americans in the South were excluded from citizenship but their presence, and more specifically slavery, was the crucial factor in southerners' imaginings of themselves as separate from the North. The existence of slavery also provided conflicting loyalties for inhabitants of the South. Loyalty to the Union increasingly competed with loyalty to the maintenance of the southern slave system as a vocal anti-slavery opinion grew in the North. Northern slavery had been gradually abolished and attacks on the peculiar southern institution painted a picture of slave-holding as a particular problem of that region. A notion which irked southerners as slavery was categorically not their invention alone.

Certainly, though, the South enjoyed the economic benefits of slavery – as indeed did northerners whose interests were linked to the institution. In the decade between 1850 and 1860 investment in slaves was as profitable as investing capital in railroads or cotton mills. Under competent management slave labour had an irresistible ability to displace free labour in competition for rich soils which were accessible to markets. The South had a valuable export surplus in cotton, rice, sugar and to a lesser extent tobacco. It was highly improbable that free white labour would have produced these crops in the quantity that the slave system did.[15] Dr Nott argued in 1851 that 'Negro slavery has become a part of our very being; our natural prosperity and domestic happiness are inseparable from it.'[16] In 1860, South Carolinian Democrat John S. Preston asserted, 'Slavery is our king – slavery is our truth – slavery is our Divine Right.'[17]

The South was increasingly fearful of abolitionist criticisms of the southern slave system and the growing power of anti-slavery feeling among northern politicians. John Brown's raid in 1859 sent shock waves through Dixie, and the rise of the Republican Party as the majority voice in the North, although it was not only committed to the non-extension of slavery, was observed with great trepidation in the South. Throughout the antebellum period the region had been prepared to defend slavery and southern rights and liberties within the Union. The South as a minority section of the nation punched above its weight in the national political arena. Parties in the South prospered by assuring voters that they protected the rights of southerners and the maintenance of slavery. The election of Lincoln in 1860, however, forced southerners to face a new difficulty in reconciling the conflicting loyalties to the Union and the South. Confronted by this tension many chose their region over the Union. This choice emerged, to an extent, from a shared belief in distinct southern interests. As David Potter argued, 'if the members of a population are sufficiently persuaded that they have cause to be a unified group, the conviction itself may unify them, and thus produce the nationalism which it appears to reflect'.[18]

Nevertheless, as a minority movement the southern secession impulse can be viewed as sectional rather than national. Motivated by the preservation of slavery the imagined political community of the South can be seen as a rebellious divergence from the American nationalism as defined by the North. The North, however, was sectional too. When Republican spokesmen attacked the economic backwardness of slavery and the South's refusal to honour the dignity of labour, they too were expressing a sectional message.[19] A sense of northern sectionalism grew out of a comparison with the South. Focussing on the powerful enemy of the despotic southern plantation gentleman allowed the diverse elements of northern identity to gain a degree of cohesion.[20] Whilst in the South sectional forces tended to pull the region further away from the Union, especially after the rise of the Republicans, in the North sectionalism generally supported the Union. The sectional impulses of the North led it towards a desire for strong Union since these sectional forces were best served by such a strong national attachment. Northern anti-slavery feeling could be confident of eventual success inside the existing polity because of its majority position, which was the reason why pro-slavery southerners were increasingly sure that secession was necessary.[21] Northern sectional interests were best served by maintenance of the Union, and northern victory in the Civil War ensured that northern sectionalism became, in large part, American nationalism.

The bonds of nationalism in antebellum America were, therefore, 'elastic'.[22] This is an apt term because of the divergence of the North and the South from the same common reference point. Neither were fully united in their distinct nationalist impulses in the antebellum period; they both experienced internal tensions. The Revolution of 1776 and the Constitution provided the cornerstone of American civic national identity, but they were increasingly interpreted differently either side of the Mason–Dixon Line. Antebellum America saw a crisis of nationalism in the sense that the nation was afflicted by two strong forms of sectionalism which stretched the fabric of American national identity. The Civil War snapped the elastic bond and the nation was then bound up by a predominantly northern interpretation of the transformed American polity.

Crucial to the development of these competing interpretations of the nation's development was slavery and it was the peculiar institution which was decisive in the secessionist impulse. Southerners were increasingly fearful of a northern attack on slavery and secessionist leaders played on and stoked this fear. Leading southern fire-eaters like Robert Barnwell Rhett came to realise that it was the slavery issue which could be best utilised to unite the South behind secession.[23] Throughout the 1850s southern political leaders put the question of slavery before the electorate of white slave holders and non-slave holders. 'The overwhelming response was that slavery and slave-holding rights should be defended with the utmost vigilance'.[24] This issue alone, however, was not decisive. Only seven southern states seceded before Fort Sumter and they failed to persuade others to join them until after that event. The peculiar institution was not in itself enough to forge a tangible nationalism.

Furthermore, the southern secessionist movement was led by a minority who had the largest stake in the maintenance of slavery. It was not a mass movement which immediately commanded the allegiance of the majority of the southern population. The minority turned secession into a ratification on the right of states to protect their sovereignty against a powerful and threatening federal government. In this way the movement saw 'a secessionist minority ... force the southern majority's hand on the expediency of secession'.[25] In many respects the secession process was one of persuasion. Although to a large degree they were all motivated by the potential threat to slavery posed by a Republican administration, the fire-eaters themselves did not share a coherent definition of southern nationalism. While men like Edmund Ruffin and Nathaniel Tucker saw the South in terms of a distinct cultural and racial identity other fire-eaters such as William Yancey and Robert Rhett realised that southern whites were not united on the fundamental issues of slavery and secession. They called for southern cohesion and secession in terms of political expediency and *realpolitik*.[26]

Inherent in the fire-eaters' rhetoric was a contradiction that revealed the internal tensions of the South. By raising fears of a slave revolt and disharmony in the South which would be the result of 'Black Republican' rule, the secession leaders were implicitly denying the harmony and homogeneity of the region which they believed constituted a separate nation. The more the secessionists warned of the tyranny of the North, the more they revealed of the tyranny of the South. The new state constitution of Georgia, which was ratified following secession, created a 'patriarchal republic'. The new governing document reduced the freedom and the democratic rights of the mass of the non-slave-holding white population of the state.[27] This change was reflective of the internal crisis of the South; it was not the homogeneous, organic nation that many spokesmen argued it was. Many southern moderates despised the virulent pro-slavery ideologues almost as much as they did the abolitionists. A significant number of southern ex-Whigs favoured a strong, industrial and united American nation and they were integral to the 'new South' movement of the post-bellum years.[28] The existence of such sentiments was a worry to secessionists who saw the possibility of ground in the South which would prove fertile for Republican Party policies. Secession was a difficult process and one which attempted to force a nation into being.

Therefore the idealised vision of a southern white nation bound together by a commitment to preserve slavery only told half of the story. A distinct southern sectional identity did exist in the antebellum period but it was during the Civil War that nationalism fully emerged. This conflict saw the disparate members of the South's imagined community brought more fully into contact as warfare and nationalism acted in a mutually reinforcing process. Furthermore, recognition of the internal divisions in the antebellum South made the leaders of the Confederacy aware of the need to build a national identity. 'From the start Confederate nationalism was self-conscious. The building of national unity, like the creation of a winning army, was a problem southerners had to meet.'[29] This construction process was inextricably linked to the experiences of war. As Anne Sarah Rubin pertinently observed, the 'Confederacy willed itself into being'.[30] The Confederate nation reached deeper into the hearts of its people as the war continued and this helps explain why the conflict lasted as long as it did.[31] America was born in the midst of a struggle against the British, competing colonies were bound together in common cause. The internal divisions of the South which had precluded the emergence of a unified response to the election of Lincoln were, to an extent, subordinated to the desire to fight on against the northern enemy.

The Confederacy inspired incredible devotion to its cause in terms of sheer human sacrifice. It mobilised 75–85 per cent of its draft age white military population and roughly one in three men died in uniform. In comparison the North mobilised 50 per cent and one in six died.[32] Certainly the northern population as a whole was larger and, except briefly when Lee invaded Pennsylvania, it did not face military occupation or significant fighting on its soil. It is also true, however, that the North did not have to contend with the need to leave a portion of men at home for the purposes of slave supervision. In this context the military effort of southern soldiers and the strong feelings of national purpose that motivated them are impressive. It was not only men who devoted themselves to the Confederate national cause. Southern women in many cases matched their men in expressions of patriotism. Although diaries and letters provide examples of women conveying war-weariness, they did not reject the Confederacy itself. Women channelled their nationalistic energies into nursing, sewing and aid societies. They also played a vital role in shaming men into doing their patriotic duty.[33] Some women even expressed their own patriotism in martial terms. In 1864, for example, Secretary of War James Seddon received a petition by 28 women angry at Sheridan's victories over Early in the Shenandoah Valley. They asked to raise a regiment of ladies armed for service and ready 'to endure any sacrifice ... for the ultimate success of our Holy Cause'.[34]

This religious element to Confederate nationalism was also important. Southerners believed themselves to be the most Godly Americans. For many southerners, nationalism was something of a crusade and the

Confederacy was seen to have the divine favour of God, replacing the United States as a new redeemer nation. Jefferson Davis called for days of fasting and prayer on nine occasions during the war as Confederate nationalism was wedded to a higher power.[35] Davis himself, however, was limited as a spokesman for, and leader of, his nation. His conservatism and the lack of a viable two-party system in the South meant that he did not have to articulate his national aims in the same way that Lincoln was required to do. Nor did Davis possess the same ability to shape public opinion as Lincoln.[36] Increasingly it was General Robert E. Lee and his Army of Northern Virginia which came to embody and inspire Confederate nationalism. A significant number of the officers of the force were young slave-holding men who had been in the vanguard of the secessionist movement. Lee and his army, in their continual defiance of northern troops, won the hearts and minds of the Confederate people. Just as Washington and his army had inspired patriotism during the American War of Independence so Lee's army evoked patriotic feelings among southerners.[37]

This focus on the battlefield and martial glory did, however – as it would later during America's post-bellum reconciliation – deflect attention from the internal struggles of the South. Confederate leaders presented their new nation as a continuance of the ideal of 1776 and 1787 whilst it appeared as a process of separation from, and discontinuity with, that heritage. More importantly, in a society where the majority of white citizens were not slave holders, Confederate leaders had to craft a nationalism which was clearly linked to the preservation of slavery. They had to make their minority interest synonymous with a national interest.[38] In this respect the construction of Confederate nationalism was a process of persuasion in the same way that the secessionist movement had been. Whilst the trials of war evoked considerable patriotic devotion among southerners for their cause against northern armies, the social and economic fault lines in southern society caused by slavery undermined the permanence of Confederate nationalism. It can be argued that this nationalism was as much, if not more, defined by the shared experience of fighting *against* a loathed common enemy as it was fighting *for* a truly shared vision of the South, because that vision was contested.

The tensions of the antebellum South had a continued impact on Confederate nationalism. Slavery was intrinsically linked to Confederate citizenship. The peculiar institution was not viewed as a stigma in a predominantly anti-slavery world but instead it was portrayed as a positive good in southern school textbooks and in popular literature. The lyrics of the Confederate anthem, Dixie, emphasised that the slaves wished to live and die in 'de land ob cotton'.[39] As the war dragged on into 1864 debate in the Confederacy began concerning the possibility of arming the slaves in order to help with the military effort. The desire to win independence, therefore, had the potential to destroy the very institution which secessionists had sought to preserve. With thousands of white yeoman dying on the battlefield, slave holders acknowledged the possibility of a sacrifice on their part, namely the potential loss of property. The war quickened the pace of confrontation between competing forces inside the South as 'Confederate nationalism prescribed change in the service of continuity'.[40] In 1865 the Confederate Congress did pass measures which allowed for some slaves to be engaged in military activity in return for gradual emancipation. This decision to make real a recurring southern nightmare – armed slaves – showed the depth of southern commitment to their nation and also the complexities of Confederate national identity.[41] Confederate leaders argued that secession was needed to protect the true ideals of the founding fathers and the uniquely southern way of life, but the nationalism that emerged during the war necessitated change in order to establish independence.

Southern nationalism had long struggled with the internal tensions of the region caused by the peculiar institution. Post-war expressions of southern identity attempted to neutralise these tensions. Celebrations of the Confederate tradition in the post-bellum era and the myth of the Lost Cause were used to stabilise the New South. National reconciliation embraced a lily-white interpretation of the Civil War and downplayed the issues of race that were central to its origins. The celebrations of the Confederacy in the period after the war embraced martial glory and the eventual victory for American nationalism. In this way defeat for the South did not provoke soul searching on the morality of slavery or the future of race relations. As a result, 'the Confederate celebration did not so much sacralize the memory of the war as it sanitized and trivialized it'.[42] The romantic, mythical vision of the Confederacy, and its failed attempt to create an independent southern nation, obscured the difficult racial issues which helped undermine that attempt.

The experience of the Confederacy, therefore, had a significant impact on the post-bellum identity of the South. During the war the popular press and the rhetoric of southern leaders had encouraged those below the Mason–Dixon Line to invest their maximum effort in the cause of independence; after the conflict a similar effort was called for to rebuild the South. As southerners embraced the Union once more and engaged politically and economically with the reunified

American polity, they did not abandon the sense of distinctiveness that bound their imagined community together. White southern identity continued to be shaped by the experience of the Confederacy as men and women of the South settled for a compromise. They ceded 'their political independence while continuing to preserve a distinctive social and cultural identity'.[43] This identity embraced a racial status quo which bequeathed a divisive legacy not only for the South but the nation as a whole.

The maintenance of slavery was the driving force behind the secessionist impulse but the war that this caused exposed the tensions inside the South surrounding the peculiar institution. The system of slavery was eventually destroyed by the conflict but an overwhelming white southern commitment to a society based on racial hierarchy survived undimmed. Southern nationalism remained incomplete. An independent South proved elusive both because of the region's internal contradictions and the military superiority of the North. This did not mean that Confederate nationalism was not real or that southerners did not display tremendous patriotism in trying to establish independence. The uncomfortable truth that slavery was inextricably linked to this southern patriotism has troubled many historians. As Gary Gallagher contends, 'the aroma of moral disapprobation envelops most arguments denying the existence of Confederate nationalism'.[44] It is, however, an appreciation of this nationalism which provides a crucial link to understanding race relations in the period since the Civil War.

8

LINCOLN AND LIBERTY

During the national emergency of the Civil War Lincoln assumed presidential powers which produced debates over constitutionality. These disputes were manifold among contemporaries of the President and have been explored by historians in the period since. The ambiguity of the Constitution has ensured that it was not only Lincoln who faced questions over the constitutional legitimacy of his actions. Andrew Jackson's frequent use of the veto and expansive view of his role as president caused opponents to call him 'King Andrew'. Before America officially entered the Second World War, Roosevelt started a quasi-war in the North Atlantic and during the conflict he authorised the internment of Japanese-Americans. Historians have explored from where he received his authority to act in such cases.[1] An open letter from scholars of constitutional law to members of Congress in 2006 seriously criticised President Bush's domestic wiretapping programme. The argument concluded, 'the President cannot simply violate criminal laws behind closed doors because he deems them obsolete or impracticable'.[2]

Scrutiny of Lincoln's policies revolves around the concepts of liberty, rights and the power of the federal government. The focus of this chapter is the impact of these issues on Lincoln's policies on the Union home front. The discussion will centre mainly on liberty, its restriction and its expansion. Given the great dangers afflicting the republic during the Civil War one cannot help but wonder at the judicious judgement and faith in democracy that Lincoln showed. He did preside over a system of domestic security which restricted liberty – certainly as it was conceived by the revolutionary generation. Lincoln, however, also played a significant part in a shifting interpretation of liberty which was to have profound consequences for the future of the United States.[3] Lincoln argued in December of 1862 that by 'giving freedom to the slave, we assure freedom to the free – honourable alike in what

we give, and what we preserve'.[4] Crucially, Lincoln's management of
the Union war effort pointed to a new conception of liberty with a
truly moral reading of the Constitution at its centre. This was to have
a significant impact on the struggle by racial minorities to attain full
citizenship in the post-bellum years.

During his presidency Lincoln was seen by many in the southern
states as the enemy of liberty. From the vantage point of those in the
Confederacy he was the leader of an oppressive regime which sought to
destroy their freedoms. Theirs was a liberty conceived in the revolutionary period which acted to limit the powers of central government
and restrict its ability to reach into the lives of the country's citizens.
Jefferson was perhaps the most vocal of the revolutionary leaders in his
support for states' rights against an oppressive federal government and
elucidated his position in the Virginia and Kentucky Resolutions of
1798. The Confederate Constitution was founded on this states' rights
heritage and ensured that the central government was expressly prohibited from interfering in the rights of the states and the liberty of
the people in them.[5] The ultimate expression of state sovereignty came
in the act of southern secession. During the secession winter there was
a widespread belief in the North that the South had the right to leave
the Union under the philosophy of the Declaration of Independence.
Several Republican newspapers expressed the opinion that the South
had the same rights as the colonies in 1776.[6]

Lincoln, however, refused to see secession as legitimate. Far from a
genuine expression of liberty, Lincoln pointed to the southern attempt
to destroy the Union as a dangerous repudiation of the self-governing
experiment itself. He argued that it was the Confederacy that chose
the path of tyranny when it attempted to secede. According to the
President, 'rejecting the majority principle, anarchy, or despotism in
some form, is all that is left'.[7] Lincoln believed it was he who was
protecting the ideas of the founders, he who was protecting the Constitution. The leaders of the Confederacy, however, viewed Lincoln as
the real tyrant – a figure who sought to forcibly reunite the country
through a war of immense bloodshed.[8] Thomas J. DiLorenzo is the
scholar who most aggressively criticises Lincoln's record. He argues
that the South had a constitutional right to secede and that Lincoln
was in no way justified in prosecuting a war which killed 300,000
citizens to bring the South back into the Union.[9]

It was not only southerners who saw Lincoln as a leader who stood
against liberty. One northern Democrat pamphlet published in opposition to Lincoln argued 'the people of this country may demand the
impeachment of the President himself for the exercise of arbitrary

power'.[10] Undoubtedly Lincoln did display an expansive interpretation of his executive authority. By imposing a blockade of the Confederacy he assumed authority previously believed to require a declaration of war. When he called for volunteers to enlarge the army he was assuming the power of Congress to raise armies. Lincoln also ordered public money be spent on defence without congressional approval and he instructed the commanding General of the Army to suspend the writ of habeas corpus. Description of this suspension lay in the article of the Constitution outlining the powers of Congress and to many commentators Lincoln was stretching its original intent by suspending the writ using executive power.[11] The President told the special congressional session that his actions were necessary to maintain the Union and rhetorically enquired, 'must a government, of necessity, be too strong for the liberties of its own people, or too weak to maintain its own existence?'[12]

Lincoln was certainly no dictator but civil liberties were infringed more significantly in the North than they ever were in the South. Jefferson Davis suspended civil liberties with the approval of the Confederate Congress and had the authority to suspend the writ of habeas corpus for only sixteen months. Indeed the Confederate President did not use his war powers as Commander-in-Chief as extensively as did his counterpart in Washington.[13] After the initial suspension of the writ of habeas corpus in April 1862, the Lincoln administration moved further in the restriction of civil liberties three months later. Secretary of War Stanton issued, with Lincoln's approval, orders on 8 August which were designed to ensure adherence to the Militia Act of the previous month. The writ of habeas corpus was suspended across the whole country and arrests were made of anyone evading the draft or trying to discourage the Union war effort in any way. Mark Neely describes the period of arrests that followed as 'the lowest point for civil liberties in U.S. history to that time, and one of the lowest for civil liberties in all of American history. It showed the Lincoln administration at its worst – amateurish, disorganised and rather unfeeling.'[14]

The orders of 8 August led to a number of judgements on the loyalty or otherwise of numerous northern citizens. One individual who was subject to this process was Dr Israel Blanchard of Illinois. He was arrested on the strength of evidence that he had attended a meeting of the Copperhead organisation called the Knights of the Golden Circle. Copperheads opposed the northern war effort. Whilst Blanchard sat in the Old Capitol prison in Washington, Lincoln read a letter from Democrat politician John Logan that testified to Blanchard's faith in the Union cause and to the physical impossibility of his having attended the Copperhead meeting. The President gave instructions for Blanchard to be released. He was a lucky member of the group of 354 civilians who were arrested in the month after the 8 August orders. The number of arrests eventually went down, though, as the orders were relaxed in early September.[15]

In March of 1863 Congress passed the Habeas Corpus Act which gave congressional approval to the suspension of the writ. The legislation was ambiguous in the sense that it did not clearly decide whether presidential actions had been legal before the Act or were only made legal by the Act. On 15 September 1863 Secretary of State Seward drafted a proclamation for Lincoln which affirmed the fact that the writ of habeas corpus was suspended throughout the country. In justifications of the policy Lincoln made no reference to the Habeas Corpus Act and in his proclamation spelled out the constitutionality of his suspension of the writ which he argued could be modified or revoked at any time during the rebellion.[16] The inference being that the President did not believe he needed congressional approval.

One of the most high-profile arrests was that of Ohio Democrat Clement Vallandigham, who was an outspoken critic of the Republican administration. He was arrested by General Ambrose on 1 May 1863 and sentenced the following day to imprisonment for the rest of the war. Vallandigham was denounced as a traitor after a pro-compromise and pro-peace speech and continued opposition to Lincoln's policies, especially emancipation. Lincoln defended the arrest in a letter to his Democratic opponents the following month. The President argued that his actions were constitutional stating that the suspension of habeas corpus was allowed by the Constitution so that 'men may be arrested, who cannot be proved to be guilty of defined crimes, when in cases of rebellion or invasion the public safety may require it'.[17] Pointing to Vallandigham's statements encouraging evasion of the draft and desertion from the Union army, Lincoln asked 'must I shoot a simple-minded soldier boy who deserts, while I must not touch the hair of a wily agitator who induces him to desert?'[18]

Although Lincoln defended the arrest of Vallandigham it was not the sort of incident which he believed the suspension of habeas corpus should lead to. Lincoln was privately disappointed that Ambrose acted as he did. The President was tolerant of the Democrat press and his political opponents. He did not wish to punish those who were guilty only of exercising free speech and providing legitimate opposition. Realising the danger of creating a martyr, Lincoln commuted Vallandigham's sentence to banishment to the Confederacy and then largely ignored the ex-congressman when he returned to the North illegally.[19] Frank Klement has argued that the Republican administration used the suspension of habeas corpus to wage political war against the Democrat Copperhead organisations which opposed Lincoln's prosecution of the conflict. He points to trumped-up charges against leading Democrat spokesmen and arrests on the eve of election campaigns in order to provide political gain for the Republicans.[20] This was not, however, the purpose of the orders to suspend the writ of habeas corpus. Their purpose was specific: to prevent draft resistance. The vast majority of the arrests had nothing to do with political opposition and dissent but it is these cases which have gained most historical coverage.[21]

Lincoln faced regular criticism of his policies on habeas corpus. Chief Justice Taney prepared a number of undelivered opinions which called into question the constitutional basis for the President's actions.[22] Nevertheless, Lincoln cared deeply about constitutional principle and he was sure of his authority to act. With this commitment as his guide he suspended civil liberties with the sole objective of improving the fortunes of the Union army. Lincoln did not, as lesser men may have, contemplate perverting the democratic process. In August 1864, with the northern war effort stalled, Lincoln wrote a memorandum in which he stated, 'it seems exceedingly probable that this administration will not be re-elected'.[23] Even at his lowest ebb he showed faith in the electoral process and was prepared to abide by the decision of the people.

The President was therefore confronted by a Democratic political opposition throughout the war as the two-party system continued in the North. The extent to which this system helped or hindered the northern war effort has long been debated by historians. Key to Lincoln's political skill, however, was the way he and his party shaped a clear message to gain public support for the Union war aims. The Republicans – known as the Union Party throughout the war – sought to build on a long legacy of anti-party feeling in the US. They adopted an 'anti-party nationalism' and mobilised support not through appeals to partisan loyalty but by calling for national political unity and therefore discrediting the Democrats as unpatriotic. Lincoln's great skill was in rallying and shaping popular support for his policies and he regularly did this through the language of anti-partisanship and national unity.[24]

This strategy was particularly important in relation to the issue of emancipation. Perhaps the most violent expression of resistance to Lincoln's wartime policies was provided by the New York City draft riots of July 1863. Described by Stephen Oates as 'a macabre episode, a three-day orgy of violence which sickened Lincoln to read about it', the riots saw poor whites burn down draft offices and hang blacks from lamp-posts before incinerating them.[25] New York Governor Horatio Seymour, already a vocal critic of Lincoln, called on the President to stop his policies of conscription and emancipation. Although part of a longer-term pattern of racial tension which was heightened by the use of black strike-breakers some months before, to a large extent the riots reflected a rage against Lincoln's policy of emancipation.[26] This policy laid the foundations for a shifting interpretation of liberty in America's future and a moral reading of the Constitution.

Lincoln's antebellum public statements had revealed him to be avowedly anti-slavery, but he was also a realist and a constitutionalist. Lincoln understood that moving too quickly would damage northern support for the war effort and may push the border states into the ranks of the Confederacy. Lincoln had disappointed radicals when he revoked the policies of Butler and Fremont which had been aimed at giving freedom to and arming slaves that were encountered by Union troops. He was aware of signs of resistance to Republican policies. In 1862 Stanton's decision to establish a contraband camp in Illinois and hire out black labourers caused uproar in southern districts of the state.[27] The President was aware he had to tread carefully. He believed, however, he had the constitutional authority as Commander-in-Chief to free slaves as a war measure and came to a decision by June 1862 that emancipation was a policy he would pursue.[28] Lincoln warned a delegation of border states' congressmen in July that if they did not agree to a compensated emancipation programme then the slaves would go free because of the 'mere friction and abrasion' of the war effort and they would receive no monetary compensation.[29]

What would happen to the slaves who went free was the subject of talks with a black delegation in August 1862. At this meeting Lincoln endorsed policies of colonisation as he had done in his earlier political career. Indeed Lincoln went so far as to ask for a constitutional amendment to facilitate colonisation of Haiti in late 1862. Since the subject of this chapter is Lincoln and the concept of liberty these proposals appear as evidence for the President's limited concept of freedom for African-Americans. They could go free but could not exercise liberty alongside the predominantly white population. This, however, ignores the purpose served by Lincoln's discussion of colonisation. His contemplation of the scheme is reflective of his own intellectual struggle with the issue of black equality and, more importantly, it served the purpose of softening the impact of emancipation on public opinion.[30]

Lincoln's letter to Horace Greeley in August 1862 again shows Lincoln attempting to shape public responses to the policy. Lincoln argued the war aims were not changing, that his 'paramount object' was to save the Union. 'If I could save the Union without freeing any slave I would do it, and if I could save it by freeing all the slaves I would do it.'[31] On the advice of Seward, Lincoln waited until after the Union victory – of sorts – at Antietam before issuing his Preliminary Emancipation Proclamation on 22 September 1862. This stated that the slaves of the states still in rebellion on 1 January 1863 would go free. In the mid-term elections of that year the Democrats accused Lincoln of breaking the Constitution and the Republicans suffered losses at the polls. Conservatives in his own party urged Lincoln to withdraw the plan but the President stood firm. He had, in fact, followed a course which steered a middle path between conservative and radical opinion and he explained that he was taking the step using his powers as Commander-in-Chief.[32] Certainly the Constitution gives the President the power during war to direct the military effort and confiscation of the enemies' slaves was legal under international law.[33]

Critics of the Emancipation Proclamation have pointed to the limited number of slaves it actually set free and the failure to define the nature or meaning of their freedom. Others have pointed to the questionable longevity of the action. Lincoln himself admitted in February 1865 that his proclamation was a war measure and therefore would not necessarily remain in effect following the cessation of conflict, at which point the courts may decide that the slaves were not free.[34] Referring to the limited reach of the Emancipation Proclamation, the British Prime Minister, Palmerston, called the measure 'trash' and foreign opinion was generally unimpressed.[35] Whilst the majority of abolitionists declared their work done after Lincoln signed the proclamation, others felt the President had done too little too late. Critics condemned Lincoln for refusing to allow anti-slavery generals to accelerate emancipation in occupied areas of the South.[36] The proclamation did not apply to the nearly half a million slaves in the border states and, because it only applied to areas under Confederate control, it did not free the three hundred thousand slaves in Union-occupied areas of the South. The Sea Islands of South Carolina were not exempt, however, from the emancipation order and here more than ten thousand slaves were indeed freed with a stroke of the President's pen.[37]

As Lincoln continued to defend his policy to the northern public and answer the attacks of his political opponents he displayed that his commitment to emancipation was steadfast. Lincoln's gradual approach was chosen because he believed that it was true to the ideas of the Founding Fathers and because he thought it was the best way of maintaining progress.[38] What was driving his approach, however, was a deep commitment to the ideal of equality expressed in the Declaration of Independence. 'Lincoln's attachment to the Declaration was neither temporary nor merely expedient.' In an extemporaneous speech to well-wishers in July 1863, the President affirmed that the Union forces were fighting for the ideal that all men were created equal and that the Confederates were the enemies of the Declaration.[39]

As the war turned further in favour of the North, Lincoln asserted more strongly his commitment to black freedom. In a letter to be read at a Republican rally in August 1863 he argued, 'if they [black men] stake their lives for us, they must be prompted by the strongest motive – even the promise of freedom. And the promise being made, must be kept.'[40] Lincoln threw support behind a constitutional amendment to end slavery which he insisted was included in the Republican platform of 1864 and saw his electoral victory as vindication of his emancipation policy. In the final draft of the Emancipation Proclamation there was no mention of colonisation and Lincoln dropped the idea thereafter.[41] The President also moved tentatively towards a plan to give at least some blacks the same political rights as white men. Furthermore, he signed a bill which set up a Bureau of Freedman's Affairs and so accepted that the government had some responsibility for the needs of the freed people.[42] In his Gettysburg Address Lincoln referred to the Declaration of Independence as the guiding light of his values on liberty and equality. He portrayed the struggle to maintain the Union as a struggle to preserve the ideal of equality and connected the promises of 1776 with the formation of the Constitution as essential elements in the self-governing experiment.[43] In his second Inaugural Address Lincoln moved to a position which saw slavery as the fundamental cause of the war and its destruction the will of the Almighty. The President asserted that God intended 'to remove [slavery] and he gives to both North and South this terrible war, as the woe due' to those complicit in the peculiar institution.[44]

Lincoln was the central figure in the changing meaning of the Union war effort and he was central to a shifting notion of liberty in America. During an address in Baltimore in 1864, Lincoln declared, 'the world has never had a good definition of the word liberty, and the American people, just now, are much in want of one'. He then told a parable of a flock of sheep stalked by a wolf but protected by a shepherd. When the shepherd drives the wolf away the sheep thank him 'as a liberator, while the wolf denounces him for the same act as the destroyer of liberty, especially as the sheep was a black one'.[45] James

McPherson, using the conceptual framework of Isaiah Berlin, has argued that Lincoln was articulating a radical shift in the American conception of liberty. A shift from negative liberty, defined as the freedom from government interference, to positive liberty, defined as freedom for the government to intervene and protect liberty. It is argued that Lincoln initiated a process which expanded the power of the federal government to protect liberty, the most visible expressions of which were the Thirteenth, Fourteenth and Fifteenth Amendments.[46]

Although his ideas have merit they are not immune from criticism, some of which hits the mark. Firstly, it is difficult to see Lincoln at the vanguard of a revolutionary change in the conception of liberty because by the mid-1870s America had retreated to a position which largely endorsed negative liberty. Supreme Court decisions in that decade through to the end of the nineteenth century restricted the power of the federal government to interfere with the states in areas of civil rights and personal freedom. Secondly, the Fourteenth Amendment especially can be interpreted in some ways as an expression of negative liberty. The amendment states that no citizen shall have their 'privileges or immunities' abridged by the state. In other words citizens were guaranteed freedom from interference. The ambiguity of the amendment's language allowed the Court to decide that states should be safeguarded from federal interference in their laws and so Congress was not given the power to ensure the freedom of citizens. It was a new twentieth-century reading of the amendment which saw the true birth of positive liberty. Finally, by seeing Lincoln and the Republicans as revolutionary, McPherson asserts that the secessionists were conservative and it was they that protected the Constitution. If this is the case then Lincoln's faith in the Declaration of Independence and its connection to the Constitution appears significantly blurred.[47]

In pointing to these criticisms of McPherson it is not my intention to reduce the important part Lincoln played in a shifting conception of liberty and the impact of this; it is merely to question how revolutionary he was and so suggest a different form of change. Lincoln extended liberty to millions of black people and so expanded freedom. Furthermore, Lincoln articulated a vision, based on America's heritage and future promise, of a nation founded less on blood and race and more on the ideals of liberty and equality.[48] This liberty was rooted in the ideal that all men were created equal and that they should be free to enjoy equal status in life. Lincoln believed the ideals of the Founding Fathers to be sacred and saw his role as President to defend both the Declaration of Independence and the Constitution. Although eleven years passed between the two documents they were inextricably linked and achieving the ideals of the Declaration meant protecting the Constitution. When Lincoln's critics argued he was restricting liberty by abridging individual freedom through suspension of the writ of habeas corpus, he believed he was working inside the parameters of his constitutional authority. He was doing so in order to save the self-governing experiment and so fulfil the promises of the Declaration. Moreover, by 'emancipating the Republic from slavery', Lincoln made it possible for Americans' devotion to self-government to 'incorporate the promises of 1776 within the processes of 1787'.[49] This is the crucial shift in the meaning of liberty that Lincoln brought.

In his Gettysburg Address Lincoln looked back to the Founders and forward to the future and expanded a 'new birth of freedom' for America. This new nation was dedicated to the proposition that liberty meant freedom and equality for all men. The history of race relations since Lincoln's death shows that not all Americans were prepared to embrace this vision. The Warren Court of the 1950s and 1960s did, however, try to make the Constitution work for liberty and equality, using a 'moral reading' of the document and a central meaning of 'equal respect for individuals'.[50] There has been no more significant moral reading of the Constitution than that provided by Abraham Lincoln. By expanding the number of those it protected and tying to it the ideal that all men were equal, Lincoln contributed to a significant shift in the concept of liberty. The struggle by American racial minorities to achieve equality in the post-bellum period is closely linked to a contested process during which this concept of liberty was not fully embraced.

9

RECONSTRUCTION
The unfulfilled promise

Twenty years ago Eric Foner wrote,

> from the enforcement of the rights of citizens to the stubborn
> problems of economic and racial justice, the issues central to
> Reconstruction are as old as the American Republic, and as
> contemporary as the inequalities that still afflict our society.[1]

His words are as true now as they were then. Reconstruction witnessed
a hugely significant episode in American history. The need to bring
the nation back together after four years of bloody civil war and to
deal with the racial questions which emerged from emancipation provided massive tasks for the American body politic and a unique epoch
in the history of the United States. One historian has referred to
Reconstruction as the 'Bermuda Triangle of American history, a place
where we lose our bearings, where the usual American stories of progress and success simply do not work'.[2] A tangled web of hope and
failure, of reconciliation and rebellion, the period produced a myriad
of questions, some answered and many unanswered. Not surprisingly
there is a mass of literature on the intricacies and impact of the
Reconstruction period. A comprehensive survey of this work would, I
fear, be beyond the brevity of this essay. As a consequence we will
focus on the impact of Reconstruction on the freedman. This spotlight
will further illuminate one of the main themes of this volume, namely
the progress of racial equality and the development of American citizenship. Furthermore, it will point to the most important area of
promise and disappointment for America during the history of
Reconstruction.

The early twentieth century witnessed the emergence of a history of
Reconstruction that would dominate the historiography of the period
for the next four decades or more. Drawing on the themes of

scholarship in the late nineteenth century, William Dunning's *Recon-struction, Political and Economic, 1865–1877* presented a negative view of the period. Of particular importance for the focus of this chapter, Dunning was extremely critical of the attempt by radical Republican 'carpetbaggers' and their southern 'scalawag' allies to force black suf-frage on the white South. Dunning was scathing in his criticism of Republican idealism, ignoring his editor's pencilling out of his attack on the radical Charles Sumner and painting a picture of Reconstruc-tion as tragic and flawed.[3] Although he was determined not to impose a master interpretation on his students, his influence was such that a 'Dunning school' of Reconstruction emerged. This school viewed the period as 'black', both metaphorically and literally in terms of African-American domination of southern Republican governments.[4]

In 1935, however, African-American historian W.E.B. DuBois interpreted 'black' Reconstruction in an entirely different way. He pointed to the important efforts to bring equal citizenship to African-Americans despite the eventual failure of Republican policy makers.[5] DuBois was the forerunner for a revisionist movement which, spurred by the events of a second reconstruction in the 1960s, dismantled the old Dunning thesis and viewed Reconstruction in much more positive terms. Revisionists replaced racist assumptions and defence of the white South with an approach that looked more favourably upon the intentions of Republican policies.[6] Scholars did, however, challenge this new school of thought, possibly influenced by disillusionment with the modern civil rights movement in the 1970s and 1980s, and sought to question the real progress made during Reconstruction whilst emphasising conservative forces.[7]

Certainly the fortunes and role of the African-American have been given increasing attention by historians of the Reconstruction period.[8] The balance of history has also tipped and the sources created by blacks themselves, often neglected by Dunning and his students, have been utilised to paint a richer picture of the African-American experience during Reconstruction and the consequence of this experience for the construction of race relations. The era of Reconstruction has been described by one historian as a 'perfect litmus test of [the] racial assumptions' of historians.[9] Responding to the burgeoning revisionist literature in the mid-1960s, Thomas Pressly counselled historians to approach the period dispassionately and cautioned that just as Dunning's racist suppositions damaged his work, so strong commitment to racial equality could also produce flawed accounts of the past.[10] Whilst acknowledging this reminder let us turn to an analysis of the impact of Reconstruction on the African-American.

If we look at the fortunes of the freedman chronologically we can see a pattern of response and counter-response between Republican policy makers and their opponents which shaped the experiences of African-Americans. The newly freed slaves were not, though, a passive presence in the Reconstruction story, tossed between Republican attempts to extend freedom and civil rights and the endemic racism of American society. At every turn African-Americans struggled to define the scope of their emancipation and strove towards an equal place in society alongside the neighbours that had enslaved them. Inspired by the revolutionary change in their status the freedmen dreamed of a new and exciting experience. An ex-slave preacher near the Lester plantation in Florida told his audience, 'from now on my brudders an' my sisters, old things have passed away an' all things is bekum new'.[11]

At the war's end the Thirteenth Amendment was passed by Congress and sent to the states for ratification. It provided a defining moment in the history of black Americans because it was this constitutional provision that forever destroyed slavery. This Amendment confirmed the revolutionary change in the status of millions of black southerners as a consequence of the war and the Emancipation Proclamation. The second clause of the amendment gave Congress the power to enforce abolition and its ratification became a requirement of reunion for the former Confederate states. This was, however, very much a beginning as well as an end. Republicans believed that the Thirteenth Amendment would protect the black position as citizens and the rights that came with this.[12] Nevertheless, the significant struggle over the extent to which these rights were going to be protected commenced with the enactment of the Black Codes by many southern states in 1865 and 1866. These codes were an attempt to restrict the mobility and prescribe the extent of the freedman's liberty. 'The inability of the freedmen to function within southern states' legal-judicial systems because of the Black Codes struck to the root of the Thirteenth Amendment.'[13]

President Johnson's plans for Reconstruction gave the southern states freedom to rewrite their constitutions and reinstate the antebellum status quo. The Black Codes which the state legislatures enacted accepted minimal levels of black freedom, which included the right to marry and own property, but importantly they denied the freedmen the right to testify in court against whites, equality before the law and political rights. They also required African-American labourers to sign year-long contracts which restricted their economic independence. Northern journalist, Sidney Andrews, reported 'the whites seem wholly unable to comprehend that freedom for the negro

means the same thing as freedom for them'.[14] The difficulty of reconciling the white majority with the dreams and aspirations of the ex-
slaves was clearly recognised by Republican policy makers. Defining
what liberty was going to mean was a central question of Reconstruction. Did it mean equality? Did it require economic assistance?
Did it mean black suffrage? These questions were not confined only to
African-Americans. There was a wider consideration of the meaning of
citizenship for all Americans. During debates on the Fourteenth
Amendment, for example, Native Americans and women were among
the groups given attention when the measure was being discussed in
Congress. Lincoln's cautious approach before his assassination meant
he had not clearly answered these questions concerning citizenship. The
'new birth of freedom' mentioned in the Gettysburg Address represented the expression of an ideal with no plan for its practical outworking. Indeed many abolitionists themselves were not agreed on
what racial equality meant or whether it was desirable.[15]

On the ground in the South the Freedman's Bureau was instituted
in order to help ex-slaves adjust to their new-found freedom. With
limited financial support and personnel it faced the massively daunt-
ing task of providing immediate relief for the freedmen and, importantly, negotiating labour contracts. With the real decision-making
power held in the hands of local Bureau officials, decisions were often
contradictory and showed deference to influential white landholders.
Although the Bureau had been in a position to make radical changes
in labour relations, invariably it facilitated the emergence of a system
which perpetuated the economic dependency of the ex-slaves.[16] The
head of the Bureau, General Howard, visited freedmen on Edisto Island,
South Carolina, in late 1865 who had taken control of land formerly
owned by planters and appointed their own simple government. Howard
informed them that the planters were to return and reclaim their land
and listened with sorrow as one woman sang the spiritual 'Nobody
knows the trouble I seen'.[17]

These practical problems and the rapid adoption of the Black Codes
by the new southern state constitutions were answered directly by
Republican policy makers when they passed the revised Freedman's
Bureau Bill and the Civil Rights Act in 1866. Congressional debates
on these measures did reveal the reluctance of policy makers to provide
land for southern blacks. Nevertheless, the measures extended federal
authority to protect the freedman. The legislation, which was passed
over Johnson's veto – he argued it was unconstitutional because eleven
southern states did not have representatives sitting in Congress – was
an effort to give meaning to the freedom enshrined in the Thirteenth

Amendment and to directly address the Black Codes' attempt to restrict the parameters of black freedom. The Civil Rights Act was an unprecedented endeavour to define the rights of citizenship. Importantly, however, the federal–state power balance was also safeguarded. The Act presented federal power as latent, only to be triggered by discriminatory state laws. It was the state that would retain its traditional responsibility for law enforcement.[18]

This tension between meaningful extension of civil equality and adherence to traditional constitutional principles was a feature of Republican policy on civil rights. The Fourteenth Amendment, which was ratified in 1868 having been approved two years previous, sought for the first time to guarantee citizenship through birthright and equal rights for all in the Constitution. It also sought to 'abrogate the Black Codes and eliminate any doubts as to the constitutionality of the Civil Rights Act'.[19] Nonetheless, it did not list specific rights and somewhat vaguely prohibited states from denying 'equal protection of the law'.[20] Historians who viewed Reconstruction as a tragic episode argued that because ratification became a condition of southern states' re-admission into the Union the Fourteenth Amendment was unconstitutional. This school of thought saw the Amendment as part of a new Constitution imposed by force.[21] This view is discredited, however, by the fact that Congress's actions were fully considerate of what was acceptable under the original Constitution. Republicans shared the concerns of Democrats about the maintenance of constitutional principles. For example, when later discussing black suffrage it was conceded that the constitutional system gave states the power to determine their own electorate.[22] Revisionist writers emphasised the tension that existed between Republicans' desires to protect the freedman whilst also respecting the existing philosophy behind the Constitution.[23] The vast majority of Republicans supported black equality and the party had been working towards policies to safeguard this for several years prior to the Fourteenth Amendment.[24] Republicans were not, however, seeking to create a radical new Constitution. Instead they aimed to complete the existing document. Through the Reconstruction amendments the principles of liberty and equality in the Declaration of Independence were more effectively implemented in a Constitution which protected the freedom which emerged from the destruction of slavery.[25] In this sense the Amendments were an extension of the moral reading of the Constitution which Lincoln increasingly elucidated during the Civil War.

As Republican policy makers struggled with southern recalcitrance and the obstructions of President Johnson in their efforts to protect black freedom and delineate civil rights, African-Americans engaged in their own grass-roots struggle to define their emancipation. Black and white Republicans lived under the threat of violence and intimidation as the Ku Klux Klan spread into nearly every southern state by 1868. The Klan instigated a reign of terror which was not tackled effectively in the late 1860s because Johnson appointed commanding officers who were opposed to Reconstruction. The local Republican governments struggled to stop the violence.[26] Nevertheless, thousands of black Republicans displayed great bravery by facing down intimidation and turning out to support their party on election days.[27]

Large-scale black political activity began in 1865 because Congress decreed that southern constitutional conventions would be elected on the basis of universal suffrage. Never in the course of human history had so many emancipated slaves been given political rights and by the 1870s previously unknown bi-racial democracies were functioning in the South.[28] In all, sixteen black men represented their southern states in Congress during Reconstruction. Proponents of the Dunning school painted a picture of black domination of politics in the South in a tragic period of chaotic and incompetent government. The blanket conclusion that the freedman was incapable of effective political participation and government does not, however, stand up to historical scrutiny.[29] In Mississippi, for example, blacks did not dominate the political process and representatives very rarely proposed legislation which was designed to gain special privilege for the freedman.[30]

African-Americans expressed their liberty with acts that would not have been possible under slavery. They organised public meetings and associations to campaign for equality and justice. Political organising inside the black community helped put the issue of black suffrage on the national agenda in 1866. Symbolically, freedmen ignored the constraints of their old existence by adopting new forms of dress, rode on horses or in carriages and often refused to step aside for white pedestrians.[31] Northern philanthropists and missionaries moved south after the Civil War in order to help the former slaves adapt to their new-found freedom. Increasingly, though, black southerners broke away from the paternalism of white institutions and created their own community organisations. In the field of religion blacks were reluctant to give up the fervent worship and preaching styles that had sustained them during the period of slavery. White missionaries often disapproved of these practices but blacks regularly chose to break free from the supervision of a white minister and created their own churches. Many ex-slaves escaped what black leader Henry McNeal Turner called the 'white man's foot-kissing party', and proudly built the black churches so central to the black community which emerged in the Reconstruction period.[32]

Whilst the white elite had used religion as a means of social control during the days of slavery they had consciously restricted any efforts to educate the black man. During Reconstruction this elite looked with disdain at the Yankee school teachers who went south to teach the ex-slaves. These educators and the activities of the Freedman's Bureau did much to help lay the foundations for black higher education in the South. Crucial to the emergence of a black school system, however, were black teachers and community leaders who were determined to lift up their race.[33] Although often extremely poor, black communities all over the South taxed themselves to support a school system.[34] It was not just children like Booker T. Washington who were excited by the prospect of learning. He told also of men and women in their seventies who were determined to learn to read the Bible before they died.[35]

African-Americans in the South played a key role in the debate over what freedom and equality should mean. The freedman understood the clear distinction between freedom and slavery. They had lived alongside free blacks in the South who were the victims of inequality. Freedom did not therefore represent equality and in order to move towards this status there needed to be economic as well as personal change.[36] Indeed many ex-slaves in the South expected, and in many cases requested, that they be given land. Writing of the freedman's plight, DuBois argued, 'he had no way to rent or build a home. Food had to be begged or stolen, unless in some way he could get hold of land or go to work.'[37] Radical Republican Thaddeus Stevens proposed confiscation of planters' land and a restratification of southern society which would benefit black and white yeomen.[38] Writing in the revisionist vanguard of the 1960s, James McPherson argued that at the war's end there were encouraging signs for the realisation of land for ex-slaves.[39]

This view, however, overstates the likelihood of land redistribution in the South. Stevens was a radical who swam against the tide of the mainstream Republicans. In fact, their free labour ideology determined an aversion to legislation which confiscated property and tried to circumvent the traditional road to equality which would be reached by natural economic growth. Even among radical Republicans there was little support for land redistribution.[40] The abolitionists who were certainly in favour of equality defined this largely in narrow terms of equality before the law.[41] This was the aim of the Fourteenth Amendment but its provisions did little to check the massive social inequality in the South. Racial discrimination was the dominant condition of southern race relations during Reconstruction and this was not only because of the prejudice of whites. Much *de facto* segregation was instituted by black southerners as they sought to build their own communities.[42]

Black leader Frederick Douglass asserted slavery would not be fully abolished and freedom guaranteed 'until the black man has the vote'.[43] Certainly Republicans stood to benefit from black suffrage as the newly enfranchised voters would overwhelmingly vote for the party of Lincoln. Nevertheless, the limited support for black suffrage among the northern white electorate meant that Republican policy makers risked political damage in the North by supporting the amendment. It is therefore likely that a significant number of Republicans were motivated by conscience to extend the franchise to southern blacks.[44] There was also an economic imperative for the extension of the franchise because the ideology of free-labour saw voting rights in economic as well as political terms.

The decision to approve the Fifteenth Amendment in February 1869 was, however, motivated by a more immediate political issue. In the summer of 1868 Alabama, Arkansas, Florida, Georgia, Louisiana, North Carolina and South Carolina adopted new constitutions and their newly elected Republican legislatures ratified the Fourteenth Amendment and so gained readmission to the Union. Almost immediately, however, the Georgia legislature asserted that black legislators were ineligible for office under the Georgia constitution and unceremoniously expelled them.[45] Just as the Republicans had responded to the Black Codes with the Civil Rights Act and then the Fourteenth Amendment, so the Fifteenth Amendment was a direct response to the actions of the Georgia legislature. Democrats decried the Amendment as a radical conspiracy to give the black man social equality and extend central power to an unprecedented level. To give ex-slaves the vote only four years after they had emerged from bondage was a massively significant decision. The amendment did not, however, make any provisions for the right to hold office and it did not spell out uniform suffrage laws throughout the whole nation. Furthermore, proponents of women's suffrage were dismayed that the amendment prohibited racial discrimination but not discrimination by gender.[46]

The Georgia legislature had hoped that their decision to exclude black legislators would be upheld by a Democratic president. The election of Ulysses S. Grant in 1868 had, however, ensured the continuance of Republican plans for Reconstruction. The Fourteenth and Fifteenth Amendments were designed to tackle discrimination on the part of state and local governments but in 1870 and 1871 Congress passed three Enforcement Acts. These measures declared certain crimes to be punishable under federal law and were used to arrest thousand of Klansmen in the South. As a result, the election of 1872 was the most peaceful of the Reconstruction era. The election, though, also revealed fissures within the Republican Party. Many of the old radicals had died and anti-Grant Republicans focussed on the problems of corruption of government in the North and the South. Increasingly calls for political reform became wedded to opposition to Reconstruction. Although defeated easily by Grant, Horace Greeley was endorsed by the Democrats and pushed for a new policy for the South. This was something which the reformers and Democrats could agree upon.[47]

By the middle of the 1870s most Republicans were resistant to extending federal power to protect the freedman and were primarily opposed to the Civil Rights Bill introduced by Charles Sumner. Indeed, but for the death of Sumner in 1874 and the Democrat electoral gains, the Bill would not have been passed.[48] Passed it was, however, and the 1875 Civil Rights Act stated that denial of access to public accommodations should not be made on account of race. The Act did represent a greater extension of national authority than previous Reconstruction civil rights legislation but Congress had omitted schools and cemeteries from its remit. Furthermore, the emphasis was placed on blacks to sue for their rights and the financial impediments associated with this, coupled with white indifference, meant that Jim Crow segregation continued to grow.[49] Subsequent Supreme Court rulings would declare the 1875 Act unconstitutional and severely limit the scope of the Fourteenth Amendment. Although we look back from the twenty-first century on *Plessy v. Ferguson* (1896) as a blow against racial equality, the principle of 'separate but equal' largely reinforced the inequality of facilities that had already emerged during the Reconstruction era.[50]

The late 1870s saw the restoration of white Democratic home rule in the South. In the following decades the black southerner was systematically disenfranchised and a *herrenvolk* democracy, which was based on a strict racial hierarchy, dominated the South. The southern white elite were threatened by black political power and the potential of a class-based movement which would confront their power. Whilst racial prejudice was a crucial element in the eventual failure of Reconstruction there were underlying class tensions which influenced both white northerners and southerners. We must not view the four million black southerners as an undivided monolith. The black elite sought to distance themselves from the poor workers of their race and economically downtrodden whites. Conservative whites and elite black cooperationists worked together to protect the southern order from lower-class radicalism.[51] Northern Republicans had been alarmed by expressions of black radicalism in the South in the summer of 1867 and the potential for class conflict which threatened their free-labour ideology. It was this outlook that led the North to acquiesce in the gradual disfranchisement of the freedman.[52]

Black southerners continued to struggle against the reinforcement of inequality as the Reconstruction effort was gradually abandoned, just as they had struggled to define their freedom in the immediate post-war period. The fact that these efforts were necessary is testament to the failure of Reconstruction to grow the fruits of freedom. C. Vann Woodward argued that the endeavours of the radical Republicans ran up a moral debt that the country was unable to pay. 'After a few token payments during Reconstruction, the United States defaulted on the debt and unilaterally declared a moratorium that lasted more than eight decades.'[53] If the period was an attempt at a second revolution then it was incomplete, its promise of equality was unfulfilled. This should not, however, mask the significant changes that occurred. Looking back from the twenty-first century it is easy to point to the inadequacy of the Reconstruction period. Nevertheless, if we compare the situation for African-Americans in the 1870s with those of the generations before 1865 then we can see significant transformation. Although restricted by Supreme Court rulings in the late nineteenth century, a more liberal interpretation of the Reconstruction amendments in the 1950s and 1960s breathed life into the civil rights movement, completing a process begun in the immediate post-bellum era. In 1865 four million freed people 'stepped onto the stage of American freedom'.[54] The struggle over the parts they would act in liberty's play was the central drama of Reconstruction and had a significant impact on the development of America.

10

CIVIL WAR MEMORY AND AMERICAN NATIONAL IDENTITY

At the 2006 ceremony to commemorate the fifth anniversary of the 9/11 terrorist attacks, along with the 'Stars and Stripes' the band played 'The Battle Hymn of the Republic'. This song was popular with Union armies during the Civil War and expressed northern sentiments of a redemptive force marching forth to end slavery. The choice of this hymn for a ceremony to remember Americans killed in a terrorist attack and to promote unified resolve against the perpetrators of that attack shows the continued importance of Civil War memory in US nationalism. It was during the Civil War that this nationalism, tentative and unclear in form in the antebellum period, was increasingly developed. The experience of the Civil War and the way it has been remembered were crucial in the formation of American nationalism. Indeed after the North's victory the term 'nation' was used, rather than the earlier 'union', to describe the American polity.[1] In his first Inaugural Address, Lincoln called for the maintenance of the 'bonds of affection' which bound North and South together and invoked the 'mystic chords of memory' to 'swell the chorus of the *Union*'.[2] Yet, by the time of his Gettysburg Address in 1863, Lincoln was dedicating the memories of the fallen to the proposition, 'that this *nation*, under God, shall have a new birth of freedom'.[3]

In the last ten years scholarship has increasingly focussed on how the memory of the Civil War evolved to bring reunion between the North and the South and promote American nationalism. Lincoln's call for a new birth of freedom pointed towards a more racially inclusive national identity that was eventually compromised in order to reconcile the northern and southern sections of the country. The 1913 gathering of Union and Confederate veterans at Gettysburg sought to ignore the racial issues of the conflict and instead focussed on the military valour of white soldiers. As David Blight observes, this was 'a Jim Crow reunion, and white supremacy might be said to have been the silent, invisible master of ceremonies'.[4] The exclusion of the freed people from an equal place in the national family was a crucial development in the process of reconciliation after the conflict as 'memories of the Civil War helped define membership in the nation'.[5]

This whitewashed memory of the Civil War that emerged in the late nineteenth century, and persisted well into the twentieth, is an important story and one which will be addressed below. It was not, however, inevitable that such a memory of the war should emerge. We must be careful not to assume that the persistent racism and the socio-economic turbulence of the Gilded Age made a racially exclusive reunion inevitable.[6] The memory of the Civil War and its place in shaping American national identity was contested. This contest was not only between those who saw a racially inclusive view of the war and those who supported white supremacy. The place of women in the memory of the conflict and in the nation was also debated. It must further be noted that the remembrance of the war was used to sustain sectional animosities and identities as well as being shaped to promote national reunification. What is presented below is a brief analysis of these contests of memory and their impact on American national identity.

The American Civil War brought death and destruction on an unprecedented scale. The total number of those who perished was more than the total fatalities in all other US military campaigns up to and including the Korean War. In the North 6 per cent of the white male population aged 13–43 died and in the South the figure was 18 per cent. Had a similar percentage of American soldiers been killed during the Vietnam War the total number of dead men would have stood at 3.72 million rather than 60,000.[7] Such was the carnage of the Civil War that a search for meaning was imperative. Also, the fratricidal nature of the conflict required sectional reconciliation if a nationalism was to be constructed from the wreckage of four years of slaughter. Union victory in the Civil War did not settle American national identity; it instead represented 'the beginning of a long and contentious struggle over who and what would represent the nation'.[8] Americans increasingly showed loyalty to the nation, which was viewed as an independent entity, rather than their state or locality. Beginning in the North during the conflict, there was an important shift in the perception of national identity as public awareness of the nation and an expanded conception of the federal government emerged.[9]

This more powerful federal government moved during the Reconstruction period to protect the rights of African-Americans and this story is outlined in the previous chapter. Our focus here is the role of race in the memory of the Civil War. In his seminal work on the subject, *Race and Reunion*, David Blight has identified competing versions of Civil War memory which contested the place of blacks in the conflict and the legacy it bequeathed them. Firstly, an 'emancipationist' view of the war recognised slavery as the sin that brought the scourge of death and destruction to the nation. Lincoln's call for a 'new birth of freedom' at Gettysburg was followed with a more forceful statement by the abolitionist Frederick Douglass two weeks later. He argued that the purpose of the war would not be completed 'until the black men of the South, and the black men of the North, shall have been admitted, fully and completely, into the body politic of America'.[10] This was a radical vision for the future of the nation and embraced an inclusive national identity, an identity which would require massive cultural changes and confront the South with a seismic shift in the social and political fabric of the region.

It was abundantly clear that black southerners would face opposition to remembrance of the Civil War which emphasised racial change. In the spring of 1866 black residents of Hampton, Virginia, gathered to celebrate the first anniversary of their freedom. As black veterans marched through the streets in their blue Union uniforms they were attacked by a white mob.[11] In Hamburg, South Carolina, in 1876 black militia celebrating the centennial of July Fourth were attacked and following the violence seven blacks lay dead.[12] African-Americans in the South saw the central meaning of the Civil War as the birth of their freedom and celebrations of this meaning played a crucial role in the contest over national identity. It was the oratory of Lincoln that had pointed to a revolutionary interpretation of the war concerning race relations and in the huge outpouring of grief following his death African-Americans were conspicuous. Indeed a logistical mistake meant a black regiment led the dead President's funeral procession to the Capitol.[13]

Throughout the South blacks had to forge an emancipationist memory of the Civil War in the midst of Confederate hostility and indifference. In Richmond African-Americans chose to celebrate Emancipation Day on 3 April, the day the city fell to Union forces. For ex-Confederates this was a day to be mourned, a moment of final defeat. Freedom for blacks was interpreted as slavery and degradation for whites. Therefore tension emerged over the commemoration of the war in the immediate post-war period. Rumours abounded in the white press that the celebrating blacks were to trail the Confederate flag in the dust and burn effigies of Jefferson Davis and Robert E. Lee.[14] The contests over the meanings of the war played out in these early struggles were portentous for an inclusive version of national identity because white southerners could not be reconciled to a new racial order. Nationalism could not be forged if a significant portion of the nation were cold to its embrace. The question remained as to how the North and the South could be reunited if the memory of the war was emancipationist in nature. 'The imperative of healing and the imperative of justice could not, ultimately, cohabit the same house.'[15]

In 1883 Douglass argued for the importance of 'keeping in memory the great deeds of the past, and of transmitting the same from generation to generation'.[16] By this point the old abolitionist was beginning to see his vision of the meaning of the Civil War slip into obscurity. Increasingly what Blight terms a 'reconciliationist' script dominated the memory of the conflict. As the immediate political struggles began to fade from view a sectional reunion developed which sacrificed the civil liberties of African-Americans.[17] As the 1870s progressed northerners were increasingly able to look on the white South with sympathy. Many viewed corrupt Reconstruction officials unfavourably when compared with the dignified planter class who had suffered so much. A marriage metaphor with northern husbands taking southern wives was used to convey reunion in 'soft and romantic tones'.[18]

It was, however, through a focus on the battlefield that the North and the South were able to reach a form of reconciliation which fostered a nationalism which could be embraced on both sides of the Mason–Dixon Line. In a compromise which proved tragic for a racially inclusive vision of the nation, white southerners committed to patriotism in return for the North forgetting the role of slavery in the Civil War and acknowledging the valour of the Confederate soldier. As will be explored below, focus on the battlefield and the commemoration of the fallen could promote a deep sense of sectional animus. Increasingly, however, veterans came together to shape a memory of the Civil War which promoted national reunion. Although born in very different circumstances and spirits in North and South after the war, decoration days which would become Memorial Day were slowly used to bring sectional reconciliation. Memorial Day orators focussed on what Oliver Wendell Holmes Jnr would later call the 'Soldier's Faith'. 'Within a decade of the war's end the soldierly virtue of devotion, whatever the cause, was well rehearsed as a means to sectional peace.'[19] Men like Joshua Chamberlain, who heroically defended 'Little Round Top' during the Battle of Gettysburg, were venerated as fine examples of men of courage, honour and chivalry. On Memorial Day in Massachusetts in 1897, Chamberlain delivered an address in which he asserted that 'everyone has in him, slumbering somewhere, the potencies of noble action ... every man has in him the elements of a hero'.[20]

Celebration of the Civil War during Memorial Day brought the North and the South closer together and also fostered a martial spirit that saw military duty as a crucial element of American character and citizenship.[21] The veteran's organisation, the Grand Army of the Republic (GAR), developed a nationalist spirit around the concepts of manliness and sacrifice and in so doing created ceremonies and invented traditions to bolster their interpretation of nationalism.[22] Reflecting the martial spirit of the reunion efforts, *Century* magazine published hundreds of articles about the War in the mid-1880s, and in 1887 it released an immensely popular series on the battles and leaders of the Civil War. The focus was solely on military experience and no causes or consequences of the conflict were discussed, and not even secession was mentioned.[23] Despite the dissenting voices of Douglass and others, and continued attempts by black veterans to be treated as equals in the GAR, the issue of race was being erased from the memory of the Civil War. Some black soldiers did march in the 1892 national GAR parade but they faced informal discrimination. At the end of the parade a vast fireworks display took place at the Washington Monument and the bright outline of two soldiers lit up the sky, 'the Blue and the Gray faced each other and shook hands, promising the reconciliation of *white* blood brothers'.[24] The spirit of reconciliation fostered by a celebration of military valour produced a memory of the Civil War and a national identity which rejected racial inclusiveness.

The contest for Civil War remembrance did not, however, only revolve around the issue of race. The place of women in the new nation, which was forged out of the fires of that conflict, was also shaped and debated in post-bellum America. This struggle was intertwined with persistent sectional animosity, which helps in part to explain the different paths taken in the construction of northern and southern women's place in Civil War memory. This memory played a crucial role in envisioning the role of women in the nationhood which was forged in the period from the end of the conflict to the dawn of the twentieth century. This nationhood was essentially masculine and women had to settle for a traditional feminine role as their dominant identity.

The place of women in the North portrayed by popular literature during the war years was somewhat different, however. The image of mother and wife was seen as a direct link to the flag and the nation. In certainly a traditionally gendered and sentimental patriotism, the tearful woman personalised the nation and supported the male soldier. The images presented, however, were not solely of a passive woman who provided a vehicle for male patriotism. Increasingly there was a focus on women's sacrifice during the war, a suffering which entitled them to a form of citizenship which recognised their civic importance. The wounds that women endured, whilst not physical, were seen to be emotionally damaging and longer suffered than the gunshot wound of a soldier.[25] In the Confederacy the role of women was expanded as they contributed to the war effort in important practical respects such as nursing, sewing and relief societies. They showed their patriotism by accepting the sacrifice of losing their men whilst also being used to appeal to male patriotism and service.[26]

Women on both sides of the Mason–Dixon Line took a central role in the burial of fallen soldiers and in the Memorial Day rituals that emerged in the post-bellum period. The gendered dynamics of these rituals, however, differed between North and South. Military defeat for the southern white man provided troubling consequences for his sense of manhood. This was compounded as southern women took the lead role in Memorial Day rituals. In the immediate post-war period southern men played a secondary role in the commemoration of the dead as their ability to glorify the Confederate cause was restricted by the occupying Union forces. Men spoke at remembrance events and defended the cause of southern independence whilst downplaying the issue of slavery, but the principal organising efforts were carried out by women. In this way Confederate resistance was given a female and consequently sentimental face which was less dangerous for the North. Men were uneasy about this situation but, as William Blair asserts, 'like it or not, the new Confederate traditions invented after the Civil War rested on a foundation of womanhood'.[27] Northerners often viewed southern women as the purveyors of a southern opposition and viewed feminine dominance as indicative of a failure of southern society. Restoring the South to the Union would remove Confederate resistance and return the correct balance of power in gender relations.[28]

The erasure of racial issues from the memory of the war, and the emergence of a nationalism which celebrated the martial spirit in a brother's conflict, impacted on the place of women in American national identity. The GAR refused to admit any of the Women's Relief Corps (WRC) as members, even those who as army nurses had given undoubted service to the nation. Nor were the WRC's tentative calls for female suffrage heeded.[29] In the masculine view of the war there was no place for women. 'In the 1880s and 1890s ... commentators and writers increasingly attached the idea of Civil War sacrifice for the nation to men only, gendering the memory of the war in a new way.'[30] As women's organisations struggled over the issue of a colour line, the reduction of race as a factor in Civil War memory impacted on the place of women in post-bellum nationalism. Focus on the battlefield allowed white southern men to embrace nationhood in the way that they could not in the years immediately after the war. As northern policy makers left race relations in their hands southern men could reassert both white supremacy and patriarchy. In the spirit of reunion northern men throughout the 1890s praised their southern brother's chivalry and his protection of a submissive southern womanhood.[31] He was, of course, protecting her from the emancipated slave man. As the colour line was violently drawn the white southern man asserted his masculinity simultaneously with his racial supremacy.

In some of the scholarship cited here, and to some extent in this survey, there is a tendency to assume that reconciliation and national reunion were inevitable with the passing of years following the conflict. The memory of the Civil War was, however, also used by some to prolong sectional animosities and provide distinctive regional concepts of nationhood. Memorial Day ceremonies, for instance, were loaded with sectional animus in many respects. 'Every gesture toward political and social reunification was coloured by memories of battlefields scattered with the soldier dead.'[32] Indeed where these fallen servicemen were to be buried provided for continuing tensions between North and South. Arlington Cemetery was created on the confiscated lands of Robert E. Lee's estate and originally served as an area for escaping slaves to camp and then as a soldier's hospital. Controversy arose, however, as the lands began to be used as an official cemetery. Union dead were buried in an area separate from the graves of blacks and Confederates who had died during their time as prisoners of war. Not until the turn of the twentieth century was a monument to the Confederate dead dedicated at Arlington.[33]

At Gettysburg, where Lincoln made his famous address, the cemetery was for Union soldiers and great lengths were taken to separate the loyal from the rebel dead. At the cemetery for those who died at Antietam the Union soldiers were buried in neat well-marked rows, whereas the Confederate dead were scattered all across the local farmlands. Union and rebel dead were segregated in a display of continued sectionalism. Controversy arose when southern protests prompted a reconsideration of the burial patterns; some northern states withheld funds for the cemetery at the thought of Blue and Gray being buried side by side.[34] National cemeteries were expanded and through the activism of the GAR became sacred sites of memory. National, however, meant Union; it was not a sectionally inclusive term. 'For at least thirty-five years, no Confederate soldier who died while under arms resisting federal authority was ever buried in a national cemetery.'[35]

The memory of the Civil War could also be used to shape divergent myths on both sides of the Mason–Dixon Line. Emerging in the wake of the War was the southern legend of the 'Lost Cause' which has received detailed historical attention. This interpretation of the conflict argued that it was a desire for liberty and constitutional principles rather than slavery which provided the root cause of the conflict. It also asserted that the Confederacy had not been conclusively defeated on the battlefield but rather was overwhelmed by the greater numbers and resources of Union forces. Defiant southern nationalists like Jubal Early waged a war for ideas with northern writers by defending the military elements of the Lost Cause myth.[36] The memory of the war which was to be passed on to the next generation was fiercely contested. The United Confederate Veterans (UCV) and other southern organisations worked assiduously to ensure that southern schoolbooks would tell the story of the war without slavery as a cause and with secession as an expression of states' rights in a struggle for self-government. Rival interpretations were purged to the extent that by 1905 a UCV leader could claim 'the most pernicious histories have been banished from the school rooms'.[37]

The myth of the Lost Cause provided something of a psychological compensation for white southerners as they came to terms with defeat in the Civil War. The celebration of the Confederate tradition helped to stabilise the New South and promoted unity among a diverse population of whites during a period of great social and economic turmoil.[38] Focus on the valour of southern soldiers and eventual defeat at the hands of an overpowering Union force was an element of the Lost Cause which helped reintegrate the South into the nation as reconciliation focussed on the military experience of the Civil War. These points should not, however, deflect from the reality that celebration of the Confederate tradition was also fused with a defiant attempt to maintain a distinct identity that resisted complete national reunification.[39]

It was not only the South that used the war to promote a memory viewed through a sectional lens. In many respects the emancipationist interpretation of the war's memory can be viewed as sectional. The ideal of a nation newly dedicated to racial equality was anathema to the South and their myth making was a direct counterattack in the struggle over the shape of national identity. Northern politicians used 'bloody shirt' rhetoric to establish southern war guilt and to justify the use of federal power to reconstruct the nation in line with the ideals of Union victors.[40] The area of ideals and especially those connected with race caused great problems for northern myth makers, however. Civil

War memory could foster sectional animosity in the North but ultimately northern remembrance had an imperative to bind the nation together. There was a 'Cause Victorious' legend in the North which projected national reconciliation long before it was actually achieved. The problem was that two distinct peoples had to be incorporated into the national identity. Blacks and white southerners, however, were not easily welcomed into the national family of reunion and so northerners 'crafted a myth of unity even as they struggled with its implications'.[41] The fact that such an effort was necessary in itself displays the continued sectional tension that the Civil War's legacy evoked.

Despite these struggles over the conflict's memory, that the final reunion of the nation was achieved largely at the expense of the social and political equality of African-Americans is undoubted. Here we move to the third of Blight's competing interpretations of the conflict, 'white supremacy'. A southern orator in 1903 delighted his UCV audience when proclaiming that the Confederacy fought to preserve the freedom of the white man and that they must struggle to ensure white supremacy in the present.[42] As northern and southern soldiers solidified the martial spirit which had emerged as a key component in the reconciliation process, by fighting alongside one another in the Spanish–American War, so both sections embraced a racist interpretation of that conflict. An expression of imperialism and Anglo-Saxon superiority, the war with the Spanish promoted a racial supremacy that would come to dominate Civil War memory and bring North and South closer together. A Darwinist-inspired outlook on national and international events meant that the nation's identity became racially exclusive and convinced northerners that white southerners were best suited to deal with their black population.[43]

What emerged was a whitewashed account of Civil War memory, a version of the past which fostered a form of nationalism white southerners could embrace. The South, therefore, may be said to have lost the war but won the peace. The struggle over how to remember their fratricidal conflict had seen Americans wrestle with issues of sectionalism, gender and race before a coalescence of memory which fell far short of a new birth of freedom. The 'emancipationist' memory of the Civil War was all but forgotten. This was expressed most clearly by two events in the early twentieth century. On the fiftieth anniversary of Gettysburg, President Wilson spoke at the site of the battle. The first southern president since the end of the Civil War spoke of a 'quarrel forgotten – except that we shall not forget the splendid valour, the manly devotion of the men who arrayed against one another, now grasping hands and smiling into each other's eyes'.[44] Wilson emphasised military experience and made no mention of racial equality. He did not reflect on Lincoln's words fifty years previous and his call for a new birth of freedom.

Two years later D. W. Griffith released *Birth of a Nation*. The film portrayed the immediate post-war period in the South as one dominated by African-American rule over a chivalrous white southern people. In a reunion drama a white woman is rescued from the tyranny of black government by the brave knights of the Ku Klux Klan. Wilson commented after watching a screening at the White House that his only regret was that it was all 'terribly true'.[45] The nation which was birthed in Griffith's film was not dedicated to the proposition that all men were created equal; it strayed far from the emancipationist memory of the Civil War. Instead a memory had been shaped to support a racially exclusive national identity. The struggle over the meaning of the Civil War continued, however, into the centenary commemorations of the conflict. Race remained the enduring issue. With Freedom Riders nursing the wounds sustained when they were attacked in the South, re-enactors descended on the battlefield of Bull Run to celebrate the martial spirit. With enlightened historians calling for a more complete memory of the war, popular magazines like *Life* produced centenary issues which focussed solely on battles and military experience. White southerners fighting to uphold racial segregation adopted the Confederate flag as their symbol.[46] It required the second reconstruction of the Civil Rights Movement to shift focus on the war's legacy to an appreciation of racial matters.

One hundred years after the Emancipation Proclamation and the Battle of Gettysburg, when Martin Luther King told the Washington crowds of his dream, he was confronting the nation's conscience with the evils of segregation. In a less direct sense he was also carrying the torch lit by Frederick Douglass and others who called for a memory of the Civil War which emphasised black freedom and promised an inclusive national identity. Those who constructed a whitewashed reunion of North and South in the post-bellum period may have won the battle over the memory of America's civil conflict. The efforts of countless others to promote an emancipationist legacy, however, means the war for memory was eventually won by those who believed in a new birth of freedom for the nation. The struggle over how America remembered its Civil War was crucial, therefore, in marking the parameters of national identity and citizenship.

11

INTRODUCING JIM CROW
The codification of segregation in the South

Henry Grady, the Georgian regarded as the spokesman for the New South, argued in 1885 that no social differences were more important than those provided by racial distinctions. Grady's critic, George Washington Cable, argued rather for a class-based social hierarchy asserting that education and civility were not the sole preserves of white southerners. He challenged his detractors, 'tell us gentleman, which are you really for: the colour line, or the line of character, intelligence and property?'[1] By the turn of the twentieth century the codification of a host of Jim Crow laws had ensured that it was a strict colour line which would prevail in the New South.[2] Revolving around opinions on C. Vann Woodward's seminal work *The Strange Career of Jim Crow*,[3] historians have vigorously debated when racial segregation emerged in the post-bellum South and the extent to which race relations could have followed alternative paths. Woodward himself, however, contended that he started the subject of the origins of segregation in the South 'on the wrong foot … what I did was to put the question *when* before the questions *where* and *how*'.[4] Certainly there was a pattern of regional differences in the growth of segregation; therefore a southern-wide blanket of *de facto* segregation did not emerge immediately after the Civil War. Nevertheless, the colour line was clearly etched in the minds of white – and to an extent black – southerners before the emergence of *de jure* Jim Crow in the 1890s. Fundamental to an exploration of racial segregation in the South then is an understanding of *why* this legal codification occurred.

Woodward's *Strange Career of Jim Crow* still remains the starting point for any discussion of racial segregation in the post-bellum South. Originally written as the text for three lectures to be given at the University of Virginia in 1954, *Strange Career* was heavily influenced by the time in which it was written. Constructing his thesis as the Supreme Court ruled in the *Brown* decision that racial segregation in schools was unconstitutional, Woodward sought to use the past to show the possibilities of the future. Explaining that strict segregation of black and white had not been the only and inevitable shape of race relations in southern history provided optimism that desegregation of the region's schools could succeed. As Woodward later explained,

> My first concern was to overcome the prevailing impression – and in southern ideology the firm conviction – that the subject had no history, that race relations in the South remained basically unchanged, that changes in law, whether associated with slavery, emancipation, Reconstruction, or segregation, had been superficial and resulted in no real change in relations between races. No changes, no history.[5]

Woodward's thesis was that there had been fluidity in the nature of race relations during Reconstruction and its aftermath. This fluidity was evidence of 'forgotten alternatives' in the southern experience.[6]

Woodward identified three forgotten alternative models to southern race relations. Firstly, the liberal philosophy articulated by George Washington Cable spoke of a 'silent South' which did not embrace a strict racial caste system. Cable called for a more class-based hierarchy which allowed prosperous and well-educated black southerners to progress. Lewis Harvie Blair also called for a liberal approach to race relations and argued that African-Americans should be allowed open access to all hotels and places of public amusement and that segregated schooling should be abandoned because of the psychological damage to the black race.[7]

Offering a less overtly egalitarian ideology, the 'conservatives' provided a second alternative in southern race relations. Drawing on the paternalism of the old master and slave relationship, conservatives sought to attract the black vote in order to help their opposition to Democratic Redeemers (so called because they attempted to end control of the South by the Republicans and restore Democrat home rule) economic policies. They placed themselves in the middle ground between the liberalism of Cable and the Negrophobia of many Democrats.[8] In Virginia the conservatives emerged in the shape of the Readjuster coalition which saw an alliance of black and white voters temporarily defeat the Democrat regime.[9] There were elements of a class-based appeal across racial lines in this model of government. It was not, however, as pronounced as that which Woodward saw in his third alternative, Populism. This agrarian movement was a radical assault on the polity of Democrat home rule which united white and black farmers in common class struggle. The leading spokesman of the movement, Tom Watson, explained that it was economic self-interest that dictated the inter-racial alliance when he stated, 'it is to the interest of a coloured man to vote with the white man and he will do it'.[10] The extent to which the Populist Party was genuine in its commitment to the black farmer is questionable, however. The 1892 platform of the Alabama Populists, for example, simultaneously supported a white primary and protection of the black vote.[11] Indeed the inability of both the Readjusters and the Populists to resist the forces of extreme racism will be discussed below.

Central to Woodward's 'forgotten alternatives' thesis, however, is that these different models of race relations offered a period of fluidity which saw several areas of significant inter-racial contact outside of any de facto segregation. He points out that segregation grew up in the North during the antebellum period and was in sharp contrast to the relatively intimate relationship between the races in the South. When Jim Crow segregation was applied to streetcars in many southern cities in the Reconstruction period blacks campaigned so vigorously against it that the authorities in South Carolina and Mississippi, for example, passed anti-discrimination statutes.[12] Woodward pointed to the testimony of Colonel Higginson who travelled the South in 1878 and found that blacks were accepted on the trains and streetcars without any problem. Sir George Campbell visited the South the following year and found that blacks shared public facilities on the basis of equality with whites. In 1885, a Boston black man, T. McCants Stewart, expecting to find visible signs of segregation as he travelled in South Carolina, saw nothing of the sort.[13]

Woodward therefore set out his thesis for a period of flux in race relations which was then attacked by historians who found exceptions to his assertions. They tried to show that segregation had emerged, especially in urban areas, immediately after the Civil War and that widespread de facto segregation disproved the 'forgotten alternative' model. A closer reading of *Strange Career*, however, shows the very narrow nature of Woodward's thesis, a narrowness that has enabled his views to deflect or successfully incorporate criticism. He clearly conceded that segregation was extended to churches, militia companies, schools, welfare programmes and a wide range of other areas of society (it is worth noting, however, that the impulse for blacks to establish separate churches and community organisations is a totally different phenomenon to the imposition of racial segregation in other social spheres).[14] Woodward's argument for a period of fluidity in which it was not inevitable that de facto segregation emerged is restricted to hotels, restaurants, theatres and other places of public accommodation.[15] Those who have pointed to the emergence of segregation in the immediate post-bellum period have not, therefore, conclusively defeated the Woodward thesis but they have helped to explain further the *where* and *how* of Jim Crow.

Close examination of the different regional patterns of the emergence of de facto segregation in the narrow area of public accommodations also fails to deliver a knockout blow to the Woodward thesis. In a study which anticipated some of the arguments put forward in *Strange Career*, George Tindall found a fluid system of race relations in the area of public accommodations with segregation by no means universally applied.[16] Joel Williamson's study of the same state argued for a more rigid application of the colour line in public life. Blacks could legally use the same facilities as whites but in practice they did not. Williamson asserted, 'physical separation merely symbolised and reinforced mental separation ... South Carolina had become two communities, one white and one black'.[17] Although there was a great deal of de facto segregation from the end of Reconstruction through to the 1890s, there were exceptions to this pattern in South Carolina. Indeed on the state railroads there was a custom of racial separation as white passengers travelled in first-class carriages and blacks bought second-class tickets. Nevertheless, middle-class black women regularly travelled in first-class accommodation. When the railroad company started offering one class of travel there were complaints from white passengers about having to share with blacks but corporate interest militated against *de jure* segregation until the 1890s.[18] Unlike many other areas of the South, schools in New Orleans were integrated during Reconstruction. Nevertheless, the Redeemer government repealed this legislation and the reaction against racial mixing in education increased the segregation of public spaces throughout the 1880s and 1890s.[19]

Woodward himself recognised the discontinuity of experience in different areas of the South. When introducing the examples of those who did not experience segregation as they travelled through the South he stated, 'it would be perfectly possible to site contemporary experiences and testimony of a contrasting character'.[20] The Supreme Court ruling in the Civil Rights cases of 1883 argued that discrimination in the area of public accommodation was a private matter. As a legal consequence individualism and private property rights reached ascendance and proprietors could make a decision to serve whom they wished.[21] This ruling contributed to the fluidity of race relations in public spaces as it left the decisions concerning de facto segregation to the owners and proprietors themselves.

Perhaps the most successful challenge to the ideas of *Strange Career* – and one which Woodward himself acknowledged as a most constructive addition to the debate – is provided by Howard Rabinowitz.[22] He argued that the real forgotten alternative to racial segregation was in fact exclusion of black people from all areas of white southern life. In the antebellum period blacks were regularly entirely excluded from public accommodations. Segregated railroads, streetcars and theatres were instituted by Reconstruction governments as an improvement on the total exclusion of blacks before the Civil War.[23] Rabinowitz argues, 'the issue, therefore, should not be merely when segregation first appeared, but what it replaced'.[24] Certainly de facto segregation emerged in many areas of southern public life from Reconstruction onwards. The colour line was most likely to be drawn in urban areas where social intercourse and public facilities provided the circumstances in which segregation might have been most required by white southerners. Jim Crow was not all encompassing and exceptions to the rules of segregation are not hard to find though. Helped by the ruling in the Civil Rights cases of 1883, however, the custom of racial segregation was undoubtedly found all across the region by 1890.

Through a survey of the Woodward thesis and its critics we have addressed the debates over the *when, where* and *how* of Jim Crow. Scholars of the period universally accept that in the 1890s there was a significant shift from de facto to *de jure* Jim Crow. The crucial question to which we must now turn is *why* this change came into being. In the last decade of the nineteenth century a number of different factors converged to ensure the legal codification of Jim Crow: the waning of northern liberal interest in the southern black man and the emergence of a racially exclusive nationalism; the political threat of the Populist revolt; fear of a new 'uppity' Negro and the danger of miscegenation; the use of history to craft a regional identity based on a romantic image of the past; and a desire to lay the foundations for a stable and prosperous South all contrived to provide the impetus for a strict and violent drawing of the colour line. To use North Carolinian Charles Chestnutt's illustration borrowed from mythology, the white South showed the characteristics of Procrustes, the innkeeper at Attica. Southern whites kept the Negro in a veritable Procrustes' bed, chopping him down when his head rose above the line, and stretching his neck when he fell below it.[25]

The economic downturn of the 1880s and 1890s had a particularly negative impact on southern agriculture. Financial mismanagement became associated with the Democratic Redeemer governments who had restored 'Home Rule' to the South after the end of Reconstruction – in 1879 Democrats in Virginia, for example, violated the state constitution by diverting funds from the public school budget to pay interest to bondholders.[26] The rise of the Populist Party in the early 1890s threatened an alliance of white and black farmers on class grounds to overthrow the Democratic machine in the South. The actual threat to white supremacy posed by the Populists was minimal and many whites who voted for the party did so without abandoning ideas of white dominance. Nevertheless, threatened by the possible loss of votes to the Populists, especially where they formed an alliance with Republicans, the Democrats played the race card. Senator John Tyler Morgan urged southerners to 'resist any movement, social or political, that will promote the unwelcome intrusion of the Negro race into the white family circle'.[27] The Democrat elite made white supremacy their rallying cry. For the Redeemers these Populists became the new carpetbaggers who must be banished from the South. By relentlessly highlighting the issue of race, and evoking fear of Negro domination, the Democrat elite sought to ensure the white and black masses would not unite against them.[28] As the South experienced a period of competitive race relations in the labour market following the end of slavery the Democrats preached the doctrine of *Herrenvolk* democracy. Poor whites could improve their position in the social hierarchy by uniting with the white elite in a statement of racial superiority.[29]

Democrats also played on the minds of white southerners who witnessed a new breed of blacks born since the abolition of slavery. A correspondent of the Charleston *News and Courier* noted in 1883 the loud and rude behaviour of young blacks that he witnessed on a railroad journey.[30] There was a growing unease concerning the assertiveness and public power achieved by some African-Americans in the South. Many observed with growing alarm the erosion of deference to whites which had been exhibited in older black generations. Remembering the old docile Negro slave, the white South was fearful of this new 'uppity nigger'. Groups like the 'Organisation of Coloured Ladies' in North Carolina challenged their men to vote and stories of informal groups of black women randomly harassing individual white women in some southern cities were troubling for white southerners.[31]

The growing sense that blacks were beginning to move out of their 'place' in society was linked irresistibly to a perceived threat to white womanhood. The Democrats spun a yarn in which all white women highly prized their chastity and should at all costs be protected from the 'black beast', thus averting the racial cataclysm of miscegenation.[32] There was a sense that the black man was rising, that he was a threat to the social order. 'Whites created the culture of segregation in large part to counter black success, to make a myth of absolute racial difference, to stop the rising.'[33] A literature of black peril emerged on the southern literary landscape. Thomas Dixon Jnr's popular fiction displayed the contemporary white obsession with the image of the Negro rapist stalking his prey, the forbidden fruit of white womanhood.[34] White men equated political power for the black man with the threat of miscegenation. In 1883 the Readjuster regime collapsed in Virginia as the political alliance between white and black broke down in the face of a controversy surrounding the appointment of two African-Americans to the Richmond school board. Democrats highlighted the image of black men giving instruction to white female teachers and played on the fears of white men.[35]

The post-bellum generation of white men blamed their fathers for losing the Civil War, retarding industry, neglecting public education and tolerating blacks in politics. White men began to see urban disorder as an indication of a failure of manhood. They were determined to put a rising black population back in their 'place' and restore stability to the region. White women came to idealise and sentimentalise the antebellum South when they had more money and more power, blaming their men for the current conditions.[36] Women like Rebecca Felton, at the vanguard of the radical racist movement, blamed white men for failing to protect women from the black threat.[37] Democrat demagogues, like Governor James K. Vardaman of Mississippi, fuelled the southern hysteria by declaring, 'we would be justified in slaughtering every Ethiop on the earth to preserve unsullied the honour of the Caucasian home'.[38] The *Wilmington Messenger* of 8 November 1898 printed a Democrat song on the eve of the legislative elections which encapsulates the appeal to the southern white man to protect his women.

Rise, ye sons of Carolina!
Proud Caucasians, one and all;
Be not dead to love's appealing–
Hear your wives and daughters call,
See their blanched and anxious faces,
Note their frail, but lovely forms
Rise, defend their spotless virtue
With your strong and manly arms.[39]

Justice was served on the black rapist by lynch mobs. Over 3,000 blacks were lynched in the South between 1880 and 1930; black men lived under a 'sentence of death'.[40] The case of Henry Smith in 1893

Texas displays the brutality of such events. Accused of raping a three-year-old girl and then murdering her, Smith was hunted down by 2,000 men and then publicly burned. Men, women and children of all social standing watched as Smith, 'helpless, writhed and the flesh seared and peeled from the bones'.[41] Fuelled by Democrat calls for the assertion of white supremacy, the southern man conquered his own feelings of vulnerability by protecting his woman and excluding the black man from society. 'Once radicalism won dominance in the social ecosphere, it jealously denied the breath of life to any alternative.'[42]

This radicalism was the driving force behind the legal codification of Jim Crow segregation in the 1890s. The force was given constitutional approval by the 1896 Supreme Court decision in *Plessy v. Ferguson* that 'separate but equal' facilities were legal. It is important to note that events in the South were not played out in isolation; the waning of northern interest in the black man played a key role in the eventual emergence of *de jure* segregation. In Louisiana any delay in the institution of Jim Crow laws on the statute book was due to uncertainty about constitutional provision.[43] The defeat of Henry Cabot Lodge's Force Bill in 1890 represented the final chapter of northern liberal efforts to protect the black southerner. It was not until after the *Plessy* decision, however, that the South felt confident about sealing *de jure* segregation. Governor Tillman of South Carolina, a rabidly racist demagogue, warned his supporters in 1895 that they had to tread carefully for fear of antagonising Congress, the Supreme Court and northern friends of the black man.[44] The hypocrisy of rebuking the South for the legal codification of Jim Crow at the turn of the century was not lost on many in the North. Fuelled by the patriotism which accompanied the Spanish–American War of 1898, the nation increasingly embraced a racial nationalism which fully accepted the inferiority of the black race.[45]

Indeed the Spanish–American conflict and romantic memorials of the Civil War helped to forge a re-unification of North and South in the 1890s. This national unity was, however, achieved at the expense of the black race. A romantic image of the antebellum period was used by post-bellum southerners to justify their comprehensive drawing of the colour line. White women played a crucial role in the construction of a public history of the South which could be used as an ideological justification for white supremacy. Reconstruction was painted as a period of corruption and barbarism only repelled by the Ku Klux Klan. Popular white female authors painted a picture of the past full of dashing planters and beautiful southern belles served by black mammies in a romantic time which contrasted with the racial mixing of the post-bellum era.[46] Stories of the Old South embraced the ideal of a Lost Cause and were used to reconstruct racial differences. These stories provided white southerners with justification for ignoring the needs of the freedman and viewing segregation as the only future for the South.[47]

It is also important to recognise that this future was a key element in the emergence of *de jure* segregation. Grady's intent to draw a colour line in the New South was designed to ensure the racial stability which would encourage economic progress and modernisation. It was in the cities of the South where segregation grew most quickly; rapidly expanding and economically prosperous urban centres like Atlanta and Birmingham became more segregated than established settlements like Charleston. Codification of Jim Crow was seen as a necessary component in the development of the region because it settled the racial contest over public spaces which emerged in the post-bellum era. In the New South segregation was viewed as part of an exciting and prosperous future.[48]

As the twentieth century dawned, the weakening of northern liberalism combined with a passionate and persuasive Democrat campaign to solidify white supremacy – and in the process their political ascendance – left the black race cruelly exposed. Southern popular history constructed an image of the past asserting an inevitable racial segregation which perverted historical reality. The colour line was clearly drawn in the South long before the end of the Civil War but the legal codification of Jim Crow laws governing almost every aspect of public life was not inevitable. Nevertheless, the instability of racially contested public spaces created by inconsistent de facto Jim Crow produced an impulse to legally institute racial segregation. The regional stability afforded by white supremacy was regarded as necessary if the South was to progress economically. Segregation offered a way for white southerners both to cling to an idealised view of antebellum race relations and create the stability to engage economically with the rest of America.[49]

12

PREJUDICE AND PATERNALISM

Assimilation and Native American identity

During the ceremony to dedicate an Indian Memorial at the site of the Battle of Little Big Horn in 2003, Russell Means, of the Oglala Lakota, argued that the indigenous peoples of the United States understood the dangers of ethnic fragmentation. Referring to the term 'American Indian' he stated, 'We put American before our ethnicity ... We know what it is to be an American and that's why we are so proud to put it before our ethnicity.'[1] In the same year visitors to the reservation of the Blackfeet Indian Nation in Montana could see a hand-made notice with the names of the Blackfeet who were fighting in the war in Iraq. The sign included a message of support for the troops and their efforts in Operation Iraqi Freedom.[2] These two instances are offered as examples of the continued complex place of American Indians in US society.

A people who were subjected to a relentless campaign to change their social, political and economic traditions have, at times, shown great loyalty and patriotism towards the polity that sought to affect their metamorphosis. As Michael Elliott has highlighted in relation to the commemoration ceremony at the site of the Little Big Horn, Indians have displayed a form of 'anti-American Americanism'. Allegiance to the US was encouraged as part of a simultaneous proclamation of 'loyalties to tribal nations and through anticolonial criticisms directed at the United States'.[3] The purpose of this chapter is to focus on the period of the late nineteenth and early twentieth century which laid the foundations for this paradoxical position of American Indians in American society. The struggle over the place of Native Americans in US society highlights a further part of the process through which the parameters of American citizenship were defined. The following discussion centres on the efforts of those who sought to assimilate the Indians, their successes and failures and the changing motivations of Indian reformers. By 1920 there was a realisation that Native

Americans would not simply melt into the American mainstream. Instead the persistence of their cultural distinctiveness proved the failure of the assimilation process and posed important questions about the place of Indians in American society.

Federal Indian strategy after the Civil War was characterised by the 'peace policy' which was designed to move the natives onto reservations. 'The peace policy was a praiseworthy effort ... a product of the idealism of the reconstruction era.'[4] Reformers believed that moving the Indians to separate lands would protect them from the advances of white society. The Indian Wars which paradoxically emerged from this peace policy were the result of resistance by several tribes to submit to the reservation system. Sitting Bull warned, 'we want no white man here. The Black Hills belong to me. If the whites try to take them I will fight.'[5] Sioux resistance to incursions into sacred lands and attempts to force them into reservations were the catalyst for the warfare from which the heroes and villains of popular histories of the West emerged. Custer, Sheridan, Crazy Horse and others joined Sitting Bull as actors in the drama of the western theatre. Throughout the 1870s many Indian tribes were forced to relocate or concentrate in smaller areas as US authorities pushed to ensure Native Americans lived on distinct reservations.[6]

In 1871 Congress ratified an act which stipulated that no new treaties were to be made with Indian tribes. The proviso of the act asserted that existing treaties stood and therefore Indians were still to be treated as a tribal unit. This reality meant that in the period immediately after 1871 a number of treaty substitutes were used to deal with the Native Americans. Bilateral agreements which were then ratified by both houses of Congress, unilateral statutes and executive orders were all used in negotiation and accords with the tribes.[7] The policy of reservations and of using treaty substitutes encouraged the practice of reinforcing the tribal identity of American Indians. This approach increasingly came under attack from competing forces. Economic gain motivated many land-hungry whites and railroad prospectors who believed the Indian tribes had too much land and were not using it efficiently. They applied pressure on the Bureau of Indian Affairs to break up the reservations and remove the hindrance to economic progress.[8]

It was, however, reform-minded Christian men and women who provided the greatest impetus for the removal of the treaty system and the fragmentation of the reservations. It became apparent that these reservations were not staging posts on the way to Indian civilisation and eventual citizenship but instead were isolating the natives from white society. Indian reformer Lyman Abbott stated in 1883, 'I declare my conviction then that the reservation system is hopelessly wrong; that it cannot be amended or modified; that it can only be uprooted, root, trunk, branch, and leaf, and a new system put in its place.'[9] Abbott was one of many humanitarian Christian reformers who were at the forefront of new organisations that emerged with the aim of ensuring the assimilation of the Native American. In 1879 the Women's National Indian Association was founded and then followed three years later by the Indian Rights Association. In 1883 the Lake Mohonk Conference of Friends of the Indian met for the first time.[10]

Emerging contemporaneous with the rise of mass immigration in the United States and a focus on the ideal of the melting pot, these reform groups sought to ensure assimilation of the Indian. The reformers believed that the Indians were culturally inferior but not racially inferior and as such they could be civilised and assimilated. As the natives melted into the white Protestant mainstream then the norms and values of the dominant culture would be reinforced. It was this culture that provided the most solid foundations for the future of the nation.[11] The reformers had minimal appreciation of Indian traditions and values and were 'intent on forcing upon the natives the qualities that they themselves embodied. It was an ethnocentrism of frightening intensity, and it set a pattern that was not easily eradicated.'[12] Tom Holm has referred to the measures promoted by the reformers as the 'vanishing policy', in which the aim was to 'kill the Indian but save the man'.[13]

Two incidents which gained widespread publicity provided the spark which ignited the campaigns of the humanitarian Christian reformers. In January 1879 a group of Cheyenne escaped from Fort Robinson. They were then pursued by mounted cavalry and killed. Over a hundred men, women and children perished. The Indians had been imprisoned at the fort after they refused to return to their inhospitable reservation in present-day Oklahoma.[14] The great cruelty of the act and the image of mounted cavalry massacring largely defenceless Indians were used as evidence of the failures of the reservation system. In the same year as the Fort Robinson incident, the 'Ponca Affair' stimulated calls for reform of Indian policy. A Ponca leader, Standing Bear, fled the reservation in order to return the body of his dead son to the Ponca homeland. He was arrested and brought into Omaha to await transportation back to Indian Territory. Several reform-minded men filed a writ of *habeas corpus* for the Chief in an effort to set him free. Judge Dundy set an important precedent in American Indian Law when he granted the writ and ruled that Standing Bear was a person and was therefore allowed constitutional protection.[15] In effect the ruling suggested that Indians could not be forced to live on reservations and confined to certain territories.

Indeed the Christian reformers of the late nineteenth century were convinced that the reservation system had to change and that tribes should not be separated from white society. The policy of reservations perpetuated an Indian tribal identity that the reformers believed had to be broken. If the natives were to be civilised and absorbed into the dominant culture then they had to be individualised. The reformers were convinced that the crucial element in this civilisation effort was the allotment of land in severalty. They increasingly pushed for an allotment policy, although initially they were frustrated. The Scales bill of 1879 had failed to pass Congress as had many other allotment schemes and the Coke bill of 1881 was criticised by the reformers because its provisions did not apply to enough tribal groups. In 1883 the Indian Rights Association published a pamphlet which stepped up the campaign to end the reservation policy.[16]

The march towards allotments was not without opposition. In 1885 the National Indian Defence Association attempted to slow down the policy by arguing that immediate removal of the tribal structure would in fact damage the attempts to civilise the Indians.[17] Leading the reform efforts in the Senate was Henry Dawes who joined the Indian Affairs Committee in 1881. In attempting to push forward plans for allotment he faced resistance from western senators who opposed interference in their states and local administration of Indian relations. Southerners too were suspicious of Republican reform efforts. With the memory of Reconstruction still fresh, Democrats were opposed to the Republican Dawes' and others' attempts to assimilate and civilise the Indians.[18] The reformers were not to be denied, however, and in 1887 the Dawes Act was signed into law. Its provisions were a direct attempt to individualise Indians and instil in them the practice of land ownership which was central to white society. Each head of a household was to be allotted 160 acres, with 80 acres given to single persons over the age of 18. The land was to be held in trust for 25 years by the Secretary of the Interior after which it could be sold by the Indians. When selections had been made for suitable allotments and approved by the Secretary of the Interior then the occupants of the land were to become US citizens.[19]

The Dawes Act did eventually lead to significant portions of Indian land being bought by white interests and the scandals involving natives being cheated out of their land were plentiful in the early twentieth century. One historian has described the policy of allotment as a mixture of the 'philanthropic' and the 'predatory'.[20] It would be wrong, however, to imagine that the Dawes Act initiated an immediate programme to divide land. In reality few allotments were actually leased before 1895 and it was not until 1898 that the Curtis Act directed the Dawes Commission to proceed with allotment with greater speed.[21] Furthermore, it is not the case that the primary motivation of the Dawes Act was an attempt by western white interests to dispossess the natives. In reality it was eastern humanitarians who were the driving force behind the destruction of communal landholding. In the reformers' mind individualising the Indians was crucial to civilising them.[22] So it was a strong paternalism that was driving the allotment policy. Certainly there was prejudice at work because the attempts to civilise the Indians were driven by an ethnocentric assumption that white culture was superior to that of the natives. The reformers were not, strictly speaking, racists, however. They had faith that under careful guidance the Indians could be absorbed into white society.

Just as traditional accounts of Indian policy as an attempt by avaricious whites to destroy native culture and exploit their land for commercial purposes are far too simplistic, so histories that ignore Indian response and negotiation are incomplete. Native American organisations like the Four Mothers Society were formed to oppose allotment of land and the destruction of communal landholdings. Much of this resistance was grounded in native religious rituals intrinsically linked to the land. Attempts by the white authorities to restrict or ban religious ceremonies like the Sun Dance saw Indians alter their rituals to satisfy whites whilst retaining a distinct native identity. Similar negotiation with the forces of assimilation can be seen in responses to allotment. At Pine Ridge the Lakota selected their land or exchanged it so that the plots of extended family members were adjoined. In this way a semblance of tribal and communal identity was maintained.[23] There is scant evidence of literary protest to allotment by Indians largely because the most strident critics were conservatives who were unlikely to be literate. The 1891 novel *Wynema: Child of the Forest* by S. Alice Callahan, of the Muscogee, does, however, provide a strong criticism of the allotment policy. Not only are Indian characters given monologues which attack the Dawes Act but a white character named Genevieve similarly objects. She argues that the real reason behind the policy is to steal Indian land and to do it under 'the cloak of an ardent desire to promote the Indian's welfare by making him like ourselves whether he will or not, is infinitely worse'.[24]

The Christian reformers who drove the policy of allotment did, however, believe that they were acting in the best interests of the

Indians and working to elevate them to the level of white society. An accompanying policy in this process was the work of the Indian schools. Indian education programmes had begun earlier than the Dawes Act and there were 231 schools with over 10,000 students by 1887. The most famous of the Indian schools was set up by Henry Pratt at Carlisle, Pennsylvania, in 1879 and was designed to facilitate the integration of natives into white society. The success of Carlisle and many of its graduates encouraged policy makers that education could be utilised to civilise and assimilate the Indians. Thomas Morgan, Commissioner of Indian Affairs 1889–93, worked to extend Indian education and to ensure that schools on the reservations, agency boarding schools and industrial establishments like Carlisle were all to be linked into one system. In the early twentieth century there was a drive to promote Indian enrolment in public schools.[25]

All these efforts, however, did not bring the successes that the reformers hoped for. It was not as easy to assimilate the Indians and then integrate them into mainstream society. The vocational education programme was inadequate on a number of levels. Female students were often taught skills incompatible with life on the reservation and many often went back to their old tribal ways. Those who had adopted white ways and decided to leave the reservation only had the skills to work in low-paid jobs in the service economy in urban centres.[26] In many respects the school system promoted 'proletarianisation' rather than assimilation. Indian pupils were taught skills that confined them to a low level in the socio-economic structure and very few moved beyond an elementary level education.[27] Indian schools were designed to breed a degree of subservience. 'Academic and professional success were not possible outcomes for American Indians because they lay too far outside a safety zone that allocated social rankings by race.'[28]

The issue of race is important. The Christian reformers of the late nineteenth century saw the Indians as cultural backward but not racially inferior, and there was optimism that allotment and education could civilise and then absorb them into mainstream US society. Nevertheless, something different began to happen in the first two decades of the twentieth century which was to have a profound impact on the future of Indians and has excited debate among scholars. Eminent historian Francis Paul Prucha has acknowledged the declining importance of the Christian reformers. The handling of Indian affairs transferred to a more pragmatic, scientific and efficient approach. He maintains, however, that the paternalism of federal policy towards the Indians continued as did a belief in Indian cultural rather than racial differences.[29] Henry Fritz argues that, although the Christian reformers' influence did wane in the early part of the Progressive era, a series of appointments to the Board of Indian Commissioners from 1906 to 1913 saw a new reforming impulse. The new members had a Christian humanitarian motivation similar to those who had supported legislation like the Dawes Act. These men laid the groundwork for the Meriam Report and the reforms of John Collier.[30]

Despite these caveats it seems clear, nevertheless, that the influence of the old reformers was significantly reduced and, importantly, policy towards the Indians came to be dominated by a more racist outlook. Social scientists saw the Indians as a backward race and Francis Leupp, appointed as Commissioner of Indian Affairs in 1904, believed the natives could not be assimilated because they were innately inferior.[31] Racism became a more central force in Indian affairs and complete assimilation was no longer the principal goal of policy.[32] In 1903 the Supreme Court ruling in the *Lone Wolf* case gave Congress plenary authority over Indian relations and discarded the idea of requiring Indian consent for the disposition of their lands.[33] Three years later the Burke Act gave the Secretary of the Interior the authority to grant citizenship to Indians with individual allotments only if he thought them competent to live in white society.[34]

These decisions reflected a more pessimistic view of the Indians' ability to be assimilated into white society and they also paved the way for the dispossession of native lands. Between 1900 and 1934 approximately half of Indian allotments had been released on fee patent but the majority had been sold or forfeited because of non-payment of taxes. Land scandals were numerous especially in the first decade of the twentieth century. By the time allotment was ended in the 1930s the Indians had lost 91 million acres.[35] The paternalism of the old humanitarian reformers was lacking as Indian policy in the early twentieth century came to be dominated by western legislators who were hostile to an assimilation campaign.[36] The Indian was deemed to be racially inferior and unfit for absorption into white society, so he could not be assimilated in the melting pot.

This is not to say that Indian policy had performed a clear and consistent turn away from the goal of assimilation. There was a complex debate in the early twentieth century over the place of the Indian in American society. Between 1900 and 1920 federal policy saw great confusion in defining what the Indian was and what he should become. Some began to fear that the philanthropy of the old reformers and the more prejudiced policies after 1900 were destroying an ancient civilisation. Some reformers sought 'to maintain an identifiable Indian presence in American society that nevertheless conformed to white values and institutions'.[37] White-educated Indians like Charles Eastman sought to show the positive elements of native culture whilst also trying to integrate with the mainstream society. Eastman, artist Angel Decora and author Mourning Dove sought to show good in both white and native society acting as 'conveyors of ancient wisdom to modern audiences'.[38] Even in the assimilationist setting of the Indian schools there were efforts to promote courses in native arts and crafts so as to maintain defined racial differences.[39]

The decline of the influence of the humanitarian Christian reformers therefore led to an end to the drive to uplift and assimilate the Indians. Instead it left their place in American society more contested and complex. The forces of assimilation meant that the Indians were not what they had been and yet they were still separate. The late-nineteenth-century reformer's optimism that the Indian would disappear in the vast American melting pot was replaced by a belief in a hierarchical society with coexisting diverse groups.[40] In the early twentieth century an 'American culture was constructed that defined Indian-ness and modernity as polar opposites'.[41] Yet still there was an inconsistency in white thought about Indian identity and their place in US society. During the First World War, for example, natives were drafted into the army and served with distinction. The pro-assimilation newsletter *The Indian's Friend* praised Native Americans, reporting that Indian troops excelled in scouting and patrol duty but in so doing actually perpetuated racial stereotypes.[42]

The competing forces which impacted on Indian policy and the changing vision of their positions in US society left a people with an uncertain place in America. Indians themselves were operating in a cultural environment in which their identity was being shaped between two competing forces: those pulling them back to their tribal roots and others requiring adaptation to the norms and values of mainstream society. The attitudes of policy makers also evolved and they began to view the Indian's place in America in new ways. Following the willingness of 15,000 Indians to fight for the US in the First World War a law was passed in 1919 which allowed Native American veterans to become citizens and in 1924 a final Indian citizenship bill followed. It was clear, however, that this legislation did not remove federal authority over the Indians. In fact the atmosphere of patriotism which permeated the era contributed to a belief that government regulation was not incompatible with Indians' personal freedom.[43]

Despite the granting of citizenship, Native Americans continued to face depressing socio-economic conditions and a series of calls for reform in the 1920s culminated in the Meriam Report of 1928. The tale of soaring infant mortality rates, illiteracy and deaths from tuberculosis provided a stinging indictment of the assimilation policy of the previous decades.[44] The campaign to reverse this policy was led by John Collier who was the architect of the Indian New Deal of the 1930s. Legislation was passed to abolish the allotment system and to promote tribal sovereignty and local self-government.[45] The work of Collier and the Bureau of Indian Affairs was a direct assault on the reforms promoted by the Christian reformers in the late nineteenth century. Although Collier's dogmatic and inflexible approach earned him many critics, and despite the fact that the Indian New Deal failed to bring improvements to the lives of many Indians, it did lay the foundations for the development of a national Indian pressure group. The forces of Indian self-determination and growing political consciousness that were expressed by the National Congress of American Indians have their roots in the renewing of tribal identity that had begun during the 1930s.[46]

A detailed exploration of the Indian New Deal and the emergence of the American Indian movement in the mid-twentieth century are beyond the scope of this chapter. The crucial point is that the policies instituted to assimilate the Native Americans from the 1880s through to the 1930s had failed. The optimistic belief that the Indians could be civilised and then vanish into the mainstream had been proved wrong and Native Americans were left in a complex and confused space in society. Despite the granting of citizenship to the Indians in 1924 they were not granted political equality and their legal status was that of 'wards of the government'.[47] This was not what the reformers who pushed for the Dawes Act had envisaged when they called for the assimilation of the natives. Looking back over centuries of federal policy towards the Indians from the vantage point of the late twentieth century, Francis Prucha argued that 'paternalism [was] abiding'.[48] The early twentieth century, however, saw a racial prejudice which viewed the natives as destined to live on the periphery of American society. As a more pluralistic view of that society developed so Indian self-determination and cultural identity was more accepted.

These competing interpretations of the Indian place in the United States, and the response of the natives to this, laid the foundation for the unique status of Indians among American minority groups. The assimilation process was not ineffective but neither was it successful. The Indians were changed but tribal identities remained. To end as we began with examples of the complex place of Native Americans in US society, a recent multi-million-dollar deal saw the Seminole tribe buy the Hard Rock Café business chain. Tribe Vice Chairman Max Osceola said, 'our ancestors sold Manhattan for trinkets, today, with the acquisition of the Hard Rock Cafe, we're going to buy Manhattan back one hamburger at a time'.[49] The purchase of the business displays Native American emersion in the mainstream culture and yet the reference to Manhattan shows an awareness of a continuing anti-colonial struggle and a strong tribal identity. The foundations for this juxtaposition were laid in the paternalism and prejudice of the reform efforts in the late nineteenth and early twentieth century.

13

AMERICAN IDENTITY AND THE AMERICAN WEST

The American West of popular culture is a place of mountain men, pioneer families, cowboys and Indian fighters. Popular stereotypes of the West reinforced the story of a people who struggled against adversity to conquer the frontier. As Ann Fabian has argued, 'politicians, fashion designers and producers of mass culture' have moulded 'popular legend into the social and economic facts of the living past'.[1] The frontier story has provided an exciting usable history which can be shaped to promote nationalism and a distinct American character. This legend was rooted in academic history for much of the twentieth century because of the influence of Frederick Jackson Turner's 'frontier thesis'. He argued that the process of settling the West explained the development of American national identity. The pioneer spirit and the victory of civilisation over savagery played a crucial part in the construction of the nation and the progress of democracy. Turner's thesis was heavily criticised, however, in the late twentieth century by 'New Western Historians', who view his paradigm as ethnocentric and ignorant of the West as a distinct region. This chapter seeks to provide a brief survey of the major elements of the historiographical debate. Rejecting Turner's interpretive framework, more recent work on the West has explored the experiences of different racial groups in the region. Their story further contributed to the evolving parameters of American citizenship and the shaping of national identity.

In July 1893 Frederick Jackson Turner addressed the American Historical Association. He drew attention to the assertion of the Census of 1890 that the American frontier line had disappeared – the continent had been settled. Turner argued, 'the existence of an area of free land, its continuous recession, and the advance of American settlement westward, explain American development'. He believed that the social development of the country had been shaped by the continuous movement of the frontier, which provided a great force for

Americanisation. Turner told his audience that the growth of nationalism and the evolution of American political institutions were profoundly affected by the frontier. In the harsh and isolated environment of the wilderness, American faith in democracy and aversion to direct and centralised control was forged. Turner closed by stating, 'the frontier has gone, and with its going has closed the first period of American history'.[2]

Turner was very keen to establish credibility for his frontier thesis and worked hard to disseminate his ideas. By the early twentieth century mainstream history courses in universities around the United States had adopted many elements of his theories. In a discussion of American historiography which was published in 1920, Arthur M. Schlesinger gave Turner credit for the vitality and new direction he had given historical research. Turner did not escape criticism, however. Charles A. Beard questioned elements of the frontier thesis and argued that Americanisation did not proceed more rapidly on the frontier than in other areas of the country. In the 1930s and 1940s a new generation of critics questioned the overly deterministic nature of Turner's thesis and refuted claims that the frontier had been a safety valve for American labour.[3] The theory of the frontier was criticised but it was not conclusively discredited. As one historian has argued, 'the power of Turner's frontier thesis derived from its commitment to the study of what it has meant to be an American'.[4] It is this which draws historians back to his ideas and forces them to engage with the frontier thesis.

In the late 1940s a 'neo-Turnerism' developed as his ideas on the West continued to have a significant influence on American history. Ray A. Billington was the most influential of the scholars who followed Turner's ideas. He argued that the critics had largely missed their mark and he published a textbook which followed the pattern that Turner had sketched out.[5] Billingon saw the frontier as a series of 'migrating zones' which represented different stages in the development of society. He asserted that 'the continuous rebirth of society in the western wilderness, endowed the American people and their institutions with characteristics not shared by the rest of the world'.[6] With a clear echo of Turner, Billington maintained that 'frontiering was a process through which imported European customs and habits were gradually Americanised'.[7]

It is a reality of scholarship that interpretations of the past are often heavily influenced by the present. Certainly the history of the West and opinions of the frontier thesis illustrate this. Turner wrote in the late nineteenth century during a time of strong national self-confidence and Billington penned his volume in the period of post-Second

World War optimism and materialism. Similarly the critics of Turner during the depression era saw little contemporary evidence for his belief in the great riches of American natural resources.[8] It is not surprising then that a 'New Western History' which sought to fully discredit Turner's theory grew out of the changing historical focus which accompanied the civil rights' movement and its aftermath. Interest in the history of minorities and rejection of Anglocentric stories of American progress impacted on the study of the West.

Arguably the most controversial of the work produced by the 'New Western Historians' was Patricia Limerick's *The Legacy of Conquest*. She retold the story of the West not as a tale of frontier and American exceptionalism but as one of imperialism and conquest. Limerick argued that there was great continuity in the history of the West and that nineteenth-century attitudes towards the environment and ethnic minorities stretched into the twentieth century. There had not been a closing of the frontier which represented a defining line in the history of the West. Limerick asserted that continuity in the history of the region was provided by conquest, which was the dominant force tying the diverse experiences of many different ethnic groups together.[9]

The New Western Historians offered a thorough critique of Turner's frontier thesis and pointed to many new avenues of research in the study of the West. Donald Worster asserted that the ecology of the region was crucial to an understanding of the West. He argued that Turner's path of development was not followed; pastoral life was not just a passing stage of settlement. The West remained a distinct region well into the twentieth century because of its unique environment, an environment which set it apart from other regions of the United States.[10] For Worster, the land was crucial to an understanding of the West. 'Confronting the land, being subdued by it, westerners have found the beginnings of an identity.'[11] Richard White focussed on a further aspect of the environment in a study of the role of animals in the history of the American West. He argued that animals of enterprise were crucial to the development of the West throughout the nineteenth and twentieth centuries.[12]

Fresh studies of different ethnic groups, the role of women, the persistent theme of imperialism and the commercialisation of the West all emerged from the New Western History of the 1980s and 1990s.[13] The juxtaposition of different racial groups and the interactions between them were a focus for a new history of the West which saw conversations going on in several different languages.[14] Tying this scholarship together was a belief that Turner's thesis had restricted the scope of western history and provided a simplistic and mono-causal interpretation of the past. Turner's attempt to portray the West as a process in which the frontier marched forward bringing progress and forging American national identity failed to recognise the diversity of the western experience.[15]

The debate between the 'new' and 'old' histories of the West was given national media coverage. The complexities of the academic contest was simplified for members of the general public into a struggle between the cherished ideal of the West as a place of adventure and pioneering spirit, and the region as a harsh environment of exploitation and racial discord. The New Western Historians were popularly characterised as a bunch of politically correct academics who were attacking the romantic images of Billy the Kid and Davy Crockett, of adventurous mountain men and courageous homesteaders.[16] The interest in scholarly work shown by the mainstream media speaks to the importance of the West in Americans' sense of history and national identity. To challenge the optimistic and unifying message presented by Turner's frontier thesis was to question the veracity of a fundamental national legend. This legend and the ideal of the frontier were invoked by presidents throughout the twentieth century. Kennedy's 'new frontier' spoke of national challenge and struggle. Reagan spoke of settlers pushing west and singing songs of daring and fairness, songs which represented the 'American sound'.[17] The history of the West and the ideal of the frontier have been crucial in the shaping of American memory.

Not all of the new history of the West received the criticism that the work of Limerick, in particular, did. In an influential collection of essays edited by William Cronon, George Miles and Jay Gatlin, scholars explored new aspects of western history.[18] This volume was not attacked by traditionalists in the same way that other work was, largely because one of its editors, William Cronon, did not fully nail his colours to the mast of New Western History.[19] Cronon offered a brief study of an Alaskan town in which he called for a new form of environmental history integrating the ecology of people and their political economy.[20] Clyde Milner II provided an investigation of the shared identity of 'westerners' and how this distinct regional sense of self was shaped. He concluded, 'a unified western region is no more likely than a monolithic western identity. But westerners do share a territory, a history, and a future.'[21]

The new western history, therefore, engaged with the Turnerian paradigm over whether the West was place or process. The development pattern of the United States has been such that the location of 'the West' has changed. It is difficult to define a region which has evolved to such a large extent. The West can be found in western

Florida and then in Oklahoma; it was then in California and also in Hawaii. Indeed some historians have argued that the Pacific deserves consideration as a place in the history of the West. The conquest of western lands was inextricably linked with a similar process in the Pacific. It was the total settlement of land that signalled the demarcation of the Pacific Ocean as the final frontier line of the West, but this was not the case during the period of expansion.[22]

For Turner the West was dominated by an experience, the process of the ever-moving frontier is what defined that experience. The great disjuncture of western history was, therefore, provided by the closing of the frontier in 1890 which Turner used as the theme of his influential 1893 address. His critics seek to break away from the idea of the West as a process dominated by the frontier and look at the West as a region, a distinct geographical place. It is, however, important to recognise that Turner himself did not neglect the concept of the West as region. His famous thesis heralded the end of the frontier and much of his work thereafter was devoted to investigating the societies that developed after the frontier had been closed.[23] Some of the New Western Historians, whilst forthrightly criticising Turner's work in many ways, have realised that there are important connections between the concept of the West as both a process and a place. Cronon *et al.* argued, in their introductory essay to *Under an Open Sky*, that the West represented 'many things, and one cannot define away its complexities by fiat ... the West may be the region lying somewhere beyond the Mississippi River, but it is also the experience of going there'.[24]

The story of the Jayhawkers of 1849 serves to illustrate this duality of the West as both process and place. A group of thirty-six white men, they headed for southern California to make their fortunes. Not all of the men stayed in California but those who did regarded the region in which they lived as a veritable heaven on earth. The Jayhawkers held reunions from 1872 to 1918 and the letters they sent to one another show a distinct shared experience of the challenges they faced as pioneers. The Jayhawkers had an emotional connection to a specific place in southern California but they were also bound together by a shared experience. For these westerners the 'development of a sense of place was connected to the perception of the frontier's passing'.[25] Both place and process played important parts in what it was to be a westerner. A western identity has been shaped not just by attachment to a particular place and collective experiences but also the connection between the region and the nation as a whole.[26]

New Western Historians who wish to move the ground of historical enquiry away from frontier process to regional identity have not fully acknowledged the connection between the two. Limerick argued that if we 'deemphasise the frontier and its supposed end, conceive of the West as a place and not a process [then] Western American history has a new look'.[27] Seeking to investigate this western place and the diversity of peoples and interactions that inhabit it necessarily requires, however, an understanding of frontier-based ideals.[28] For example, Turner's frontier thesis neglected the role played in the West by blacks and other ethnic minorities, focussing instead on the pioneering spirit of Euro-Americans who conquered virgin lands. Many of the ethnic minority westerners that new histories of the West have thrown light on, however, shared a sense that the frontier experience had shaped an environment which offered greater opportunity.[29] The study of the West needs to engage with region and place and the diverse peoples that inhabited them but the concept of frontier and the process of becoming West are also important. There are therefore significant overlaps between the Turnerian 'old' western history and the 'new' western history of the last thirty years. Such is the significance of the place of the West in the American past, that the field of western history has room for a myriad of differing interpretations.

One of these interpretations has focussed on the history of border-lands in explaining how different communities developed in the West. Herbert Bolton, a pupil of Turner, adapted the ideas of space and frontier when focussing on the border of the south-west where the United States meets Mexico. Writing in the 1920s, Bolton argued that Spanish institutions, culture and personnel had shaped the develop-ment of the south-west frontier in a hierarchical pattern which reflected Spanish society. Border studies scholars, or regionalists, who moved the debate forward, saw places such as Los Angeles and Dallas as centres of vibrant cultural interaction and invention.[30] John Faragher has called for a cross-cultural approach to the study of different communities along the American frontiers. He argues that the eventual dominance of Anglo-American patterns of settlement should not lead historians to neglect community groups of different ethnic background that came before that Anglo-American model.[31]

To return this discussion of historiography back to where it started, with Frederick Jackson Turner, it should be noted that his ideas remain relevant. A narrow frontier-based reading of the West is too simplistic but the ideal of the frontier remains important when seek-ing to understand western history, a history which offers a labyrinth of paths to explore. Indeed as one historian has remarked, 'a place as diverse as the West is certainly capable of handling a multiplicity of perspectives, or paradigms, and even combining seemingly polar opposites on occasions'.[32] The major themes of this volume are American national identity, race and citizenship. In the final section of this chapter, therefore, we briefly address the place of ethnic minorities in the West and the contribution they made to the identity of the region. Turner's frontier thesis provided for an Anglocentric picture of the West which reinforced the racial exclusivity of national identity. He wrote at a time when white northerners and southerners were reconciled following the sectional strife of Civil War and Reconstruction. The experience of ethnic minorities is, however, a crucial element in the history of the West.

It is important to note that whilst there were many ethnic groups who came to live in the West theirs was not the same experience as those who were of the West. 'The ethnic group becomes central to the region's history when and where and to the extent it becomes altered by that region, or develops an active voice in defining the region's intractable diversity.'[33] No western history, therefore, can ignore the place of Native Americans. A celebration of the march of progress as the continent was settled is also a celebration of an invasion and a humanitarian disaster.[34] The ravages of disease had brought death to multitudes of Indians from the time of Columbus, but the violence of the Plains Wars was a crucial element in the advance of the frontier. Despite the popular images of warriors fighting US cavalrymen it was the elderly and women and children who suffered more deaths.[35] Nevertheless, the experience of Native Americans was not a simple story of conquest, of being vanquished by European settlement and the movement of the frontier. A complex process of interactions left a legacy on both native and European peoples.[36] In the period before British victory over the French in 1763 there was a shared Euro-Indian world where parallel lives were possible but after this point Euro-Americans sought to remove Indian nations from the American future.[37]

This was not, however, a process dominated by assimilation and extinction. Native Americans experienced progress and disaster, and new as well as restricted opportunities. This reality is, however, often overlooked. Even popular works like Dee Brown's *Bury My Heart at Wounded Knee*, which aim to tell history from the Indian point of view, still fall back on a tone which reinforces a discourse in which Indians are victims.[38] Historians must seek to explore the ways Indians were shaped by the experience of the West and, importantly, helped to shape that experience. Indian voices have been articulating their interpretations and contributing to the history of the West for centuries. The *Cherokee Advocate*, an Indian newspaper in the English language, for example, campaigned against removal policies and sought help from sympathetic whites. There are different strands in Indian historical interpretations which offer competing views of American history.[39] These voices are part of the western experience and must be heard if we are to fully understand the character of the West and its impact on the nation.

The work of borderland studies mentioned above highlighted the important place of Mexican culture in the development of western identity. Like Native Americans, Mexicans experienced the advance of Euro-American civilisation and the cultural and economic exchanges this brought. A pioneering study by Carey McWilliams in 1949, the themes of which were picked up by scholars in the 1960s, identified a 'fantasy heritage' in relation to Mexican-Americans. This fantasy enabled Anglo-Americans to glorify the south-west's Spanish heritage whilst simultaneously ignoring discrimination against Mexicans and Mexican-Americans. These historic and cultural roots were, however, vital to the development of the West and the continued flow of Mexican immigrants means that Hispanic culture remains a constant element of American identity, especially in the south-west.

The conclusion of the Mexican–American War in 1848 saw large areas of land and population ceded to the US. In the New Mexico territory in the late nineteenth century Hispanic farmers faced battles with corporations and railroad lines that encroached on their lands. Despite the advances of American capitalism and culture, the Mexicans in the region were able to maintain their own cultural heritage.[40] For much of the twentieth century Mexican immigrants provided a constant flow of peoples into the West. Not only has this promoted continual debate among white Americans about the desirability of such immigration but there was also tension in the Hispanic communities of the south-west between Mexican-Americans and new arrivals from across the border. Debates concerning the admission of New Mexico and Arizona into the US were marked by discussion of the large Mexican populations of the states.[41] The ever-increasing number of Hispanic immigrants means that their cultural influence remains crucial to an understanding of the West. The cultural landscape of the region was significantly shaped by Mexicans and Mexican-Americans both before and after the official closing of the frontier that Turner highlighted.

Regional identity was also shaped by ethnic minorities who moved to the West and whose experiences there in turn moulded a distinctly western ethnic identity. African-Americans who arrived in the West faced a situation in which they were not the only peoples of colour. They lived in communities which were characterised by racial diversity in a way that other regions of the US were not.[42] The West offered the promise of a new racial frontier with greater opportunity for an egalitarian society than elsewhere in the nation. Throughout the 1850s and 1860s black community groups petitioned the California government to repeal prohibitions against black testimony in court cases, discrimination against black access to open lands and poor educational opportunities for black children. Concessions were eventually won from the California assembly, which modified some of its racist legal codes.[43] On the frontier in the latter half of the nineteenth century, however, blacks faced similar racial restrictions as those existing in the rest of the county. Jim Crow segregation, both legally codified and de facto, prevailed in the West.

Nevertheless, racial prejudice was more fluid and inconsistent in the West than it was in other regions of America. By the early twentieth century black homesteaders and soldiers had faded from view, with black urbanites in Los Angeles, Seattle, San Francisco, Oakland and Denver providing the most visible African-American element in the West. The Great Migration brought a concerted move West as well as North. In the period 1890–1940 residential opportunities were better in the West than in the North or the South, with black home ownership higher than elsewhere.[44] Still, economic opportunities were restricted by a racial hierarchy in the West which reflected white supremacy across the nation. Where the South met the West there was racial violence in places like Oklahoma and Texas, whereas on the West coast there was a form of 'polite racism' which constituted relative progress.[45] 'The myth of western opportunity had a shaping impact on the region ... because newcomers brought ... fears and mythic expectations with them to the West.'[46] When hopes of a better life in the region were met with a firm pattern of white control and racism, black leaders adopted a distinctive western civil rights language. They used the ideals of opportunity and the pioneer spirit to criticise the racism of whites in the West who prevented the realisation of such an ideal.[47]

The fourth main minority ethnic group which made up the racial diversity of the West were Asian-Americans. The majority of the Chinese immigrants who arrived in the US in the mid-nineteenth century did so with the vision of a better life and the commitment to work to achieve this. Despite popular stereotypes they were not 'coolies' and did not represent a new form of slave labour. Most of the Chinese arrived as free agents who could go their own way once they had repaid the debt incurred gaining passage to America.[48] The Chinese were, however, exploited as cheap labourers by railroads and other businesses and this created animosity among the white working class who saw them as the tools of big business. This economic conflict as well as the obvious racial differences led many to argue that the Chinese would never be assimilated and drove a campaign which culminated in the 1882 Chinese Exclusion Act.[49]

This is not to argue that the Chinese suffered suffocating injustice which denied all opportunity. Farmers were able to buy and lease lands from Anglo-American corporations which far exceeded possibilities in their homeland.[50] Whites in the Boise Basin Rocky Mountain region hoped their Chinese neighbours would help grow the local economy. Chinese miners enjoyed good material wealth and relatively peaceful race relations in the area from the 1860s through to the 1880s.[51] Japanese immigrants in the West were able to progress economically and worked tirelessly to establish prosperous businesses. The concentration camps of the Second World War, however, provided a graphic illustration of the limits of their acceptance in white society.

The story of racial diversity in the West deserves a much fuller elucidation than that provided here but this brief discussion illustrates the incomplete image of the West in popular memory. Turner's thesis, that the advance of the frontier melted Americans of different European ancestry into one people, fails to acknowledge the place of ethnic minorities in the development of the West and consequently the nation. The frontier was shaped by Americans of all races and creeds. Turner was right to assert that the experience of moving west played a crucial part in the development of the American nation. What he failed to acknowledge was both the promise and racial prejudice at the heart of this process and the nation as a whole.

14

IMMIGRATION AND ASSIMILATION
Melting pot or salad bowl?

Robert Kennedy wrote, 'our attitude towards immigration reflects our faith in the American ideal'.[1] That ideal being that immigrants of all ethnic backgrounds could prosper in US society; that talent and energy and not race or creed would decide their fate. To a certain extent the reality of the American past has reflected the ideal. Many who entered the country prospered and made a vital contribution to the development of their new homeland. This, however, tells only half the story because ethnic identity so often determined the extent to which immigrants were included in American national identity. Indeed from the beginning Americans worried about how this identity could be constructed by such a diverse array of new arrivals. Washington wrote to John Adams in 1794 expressing concern that immigrants 'retain the language, habits and principles (good or bad) which they bring with them'.[2]

Central to the debate concerning immigration and the development of America – which continues today – is the issue of assimilation. If immigrants retain their native culture and if they pass this on to their children then what is to be the American culture? The extent to which it is vital to the success of the United States that newcomers are assimilated is an issue with profound implications for the national character and one which has regularly captured the nation's attention. The brevity of this chapter does not allow for a detailed investigation of American immigration. Indeed such is the rich variety of this huge topic that even a massive volume in comparative history would struggle to do it justice. Instead what is presented here is a summary spanning the turn of the twentieth century to the present. The aim is to show how the pattern of immigration and immigrant experience, theories of assimilation and ethnic identity, and government legislation have interacted and evolved in that period.

The ideal of an American melting pot where different ethnic groups were smelted into a new people was expressed in the work of French immigrant, Crèvecoeur. In a much cited passage from 1782 he answered his own question: 'What is an American? He is either a European, or the descendant of a European ... here individuals of all nations are melted into a new race of men.'[3] Importantly, Crèvecoeur focussed on Europeans, among whom there was a gradual crumbling of distinctive identity throughout the nineteenth century. During this period, which is often termed 'old immigration', assimilation was taken for granted among European groups and seen as inconceivable and unimportant in relation to other races. A largely decentralised America meant that ethnic groups often avoided major contact. It was not until the turn of the twentieth century that assimilation became a major national concern.[4] Up to this point immigrant groups who were not easily absorbed among the existing Anglo-Saxon population were effectively isolated. From 1820 to 1860 the Irish were never fewer than at least a third of all immigrants and they faced consistent oppression at the hands of nativist forces. Nevertheless, they gained acceptance by highlighting their whiteness, which set them apart from black, Mexican and Asian peoples.[5] This latter group was largely represented by the Chinese who were labelled 'coolies' entering America as unskilled contract labourers, little more than slaves. Although this characterisation did not tell the full picture, the Chinese were the victims of persistent racial discrimination and violence. Their social spaces were isolated from whites and the government eventually curtailed their arrival with the Chinese Exclusion Act of 1882.[6]

As the nineteenth century closed in the midst of an explosion of new immigration and the advance of industrialisation, the localism and separatism which had allowed Americans to avoid the issue of assimilation crumbled. It was the Progressive era which exposed 'the challenge that a divided heritage and an ambiguous, dualistic national identity posed to the American people'.[7]

Over 20 million immigrants arrived in the United States between 1890 and 1920. By the end of that period a little over 13 per cent of the nation's population was foreign born. Not only did the volume of immigration in these years increase but so too did the variety. Approximately twenty-six ethnic groups arrived from the area north of Greece and east of Germany alone.[8] There was also a more significant Asian and Pacific Islander presence in the immigration figures, including Japanese, Filipino, South Asian and Korean newcomers. As the US economy grew rapidly in the early twentieth century, immigrants flooded into the labour market from Latin America in greater numbers. By 1920 Puerto Ricans had migrated, either as contract labourers or as free agents, to forty-five American states.[9] Immigration in the south-west was swelled by the increase in Mexicans who crossed the border. Their numbers grew almost four-fold in Texas between 1900 and 1930, and from 8,000 to 191,000 in California during the same period.[10]

The majority of the immigrants who arrived in the US during this period of 'mass' or 'new' immigration were young males who came initially as migrant labourers. Their aim was to earn enough money to support families at home before returning there having improved their long-term economic prospects. Although most did eventually stay in America the numbers who returned are greater than popular imagination acknowledges. To give some examples, 35 per cent of Poles, Serbs and Croats, 40 per cent of Greeks and over 50 per cent of southern Italians returned to Europe.[11] Oscar Handlin's influential work of the 1950s described the typical European immigrant as an 'uprooted' peasant. Longing for land to start a new life, Handlin argues that these immigrants were shocked to find themselves in American cities, alienated from the rest of society and faced with hardship, squalor and oppressive landlords.[12] This view, however, ignored the fact that many immigrants were not from a monolithic socio-economic background in their native countries and were shielded from the harsh realities of America by extensive ethnic communities. There was a collectivist nature to much of the immigration at the turn of the century as family connections decided the destination of many new arrivals. These connections played a crucial part in supporting ethnic communities and economies.[13]

This massive and diverse influx of immigrants, and their experiences as they adjusted to a new life, stimulated a concerted national debate on how these arrivals were to be absorbed by the existing American society. A Jewish-English writer, Israel Zangwill, produced a drama in 1908 entitled *The Melting Pot*. The play's protagonist declares that America 'is God's crucible, the great melting pot where all the races of Europe are melting and re-forming'. Although the main focus is on Europeans, both black and Asian peoples were specifically mentioned as elements in this emerging crucible of race.[14] Explicit in the melting pot ideal was that immigrants would be assimilated and Americanised; they would lose their old culture and become Americans. President Theodore Roosevelt explained, 'we must Americanise them in every way, in speech, in political ideas and principles … above all, the immigrant must learn to talk and think and be United States'.[15]

Roosevelt did not believe that the newcomers should be allowed to maintain their cultural heritage, a situation which was tacitly endorsed by those who saw the issue of immigration through a more pluralistic lens. In an article for the *Nation* in 1915, eastern-European immigrant Horace Kallen pointed to the persistence of a distinct cultural identity among immigrant groups and argued for a multicultural society. For Kallen, America was to resemble an orchestra with many different instruments blending to produce one piece of music or a salad bowl where distinct flavours remained within a larger fusion of tastes.[16] From this perspective, diversity was to be embraced as a positive good rather than as a threat to the unity of the nation and the perpetuity of its cultural heritage. It was the ideas of Theodore Roosevelt, however, which were reflective of the dominant mood of the era; it was assimilation that was to be encouraged, even demanded.

The Dillingham Commission on Immigration which held hearings between 1907 and 1911 recommended that restrictions to immigration should be applied. In arriving at this conclusion, however, it used flawed data and logic in its simple categorisation of immigrant groups and unflattering comparisons between 'old' and 'new' immigrants. The IQ testing scales were biased in favour of native-born Americans and only perpetuated racial stereotypes which portrayed the arrivals from eastern and southern Europe as intellectually inferior and therefore damaging for American society. In 1917 legislation was passed which virtually excluded all Asian immigration – Roosevelt's 'Gentleman's Agreement' had already curtailed arrivals from Japan. The legislation also implemented a literacy test, although it was not applied to those fleeing religious persecution or joining family members already in the US. Finally, with nativist sentiment significantly in the ascendant, the 1921 Quota Act and then the 1924 Johnson–Reed Act were passed and set a limit on annual immigration whilst also instituting blatant biases which restricted the arrival of those from nations who were regarded as racially inferior.[17]

This legislation, which went into effect in 1929, saw institutional approval of the ideal of Anglo-conformity. More racially exclusive than the concept of the melting pot, this theory openly regarded those of non-Anglo-Saxon stock as inferior and aimed to protect the racial integrity of citizens of north-western European descent who represented the majority of those who populated the US.[18] Theodore Roosevelt had already indicated that he would support coercion to force hyphenated Americans to become simply Americans and he was also clear that non-white peoples were not capable of self-government and therefore never going to be fully assimilated into the American nation.[19] In the legislation of the 1920s the belief in the difficulties of assimilating 'inferior races' was clearly displayed. The aim was to curtail immigration to such an extent that the forces of assimilation could work more swiftly and without the interruption of consistent advances in the arrival of immigrants who strayed from the white Anglo-Saxon Protestant dominant stock.

The forces of assimilation had an impact on the community organisations of the new arrivals and naturalised American citizens of different ethnic groups in important ways and indeed battles between assimilationists and pluralists were fought at a local level. In New York the Jewish Educational Alliance sought to Americanise newly arrived Jews. The Alliance had Israel Zangwill as one of its most notable members and helped immigrants adjust to New York whilst also encouraging assimilation through involvement in 'patriotic' events and activities such as readings of the Declaration of Independence and singing of the national anthem. The Alliance gradually mellowed its approach towards assimilation but it was faced by rival organisations such as the Educational League, which was set up by Jewish intellectuals and sought to cultivate Russian-Jewish pride.[20] In the Mexican-American community the League of Latin American Citizens (LULAC) emphasised the American side of their identity and subscribed to the ideal of the melting pot. The Americans of Mexican descent who led LULAC attempted to gain greater acceptance in US society by insinuating that they were different from Mexicans on the other side of the border. They supported restrictions to immigration because they believed it would stop them being negatively labelled in the same way as the new immigrants. LULAC did, however, arouse opposition from those who rejected this form of assimilation and desired to develop a distinct Mexican-American culture in the south-west.[21]

Although the restrictive legislation of the 1920s did not apply to the western hemisphere, Mexican immigration was significantly reduced by the forced repatriation schemes during the depression. Only when economic conditions necessitated cheap migrant labour during the 1940s did the doors open more fully again under the Bracero Agreement. For many non-Anglo-Saxon groups, however, entry to the US in the period from the end of the 1920s through to the 1960s was nothing more than a trickle. Scholars in the 1960s therefore focussed on the extent to which assimilation had occurred; the extent to which the melting pot had smelted away the cultural distinctions of the immigrants and their children and grandchildren. The seminal study of assimilation was produced by Milton Gordon. He concluded in 1964 that neither the melting pot nor the Anglo-conformity model had been successful. Instead, the experience of immigrants was dominated by widespread acculturation or behavioural assimilation. This meant that they adopted the language and cultural behaviour of the host society. Nevertheless, what had not been achieved was structural assimilation, which saw entrance of ethnic groups into the social cliques and institutional activities of American society. Only when this occurred would all other elements of assimilation follow.[22]

First published a year before Gordon's work, Nathan Glazer and Daniel Moynihan concluded in *Beyond the Melting Pot*, a study which focussed on New York, that native language and culture were lost in the first and second generations after immigration but that the melting pot had not successfully assimilated new arrivals. It was asserted that 'the assimilating power of American society and culture operated on immigrant groups in different ways, to make them it is true, something they had not been, but still something distinct and identifiable'.[23] According to Glazer and Moynihan neither the melting pot nor the salad bowl successfully described the immigrant experience. Inherent in their conclusion was that all groups had been changed in some ways and there was scope for further assimilating progress in the future. It would seem obvious that the problems faced by blacks and Puerto Ricans in Glazer and Moynihan's study were significantly impacted by the institutional racism of American society. Writing in 1965, Shibatuni and Kwan used the framework of symbolic interactionism to explain that the treatment of a person in a society depends on how he is defined by that society. One of the great barriers to assimilation then was the colour line which segregated minorities.[24]

The 1960s brought significant civil rights' legislation in order to improve the lives of these racial minorities and it also saw changes in immigration policy which embraced a more pluralistic conception of American identity. A subtle change in approach can be noted in the McCarran–Walter Act of 1952. Although its author, Senator McCarran of Nevada, favoured limits to the flow of immigrants to ensure that the arrival of aliens was not such that it threatened successful assimilation, he did lift the ban on immigrants from Asia in place since 1924. The Act of 1952 allowed for one hundred immigrants per year from countries in a clearly defined Asia-Pacific area and those of Asian descent and any new arrivals were to be eligible for naturalisation.[25] In 1965 the Kennedy–Johnson Amendment to the McCarran–Walter Act was passed. Scheduled to go into effect in 1968, the legislation lifted the old quota system and set the annual limit for Europe, Africa and Asia at 170,000 with no stipulation concerning national origin other than a limit of 20,000 per country. Immediate relatives were to be exempted from these figures. The success of repealing the restrictive quota systems came at a price, however. The legislation fixed the number of immigrants accepted from the western hemisphere for the first time – the figure was to be 120,000 a year. This limit was included in the law at the insistence of those who supported traditional restriction and who sought to put a cap on the potential number of blacks from the Caribbean and Latinos from south of the border. Republican minority leader, Everett Dirksen, conceded that these western hemisphere restrictions were the price administration reformers agreed to pay for his support of the abolition of quotas.[26]

Nevertheless, the legislation did open the doors to more immigrants from Africa and Asia. There was increased diversity from the mass immigration of the turn of the century and there was also a continued increase in sheer numbers. There were 7.3 million new arrivals in the 1980s and the immigration legislation of 1990 allowed for a further increase in the following decade.[27] Contemporaneous with the growth of immigration was an increasing pride in ethnic identity. The most overt example of this grew out of the late 1960s and the development of the Black Power movement. This type of ethnic distinctiveness obviously raised further questions about the possibility of assimilation in America. Milton Gordon, writing in the 1970s, reflected that he had not foreseen the development of such a movement in his earlier work and argued that its existence furthered a structural separatism driven by minority groups themselves as well as the racial prejudice exhibited by white society.[28]

The greater acceptance of ethnic diversity in the post-1960s led to changes in the way ethnic groups perceived themselves and their place in American society. The Chicano movement in the Mexican-American community led to a rejection of the assimilationist model which had been embraced in earlier decades and a greater emphasis on Mexican culture. The increased prominence of ethnic identity also led to greater sympathy among Mexican-Americans for illegal undocumented Mexican immigrants, even LULAC increasingly identified with these arrivals as their 'brothers'.[29] With the fading of assimilation and the rise of racial pride and distinctiveness, ethnicity increasingly became a strategic choice for individuals, a way of gaining power and pressing for social change.[30] Herbert Gans argued that late-twentieth-century America was experiencing the existence of 'symbolic ethnicity', which was a voluntary concept often expressed as a nostalgic allegiance to the culture of an immigrant generation or old country. Mary Waters' study of suburban California in the 1980s found a pattern whereby ethnicity was individually constructed as people sought to embrace their ethnicity because assimilation had proceeded to the extent that just being a simple unhyphenated American was too bland.[31]

It is important, however, to note that there is a crucial difference between white Americans embracing their ethnic heritage and exhibiting this kind of symbolic ethnicity and the peoples of colour in the nation encouraging racial pride. The latter were much less likely to be assimilated into mainstream American society. The melting pot absorbed the ethnic identities of immigrants of European descent much more easily than those of Asian, African or Mexican origin. Nathan Glazer asked in 1993, 'is assimilation dead?' He found that the term had fallen into disrepute and was associated with unhelpful ethnocentric prejudices against non-whites. Whilst acknowledging that assimilation forces had impacted on the immigrants of European descent with high levels of inter-marriage, Glazer pointed to the lower rates of inter-marriage for Asians, Hispanics and especially African-Americans.[32] Reconsidering the immigrant experience in New York City since the publication of *Beyond the Melting Pot*, scholars in 2000 concluded that blacks and Puerto Ricans whilst having made progress were still in a disadvantaged position as part of an underclass. They were victims of the reality that race remained a barrier to progress.[33]

As already noted, the immigration legislation passed during the 1980s and the 1990s did not significantly restrict the number of legal immigrants entering the country and therefore continued to fuel the debate between pluralists and assimilationists. On the American south-western border the debate has centred more specifically on the balance between legal and illegal immigrants. In 1976 Congress extended the 20,000 per country annual limit to the western hemisphere, which made things worse for Mexicans whose average flow in the previous years had been 60,000. The 1986 Immigration Reform and Control Act failed to close the 'back door' of America as restrictionists gained employer sanctions for employing illegal immigrants. Meanwhile civil liberty groups and Hispanics approved of the amnesty regulations which gave aliens a route to citizenship.[34] The political struggles over the issue of illegal immigration from south of the border have continued to raise questions about how native-born Americans respond to new arrivals. In 1994 there were complaints and threatened lawsuits from the governors of California, Texas and Florida who claimed the federal government had lost control of the nation's borders. In the same year nearly 60 per cent of the California electorate voted in favour of Proposition 187, which included requirements for the removal of 500,000 students from school and the refusal of antenatal and immunisation services to illegal immigrants, who were blamed for the problems of the Californian economy. Targeting immigrants from Mexico and Central America most strongly, some of the provisions of the initiative were included as part of the 1996 welfare reform act passed by Congress and signed by President Clinton.[35] In 2004 conservative congressmen from south-western states warned President Bush of a voter backlash over his programme which would give guest-worker status to undocumented aliens and both Arizona and California saw grass-roots movements to enact measures similar to Proposition 187.[36]

Much of this white identity politics is connected to fears over the impact on labour relations and social services of illegal immigration, but there is a wider concern associated with the continuance of mass immigration into the US. The potential threat to the cohesion of American society has been heightened by Census Bureau projections of the changing racial landscape likely to be brought about by the continuance of current immigration patterns. Projections in the mid-1990s predicted a non-Hispanic white population of 53 per cent by 2050. Certainly by 2004 the figure stood at 67 per cent which was reduced from the 75 per cent figure of 1990 records.[37] The numerical dominance of white Americans is being eroded and during the twenty-first century whites may become a minority. It is within this context that there has been a renewed conflict between the forces of pluralism and assimilation. With greater and greater diversity among the new arrivals to the US there has been a growing debate over multiculturalism and its meaning. Most now concede the need to accept greater diversity in America, but there is a continuing struggle over how, the extent to which and under what standards this should be done.[38]

Certainly the old models of assimilation and the simple concepts of the melting pot and the salad bowl are as inadequate when explaining immigration in the early twenty-first century as they were one hundred years ago. The patterns of immigration today differ significantly from that period. Many of the immigrants now come with higher educational qualifications than native-born Americans and they bypass life at the bottom of the socio-economic structure. Overall the economic assimilation of late-twentieth-century immigrants progressed more rapidly than it did for those who arrived in the US in the early 1900s. The pattern does not, however, apply to all and black and Hispanic groups continue to dominate the poorest sectors of society.[39] These groups continue to face discrimination and prejudice and are less than optimistic about their prospects. In fact research has shown that for many groups a degree of assimilation into American society can have negative effects on health and well-being and family stability – thus turning on its head the ideal of assimilation as a positive good.[40]

The United States seems set to continue to struggle with the questions of national identity raised by immigration that it has faced to a greater or lesser extent since its beginning. Clearly the nation has absorbed millions of immigrants from all over the globe who have made a significant contribution to what America is. The evolving national identity is faced with the paradox that the common American culture is increasingly multicultural. Educationalists need to teach about America's past in terms of plurality and unity, to show diversity of experience in all its rawness whilst also looking forward and building towards the common purposes enshrined in the Declaration of Independence and the Constitution.[41] The pluralist assimilationist debate is a significant part of the United States' past, present and future and its outcomes have previously defined and will in the future define the parameters of American national identity.

15

GENDER, RACE AND THE VOTE, 1865–1920

We cannot forget, even in this glad hour, that while all men of every race, and clime, and condition, have been invested with the full rights of citizenship under our hospitable flag, all women still suffer the degradation of disfranchisement.[1]

These were the words of female suffrage supporter Elizabeth Cady Stanton at an address celebrating the American Centennial. Her assertion that 'men of every race' enjoyed the rights of full citizenship disguised the erosion of the rights of black men as the era of Reconstruction came to an end. The citizenship rights of all women were being debated as the parameters of Reconstruction were contested. The year before Stanton spoke, the Supreme Court ruled that the vote was not the right of citizens and as such female suffrage was not guaranteed by the Constitution. The intersection of racial and gender issues during the era of Reconstruction had a profound impact on the shape of female political life and the campaign for suffrage which culminated in the Nineteenth Amendment.

Feminist scholars have, since the 1980s, increasingly placed the female experience at the centre of historical research. Previously unheard voices and neglected events have been recovered in an effort which has enriched the study of the American past. A traditional feminist approach which seeks to protect women's place in history by forging a common womanhood and protecting a female autonomy, however, fails to fully explain the position of black women. The homogeneity of female experience implicit in a traditional feminist perspective, which focusses on how gender has constructed that experience, fails to deal with the issue of racial identity. It is race and community that has provided a greater influence on black women's identity than their position as females.[2] An investigation of women's history must embrace the significance of racial identity. This chapter seeks to outline some of the ways in which black and white women attempted to exercise political influence and campaigned for the vote in the period 1865–1920.[3] They sought to expand their rights as citizens of the United States. It is important to recognise at the outset, however, that simply focussing on the suffrage movement is to impose a Euro-American paradigm on the development of female political involvement.[4] African-American women, and indeed their white counterparts, often conceived of political influence outside of the mainstream of the electoral system. Denied the vote during the Reconstruction period, women forged a new kind of political involvement in the Progressive era which brought traditional domestic concerns into the public arena. In so doing they helped prepare the ground for the eventual coming of votes for women. Persistent throughout these developments, however, was the reality that shared political concerns were compromised by the divisions of race. It was 'tragically ironic' the fact that activism by black and white women to expand their rights grew alongside significant racial dissonance.[5]

The African-American experience during the Reconstruction era was affected at every turn by the role of women. They accompanied their menfolk in substantial numbers to the 1867 Republican state convention in Virginia and participated in debates and discussions from the public gallery. In 1869 Louisa Rollin addressed the South Carolina House of Representatives to speak in favour of female suffrage.[6] White women too sought to forward their political position during this period. Following the passage of the Fourteenth and Fifteenth Amendments, hundreds of women attempted to register and vote. In New Jersey in 1868 two hundred women of a small spiritualist town cast their votes in a separate ballot box and tried to get them counted with the men. In 1871 Philadelphia an unmarried tax-payer, Carrie Burnham, managed to get her name registered on the electoral roll only to have her vote refused.[7]

The movement for greater women's rights saw in the Reconstruction amendments the opportunity to press claims for female suffrage. The issue of race, however, had a crucial impact on the tactics that were adopted. Women's rights advocates who had participated in the abolitionist movement, such as Susan B. Anthony, Elizabeth Cady Stanton and Sojourner Truth, were appalled by the inclusion of the word 'male' in the Fourteenth Amendment. Lucy Stone, Henry Blackwell and Frederick Douglass were among those who argued that pressing the issue of female suffrage could threaten the passage of this amendment, and the Fifteenth, to follow, which were crucial to the rights of African-American men. Anthony and Stanton formed the National

Woman Suffrage Association (NWSA) in 1869 and demanded that the Fifteenth Amendment included the right of women to vote. In doing so they broke with the Republicans who were intent on securing the black vote. The NWSA received funding from Democrats who believed that the white female vote would be a useful counterweight to the potential strength of the African-American ballot. Rejecting this position, Stone and Blackwell formed the rival American Woman Suffrage Association (AWSA). They threw support behind Reconstruction amendments which conferred full citizenship on black men. The AWSA argued that women should campaign for the vote at state level.[8]

Central to the arguments of the NWSA was what suffragists referred to as a 'new departure'. Abandoning assertions that the Reconstruction amendments were restrictive of women's right to vote, they instead contended that they could be interpreted in a way which was wide enough to include female suffrage. The Supreme Court, however, denied this right. In the 1875 *Minor v. Happersett* case the justices ruled that, while women were citizens, the Fourteenth Amendment did not assert that suffrage was a privilege of citizenship. The Fifteenth Amendment also did not confer voting rights on women as it was aimed only at stopping states from disenfranchising citizens on account of race. The Court increasingly narrowed the parameters of political protection afforded to the freedman by the Constitution, however. In the *United States v. Reese* it ruled that the Enforcement Act (passed in 1870) was unconstitutional and so could not be used to protect the black vote.[9] Side by side, the protestations of women's rights activists and demands of those who supported African-American civil liberties were defeated by Supreme Court decisions which narrowed the definition of citizenship and restricted the number of Americans who were eligible to vote.

When studying black women's political influence and activity in the Reconstruction era, though, we should look beyond formal rights such as legally granted franchise. In the African-American community during the post-bellum years, women supported their men in a number of important ways as they struggled to exercise their political rights. Working within a conception of the vote as a community possession, black women emphasised the theory of responsibility rather than gendered autonomy. 'African-American men and women understood the vote as a collective possession not an individual one, and furthermore that African-American women unable to cast a separate vote, viewed African-American men's vote as equally theirs.'[10] Being denied the formal right to vote did not disallow African-American women political influence. Similarly, white women engaged in political activities which allowed them to exert influence even though they could not exercise the right to vote. During the anti-Chinese movements in California in the late 1870s and 1880s, white working-class women played a significant role in street protests, unions and political meetings. Emphasising both their racial and gendered identity, these women protested about the influx of Chinese labourers who took traditional women's work in the domestic and service economies.[11]

The political activity of these white women involved a coalition of interests with white men in a racially motivated campaign to exclude Chinese immigrants from the economy and then eventually to exclude any further arrivals in the US. For black women, as the dark night of segregation settled over the South, a coalition with black men provided a union for survival. Segregation and racial violence increasingly affected an emasculation of black men but they also threatened black femininity. African-American women attempted to adopt an invisible womanhood and sexuality in order to protect themselves and their communities. In the process they were removed from public discussions and memory. This has led to a dominant reading of history which views the racial oppression of the post-bellum South from a masculine perspective.[12] This is not to say that African-American women did not participate in political activity, just that the story of struggle against racial oppression in the popular imagination has been conceived of as masculine.

Women in the late nineteenth century were involved in diverse political action outside of the mainstream of the democratic election process. By embracing a different concept of political activity, women played a crucial role in the domestication of politics.[13] The civic action through which women forged a theory of citizenship and engaged in a political discourse was, however, heavily affected by the issue of race. Black women's ability to embrace this form of citizenship was restricted. When the changes in American society at the turn of the century, and the domestication of politics, eventually led to the breaking of the traditional separate spheres ideology, women were given the vote in the Nineteenth Amendment. Black women in the South especially were, however, swiftly disenfranchised. Whether it be through civic action or as part of the formal system of representative democracy, black women's freedom of action was contested at every turn. This illustrates further that historians must move beyond a traditional feminist narrative of the past and explore the way in which race above gender shaped black women's identity.

Excluded from the formal arena of electoral politics, women in the late nineteenth and early twentieth centuries formed a new type of influence away from the mainstream party system. In organisations like the Woman's Christian Temperance Union (WCTU), and missionary and labour societies, women were able to critique the efforts of men to manage the local and national political sphere. In this way they used privatised identities to comment on public matters. This development offers a new way of thinking about the way in which citizens are educated.[14] Women's involvement in voluntary associations allowed them to use their private identities to make an impact in public life.

The Progressive era brought significant changes to the make-up of the American social order, with rapid industrialisation, urbanisation and immigration, and provided the opportunity for women to engage in civil society more fully. Women were moving outside of some of their more traditional roles. There was, for example, a significant increase in the number of women in higher education. By 1880 33 per cent of all students enrolled were female. Many of these women moved into the field of social science and began to have an impact on the civic life of America. One such woman, Florence Kelley, graduated Cornell and went on to work with the Illinois Woman's Alliance and then the National Consumer's League. Kelley was instrumental in building pressure on legislators to pass minimum wage laws for women.[15]

The temperance movement provided one important area in which women brought together traditional female concerns and political activism. The issue was linked to the natural domestic concerns of women who were worried about violence in the home. Reflecting the growing influence of voluntary organisations and women's societies, the temperance movement developed beyond a call to regulate the distribution and consumption of alcohol. The WCTU, under the leadership of Frances Willard, developed a wide-ranging critique of American society and became involved in a diverse range of projects designed to fix the problems of that society. Far from being a conservative organisation, the WCTU had strong links to radical populist parties.[16] Reform-minded women founded settlements like Hull House in Chicago and Henry Street in New York where they could work with fellow activists to push their social agenda. There reformers lobbied the federal government to take more responsibility for children and healthcare issues. Hull House resident Julia Lathrop was appointed the head of the Children's Bureau after its inception in 1912. When Congress tried to limit the appropriations to the Bureau in 1914, Lathrop organised women's clubs and reformers to lobby for more funds.[17] By engaging in voluntary organisations and lobbying groups to further the cause of issues traditionally viewed as female concerns, women were bringing their private identity into the public sphere. In so doing they contributed to a distinct concept of citizenship which was political even though it functioned outside of the realm of electoral politics. Denied the political right of suffrage in the Reconstruction amendments, women contributed to the domestication of politics, which eventually saw government take on moral and social responsibility usually associated with the traditionally female sphere.[18]

Such was the importance ascribed to women's ability to provide a force for the moral uplift of society that many argued that only by not getting the vote could they continue to be an effective political force. Most have regarded the anti-suffrage campaign amongst women as a conservative force, a desire to retain the separate spheres ideal of gender relations in which women dominated the private sphere and men the public. In fact the anti-suffragists believed that women should have a visible presence in public life; they were not advocating a restrictively private and domestic role for women. The anti-suffrage campaign argued that only by staying outside of electoral politics could women effectively use their position to provide leadership in the pursuit of moral and philanthropic causes. Anti-suffragists provided evidence to show that in some western states that had given women the vote by the turn of the century there was less effective philanthropic work than in the East where women were still excluded from the franchise.[19]

During the Progressive era, therefore, women forged a concept of political action which brought domestic issues into the public sphere and positioned themselves as the guardians of the social and moral health of the nation. So much so that some believed if women were given the vote it would compromise their ability to exercise such responsibility. African-American women also engaged in political activism during this era, though they had to struggle against prejudice and racial segregation. Much of the reform impulse of Progressivism had an inherently racist character. Fighting against this racism was a crucial element in the experience of African-American women who tried to advance their community. In 1908, for example, Lugenia Hope Burns oversaw the creation of the Neighbourhood Union in Atlanta. The Union campaigned tirelessly for better facilities and increased funding for the city's black schools. The activities of this organisation and the women who worked for it were essential for providing the basic needs of black Atlantans, especially children and the elderly. Activists lobbied wealthy white women for support and invited them to look at the condition of black schools. Some concessions from the board of education were received. For the most part, however, problems were ignored as funding for reform was spent on white education.[20]

As women moved from the private sphere into the public realm they enlarged their traditional role as home keepers. Race continued to be a key determinant in the execution of this role, however. Women of different racial identity who advocated social reform did so 'more often in tension than in tandem'.[21] The erosion of the reach of the Reconstruction amendments showed black women that suffrage, either male or female, was not going to provide the avenue through which they could improve their community. As a consequence black women fell back on self-help and improvement organisations.[22] These groups had to rely on familial support and neighbourhood contacts because they found great difficulty in accessing funding outside of the black community. The civic improvement and social justice agenda of white women reformers left little room for the concerns of their black counterparts.[23] Nevertheless, in the tense atmosphere of Jim Crow segregation it was women who were more able to forge links across the racial divide. In North Carolina, black reformer Charlotte Hawkins Brown elicited the support of some influential whites and there were integrated county councils whose representatives were carefully chosen from clubs and social service programmes. When thoughts turned to the possibility of women gaining the vote, though, white women called for 'qualified' voters and so chose to further the political role of white women only.[24] The fact remained that 'few white middle-class women were able to shed the blinders of race and class privilege in order to make common cause with African-American, working-class, or immigrant women'.[25]

In the early twentieth century the campaign for female suffrage picked up pace. Denied suffrage during the Reconstruction period, women had responded to the changes in late-nineteenth-century American society with a form of political action which brought traditionally private concerns into the public arena. The campaign for social improvement became associated with a multitude of women's organisations during the Progressive era. As a consequence, women's suffrage was no longer seen as a challenge to traditional separate spheres ideals because the issues of politics and the home were intrinsically linked.[26] In 1890 the two leading women's suffrage organisations combined to form the National American Woman Suffrage Association (NAWSA), though internal divisions emerged over whether to campaign for a constitutional amendment or focus on state action. After 1900 younger women in the NAWSA found influence and initiated more grass-roots activism including door-to-door campaigns and mass meetings.[27]

A key part of this change in the tactics of the suffragist movement was the greater working-class involvement in the struggle for the vote.

Working-class women became active in other reform organisations such as the Women's Trade Union League, which was founded in 1902. In New York, Harriot Stanton Blatch played a crucial role in uniting industrial and professional women workers. Through the Equality League of Self-Supporting Women, formed in 1907, Blatch and her supporters engaged in a more militant and direct form of campaigning for the vote.[28] These changes lay the foundations for the influence of the tactics used by suffragettes in Britain. This mass radical suffragism provided a final and dramatic challenge to the separate spheres of ideology which had been slowly eroded by the domestication of politics. American suffragists were inspired by the example of the British militants. By 1913 there were tens of thousands of women in suffrage parades which marched through New York. In the same year there was a huge procession through Washington DC and the creation of a national suffrage society, the National Woman's Party (NWP).[29]

The national campaign for female suffrage did not, however, fully embrace women of colour. Harriot Stanton Blatch was among those women's leaders who did support the rights of African-American women, though this was not the dominant pattern.[30] White suffragists did not include the position of black women, the racial oppression and disfranchisement they faced in their calls for reform. Mainstream suffragists did little to counter the attempts of southern whites to write black women out of state or federal proposals to amend constitutions to grant female suffrage. There were attempts to keep black women disenfranchised right up until Congress passed the Nineteenth Amendment. Black women did vote in 1920 but within a decade they had been disenfranchised in the South and lost any political influence elsewhere in the nation. White women largely ignored their plight as race continued to shape experience more than gender.[31] In the South anti-suffrage campaigners tied the female vote to a threat to white supremacy. In Virginia, for example, the suffrage campaign had to face the issue of race. Suffragists could distance their aspirations from those of black women and preserve some chance of victory or they could embrace the interests of black women and by so doing completely doom any hopes of winning. In seeking to avoid the issue of race most white suffragists simply did not talk about it, implicitly signalling that white supremacy was safe whether women got the vote or not.[32]

That they did finally get the vote was down, in no small part, to the new leadership of the NAWSA and the disciplined and skilful political campaign it operated. Women like Alice Paul and Lucy Burns had spent time in England and they brought a more urgent and radical approach to the suffrage movement. Responding to this pressure the NAWSA elected Carrie Chapman Catt as its President in 1915 and she pursued new tactics and used considerable skills of organisation to push the issue of women's suffrage to the centre of the political arena. In 1916 both the Republican and Democratic conventions were inundated by women eager to secure the vote. The suffrage movement benefited from the visible support of women for the war effort and their role in the war industries.[33] Not all campaigners fell into line with the wave of patriotism and the NWP picketed the White House and was tried under anti-sedition laws. Nevertheless, 'the war provided time (and a suprapartisan environment) for the maturation of the political forces necessary to enfranchise women'.[34]

The passage of the Nineteenth Amendment was the completion of a process through which women had brought the private and domestic sphere into the public political arena. The old notions of separate spheres of gender influence had been eroded by the domestication of politics to the extent that giving women the vote was no longer seen as a radical or undesirable event by mainstream American political thought. It is important to note that women of all colours did get the vote. In the North and the West black women voted alongside their menfolk and white women. In the South some black women were able to exercise their new constitutional rights. Charlotte Hawkins Brown helped several African-American women register in North Carolina during her campaign of 1920.[35] In the areas of Virginia with a relatively small proportion of black females compared with whites, the numbers who were registered to vote was significant. Black women did vote and they were able to forge some tentative inter-racial alliance organisations. White suffragists stopped short, however, of supporting an enlargement of voting rights for black people.[36] In the years between the passage of the Nineteenth Amendment and the civil rights movement of the 1960s, black women struggled to establish organisations for effective political action when faced with the continued racial hostilities of mainstream American society. Their struggle continued to be shaped not primarily by gendered identity but by the racial identity, which restricted their access to full citizenship.

16

ORIGINS OF THE CIVIL RIGHTS MOVEMENT

Southern black protest, 1900–1945

At the dawn of the twentieth century African-American leader W. E. B. DuBois wrote, 'through all the sorrow of the Sorrow Songs there breathes a hope – a faith in the ultimate justice of things'.[1] Black southerners lived with the daily injustice of legally sanctioned segregation and ubiquitous racial oppression. Traditional narratives have viewed the period leading up to the Second World War as one dominated by African-American quiescence in the strictly enforced apartheid of the South. Certainly the unforgiving grip of white supremacy severely constricted the advancement of black southerners in this period. They continued, however, to breathe the hope to which DuBois referred. Black resistance and protest in many differing forms brought slow and tentative progress towards an end to racial injustice. By the 1940s cracks in the foundations of the 'solid South' had begun to show through.[2] African-American men and women had begun to carve tiny chinks of hope in the great mountain of despair. It was this action that provided the genesis of the civil rights movement. This movement played a key role in the evolving parameters of American citizenship and will be explored from a number of different angles in this and the following two chapters.

Traditional accounts of the civil rights struggle in America focus on a specific time period dominated by the 1950s and 1960s. Manning Marable argues that a 'Second Reconstruction' began in February 1960 with the first sit-in and, like the first Reconstruction, saw a 'series of massive confrontations concerning the status of the Afro-American … in the nation's economic, social and political institutions'.[3] Taylor Branch, in *Parting the Waters*, focusses on 'America in the King years' which he designates as 1954–63. In his concluding comments Branch argues, 'Kennedy's murder marked the arrival of the freedom surge, just as King's own death four years hence marked its demise.'[4] In his survey of the fight for black equality from 1890 to 2000, Adam

Fairclough devotes three chapters to the 'non-violent rebellion' starting in 1955 and ending with the signing of the Voting Rights Act of 1965. He then examines the rise and fall of Black Power, beginning in 1965 and ending with the first years of the Nixon administration.[5] Marable's central chapters are entitled 'We Shall Overcome, 1954–60' and 'Black Power, 1965–70'.[6] The civil rights movement has therefore been traditionally framed as the period from the *Brown* decision to the collapse of non-violent resistance at the hands of a rising militancy and Black Power agenda. This provides the dominant narrative of the civil rights movement.

There are, however, dangers associated with such a narrative. Jacquelyn Dowd Hall argues that by limiting the civil rights struggle 'to a single halcyon decade, and to limited, non-economic objectives, the master narrative simultaneously elevates and diminishes the movement'.[7] Hall argues for a different chronology, for a 'long civil rights movement' which provides a more complex and complete picture of race relations stretching back to the 1930s. Indeed the forerunners in the fight for civil rights in the 1950s and 1960s can be observed even earlier than this decade. The tactics of the civil rights struggle and the will to engage in them was not simply a post-1945 phenomenon. The purpose of this chapter is not to diminish the importance of those efforts associated with traditional accounts of the civil rights movement but instead to show where their roots lay and that the black struggle for justice was a long-term process – one which continues today.

Indeed one conception of a civil rights movement could be traced right back to the Reconstruction era. The unprecedented federal power exercised in this period and the attempts to grant and protect black citizenship in the Thirteenth, Fourteenth and Fifteenth Amendments was a beginning. The effort to enjoy the full measure of these rights was the focus of a civil rights struggle which spanned the century after the 1860s. It was the liberal interpretation of the Reconstruction amendments by the Warren Court in the 1950s and 1960s which breathed life into the civil rights movement of those decades. We need to move the traditional chronological parameters of the struggle for equality in order to fully appreciate the wider narrative of the civil rights movement. As such the following pages will focus on the first half of the twentieth century, showing an important and often overlooked phase of the story of this movement.

As mentioned above 1954 is often regarded as the starting point of the modern civil rights movement. In that year the National Association for the Advancement of Coloured People (NAACP) won a landmark decision in *Brown v. Board of Education* which found that separate but equal educational facilities were unconstitutional. This began the slow dismantling of Jim Crow segregation. Within two years of the *Brown* decision Martin Luther King was catapulted onto the national stage and based his campaign for civil rights on shaming America to live up to its ideals, appealing to the soul of the nation and the conscience of its white population. The roots of these developments, however, can be traced back to the early twentieth century. Founded in 1909, the NAACP had been chipping away at the wall of legal segregation for decades before *Brown* and like King's the organisation's message was a moral one. In its tenth annual report the Association laid out its goal to 'reach the conscience of America'.[8]

In the early phase of its development the NAACP faced criticisms from Booker T. Washington, who favoured an accommodationist approach to race relations, and from the black nationalist leader Marcus Garvey, who disliked the inter-racial make-up of the organisation and criticised its foremost spokesman, W. E. B. DuBois, for being a 'white man's nigger'.[9] Yet the Association increasingly became the most important defender of black rights, tackling numerous problems in its attempt to ensure that black people were protected in the way the Fourteenth and Fifteenth Amendments had intended. In one case in South Carolina in 1925, the organisation secured acquittal or retrial for three black children. They had been convicted of murder after a fight which resulted in the death of their mother and the white sheriff who had come to arrest their father. The acquitted youth was immediately arrested on new charges and that night a white mob stormed the jail where the children were being held, took them away and shot them. For the NAACP setbacks were often more commonplace than victories. Despite the unsuccessful conclusion to this and many other cases, though, even the organisation's critics conceded that 'its outstanding victories ... have been in court'.[10]

Indeed in 1915 the Association had won a decision which struck down the Oklahoma 'grandfather clause' and two years later the Supreme Court ruled against residential segregation laws in Kentucky. In 1920 the NAACP held its first meeting in the South, though it remained a primarily northern organisation. Increasingly the NAACP worked to lobby the federal government, exercising considerable pressure on senators in 1930 to vote against the confirmation of Judge John Parker to the Supreme Court. Parker supported black disenfranchisement and the NAACP celebrated after vigorous campaigning saw two of the four senators who had voted for him lose their Senate seats.[11] In 1936 legal assistance was given to black teachers seeking equal salaries in both the North and the South. Branches of the Association functioned in every southern state and their existence provided the most visible expression of a protest movement. By 1946 nationwide membership had expanded to 450,000.[12] Furthermore, during its anti-lynching campaign of the 1930s the NAACP learned the lessons of modern public relations, fund raising and lobbying. This professionalising of the civil rights movement laid the foundations for the struggle to come.[13]

African-American organisational struggle against inequality in the first half of the twentieth century was by no means limited to the NAACP; there were examples of grass-roots movements in the South. In Arkansas, for example, black activist W. H. Flowers was frustrated by the lack of resources supplied by the Association in his state. He argued there was a 'blackout of democracy' in Arkansas and decided to make an effort to organise the African-American population. In 1940 he founded the Committee on Negro Organisation (CNO) and began to release a bi-monthly leaflet to inform citizens of the organisation's activities. Poll tax drives in the black community saw voter registration rise 16 per cent by 1947.[14] As well as founding their own movement institutions, black activists had a profound influence on existing political agencies. The Communist Party of the United States held an official policy of inter-racial action in a world-wide class struggle. Especially in the South, however, working-class black activists brought their race-conscious traditions to the party, transforming old spirituals and protest songs into communist verses. During the 1930s thousands of African-Americans were attracted by the communist movement and brought with them a racially distinct protest culture.[15]

A crucial organisation in the civil rights struggle of the 1950s and 1960s was the black church. Its role in supplying black leaders and in mobilising people has been well documented, as has the ideological contribution they made to the drive for racial integration.[16] The importance of the black church to the development of the African-American community emerged during the Reconstruction period when black southerners shook off the paternalistic and philanthropic grip of white religious institutions. It was by no means axiomatic, though, that religious leaders would get involved in civil rights struggles and many provided a conservative force in black society. One young writer in the *Crisis* publication of the NAACP complained in 1935 that southern blacks were 'hog-tied by the fundamentalist, do-nothing coloured churches'.[17] There was, however, a role for church leaders to push for racial change long before Martin Luther King. A particularly extreme example was Bishop Henry McNeal Turner. The Methodist minister was an outspoken black nationalist who was active in attempts to end disenfranchisement and lynch mobs in the turn-of-the-century

South.[18] The southern labour movement was also influenced by the black church and religion provided a moral foundation for working-class unity. Even when not involved in overt racial protest, church groups and other grass-roots societies were important in black people's struggle for survival.[19]

In many instances, however, it was these community groups which helped to mobilise the thousands of black southerners who took part in the direct action of the 1950s and 1960s. Images in textbooks and on newsreels show sit-ins, boycotts and marches to register voters and end segregation. Nevertheless, this direct action tradition emerged in the early twentieth century and laid the foundations for the efforts which were to come later. The emergence of Jim Crow segregation was consistently challenged by black southerners. In the period from 1900 to 1907, for example, there were boycotts of streetcars in Montgomery, Mobile, Little Rock, Atlanta, New Orleans and Memphis. In Virginia, John Mitchell Jnr, the editor of the *Richmond Planet*, led an almost year-long boycott of the city's streetcar company from 1904 to 1905. The company was eventually forced into bankruptcy.[20] Despite the problems of civil rights activism in South Carolina because of black fear of white reprisals, in Greenville in 1931 the National Textile Workers Union organised a bi-racial unemployed council. Thousands of Greenville's jobless took part in militant action, black and white stood side by side in the face of Ku Klux Klan violence and intimidation.[21]

During the depression the black community organised 'don't buy where you can't work' campaigns in cities across the country including the South.[22] This economic dimension to direct action was a continuing theme. Organised unionism was also touched by civil rights activism. Local studies have begun to show the extent to which unions in the South were bi-racial. There was in fact a strong civil rights influence on the Congress of Industrial Organisations. The Steel Workers Organising Committee was portrayed as a 'nigger union' because blacks held office and were appointed to significant positions within the organisation. Nevertheless, the union gained a foothold in Alabama and many white workers joined. This bi-racial element to union organisation did not change racist attitudes but it did force recognition of black rights and a forum to redress some of their grievances.[23]

The dominant narrative of the civil rights movement of the 1960s sees a period of non-violent direct action slowly give way to a more aggressive and violent black militancy. This black militancy and the willingness of some individuals to meet racial oppression with violence had deep roots in the South. Although faced with the constant threat of white brutality black southerners did occasionally resort to violent protest despite its obvious dangers. In Birmingham during the Second World War racial confrontations on public transport which often led to violence were commonplace on Friday and Saturday nights. From 1941 to 1942 there were reports of 176 racial conflicts including forty which involved fights between black and white passengers or black passengers and white operators.[24] It was blacks mainly who were the victims of racial riots in 1918–19 following the conclusion of the First World War, although violence was not always instigated by whites against blacks. Two years earlier, with the war in Europe still being fought, a hundred black soldiers of the 24th Infantry stationed in Texas went on a violent and drunken rampage in Houston. Outraged at being subjected to Jim Crow rules, they seized weapons and fired on the downtown police station killing five policemen and twelve other white people.[25] Individual acts of violence were also a part of the daily struggle against oppression in the South. South Carolina newspaper reports from 1925 to 1928 show evidence of eighty-nine interracial homicides including thirty-two whites killed by blacks. In New Orleans in 1900, Robert Charles shot a white policeman and then held off a mob of more than a thousand killing seven whites and sparking a race riot.[26] The willingness of black southerners to defend themselves and their families and to fight oppression with violence stretched back several decades from the movement of the 1960s.[27]

Arguably the most symbolic act of the civil rights struggle of that decade came with the March on Washington in the summer of 1963 when King delivered his iconic 'I Have a Dream' speech. Yet the concept of a protest assault on the nation's capital and the choice to stage the rally on the steps of the Lincoln Memorial were derivative of a previous era. When in 1939 black singer Marian Anderson was denied the use of Constitution Hall for a concert because it was open to whites only, NAACP secretary, Walter White, led the plan to stage the concert in front of the Lincoln Memorial. The symbolism and irony were palpable to all present as Anderson sang 'sweet land of liberty'. So 'by invoking and reinterpreting a national icon, black protestors explored the ambiguities and possibilities of American society'.[28] This process, which reached fruition in 1963, began in the 1930s. Although never realised, the idea of a march on Washington also emerged in an earlier period. In 1940 and 1941 black leaders held protest rallies around the country aimed at putting pressure on President Roosevelt to end discrimination in the defence industry. A. Phillip Randolph then called for a 'March on Washington' to force the government to listen to black demands. The idea captured mass support and the number set to march stood at 50,000 when Roosevelt's executive order creating a Fair Employment Practices Committee led to a cancellation of the event.[29]

It is a central contention of this essay that attempting to fix the civil rights movement inside a narrow chronological framework is misguided. The original March on Washington Movement, however, highlights a significant period of change in the consciousness of black America and a quickening of the civil rights impulse, namely the Second World War. The hypocrisy of a war for democracy and freedom against the fascist tyranny of Japan and Germany when segregation continued at home was not lost on many blacks – nor whites. One African-American columnist argued, 'our war is not against Hitler in Europe, but against the Hitlers in America'.[30] During the war years black servicemen gained a particular reputation for opposing Jim Crow laws. Their uniform signified a fight against fascism and Aryan supremacy, which is exactly what they faced in the South. Just as the soldiers of the 24th Infantry and many others had objected to segregation in the years of the First World War, black troops tested the limits of Jim Crow in the years of the Second World War. Most often this took the form of contesting segregation ordinances on public transport.[31]

We have already noted that the membership of the NAACP increased markedly during the period from 1940 to 1945 and this reflected a growing commitment to protesting racial oppression. Indeed among the black professional classes, who had found security and prosperity in their parallel institutions during the period of segregation, the Second World War provided a great catalyst for increased civil rights activism. Black nurse Mabel Staupers was among those who led the way calling for the desegregation of the US army's nursing corps. The work of Staupers and others prepared the ground for the civil rights progress of the 1950s and 1960s.[32] The Second World War gave African-Americans the opportunity to point out the hypocrisy of the American dream and they did so with increasing confidence and militancy. 'When the expected white acquiescence in a new racial order did not occur, the ground was prepared' for the civil rights movement of the 1950s and 1960s.[33]

The development of white America's response to black protest efforts is another important element of the wider narrative of a long civil rights struggle. In the 1930s and 1940s a gentle breeze of change did stir the southern landscape and important seeds were sown for the progress of white liberalism. As with earlier efforts to organise a 'silent South' – moderate and liberal whites who wanted improvement and modernisation for the region – the struggles of the New Deal era brought failure as disunity and poor organisation stymied progress.

This white dissent, however, laid the foundations for the future and showed that some southerners were prepared to abandon a strict racially segregated order.[34] Emancipated white southerners like Will Alexander and Clark Foreman were stirred and inspired by the New Deal and worked to improve their region. These liberals did not overtly challenge the Jim Crow system but they recognised that the rigidity of racism existed to the detriment of economic and political progress. It was these priorities which led to a de-emphasising of racial issues to win broad support for reform programmes.[35]

These reforms were given impetus by President Roosevelt, who announced that the South was the nation's principal economic problem. FDR intervened in the 1938 primary elections to support liberal candidates who shared his effort at social and economic reform. In response southern liberals organised the Southern Conference for Human Welfare, which invited black and white people from across the region to discuss change and prepare for political action. During one of the group's meetings in Birmingham, police commissioner Eugene 'Bull' Connor entered the hall and told the delegates that they were sitting in violation of an ordinance which banned racially mixed meetings. Whites were moved to one side of the hall and blacks to the other – the first of many public confrontations between Connor and the forces of integration.[36] Although the voice of these southern liberals was frequently drowned out by the segregationists' message, there were signs of progress. The SCHW could not list tangible achievements but it was significant because it attempted to shake the South and bring change. Although in the South the administering of the New Deal at the local level was influenced by a large degree of racism, African-Americans did gain from the economic and social reforms. A delegation of black social workers articulated a new mood of black America in 1939, stating that 'for the first time Negro men and women have reason to believe that their government does care'.[37]

A growing sense of black consciousness was a further element in the origins of the civil rights movement. A sense of racial pride and a refusal to submit to the oppression of segregation and prejudice provided a psychological resistance which laid the foundations for the mass movement of the 1960s. Black southerners engaged in subtle forms of resistance on a regular basis. They 'relentlessly, joked, jibed, questioned and vigorously rejected the unethical, immoral, illogical, and crude character of the system'.[38] African-Americans venerated folk heroes, black bandits and 'bad niggers' who outwitted the white man. An example is the story of a mythical hero named Shine. The sinking of the *Titanic* in 1912 was seen by many in the black community as divine retribution for the refusal to carry black passengers. In folklore Shine came on deck to warn the Captain of rising water. He is told to get his black ass back down below; he consequently jumps overboard and swims to safety.[39] Stories such as this and black jokes and folklore which laughed at the white man when Jim Crow backfired were a crucial element in a hidden resistance to white supremacy.

This form of resistance was combined with economic struggle. Black workers were regularly engaged in acts of foot-dragging, theft and the destruction of property. In North Carolina tobacco workers were involved in a variety of activities aimed at controlling the pace of the work they were expected to complete. Black domestic servants organised 'slowdowns', left work early or stole food from their employers. In Durham black workers fixed the clock so they could steal time and in the coal mines of Birmingham they pilfered fuel for their own homes.[40] This form of resisting the system of racial and economic oppression had roots in the slave experience of feigning illness, working slowly and destroying the master's equipment.[41] Refusal to submit to the repression of the Jim Crow South gave black southerners a sense of dignity and provided a psychological revolt against white oppression which was an important foundation for the mass displays of organised public disobedience in the 1960s which finally brought segregation to an end.

For some southern blacks the most physical form of protest was to leave the region. During the first half of the twentieth century thousands left the South and migrated northwards in search of liberation from the restrictions of white supremacy.[42] In their own way many of these men and women would contribute to the progress towards civil rights as the Democratic Party broke free from the solid South and courted the northern urban vote. In a more direct sense their actions were one manifestation of a continuing struggle against racial injustice in the first half of the twentieth century. This struggle was a crucial element of the civil rights movement in the South which developed before the increasing direct action protest of the period from 1955 to 1965. It is an important story that needs to be told in depth, not only because it laid the foundation for the civil rights breakthrough of the 1960s but also because it ensures a more comprehensive appreciation of the struggle for equality, a struggle which continues to this day. If we reduce 'the movement' to a narrow time period then we limit its impact and minimise the scope of the change it demanded. The danger then is that conservative forces can work to narrowly define civil rights advances and consequently neutralise the continuing movement for equality.[43]

17

KENNEDY, JOHNSON AND CIVIL RIGHTS

By the time of his death in 1963 many black Americans had come to see John F. Kennedy as the 'white knight of the modern civil rights movement', a movie star president with a deep moral commitment to equality which allowed him to bridge the racial chasm in American society.[1] As early as the first year of his term in the White House, Kennedy himself claimed, 'I've done more for civil rights than any other president in American history.'[2] Kennedy is the slain hero of the New Frontier whose violent death signalled the descent into the bloody turmoil of the 1960s when US society itself seemed to be disintegrating. The man in the Oval Office during this tumult was Lyndon Johnson. It was during his presidency that the landmark civil rights legislation of the 1960s was passed. The dominant images of those years, however, are flaming cities and burning Vietnamese villagers. The sunlit promise of Johnson's Great Society was increasingly clouded by the national trauma wrought by the conflict in South East Asia.

Even before the war in Vietnam took its toll on the Johnson presidency it was evident that he was not admired in the same way Kennedy was. One commentator said of Johnson, 'the sacerdotal, priestly, almost mystic quality of the Presidency eluded him'.[3] Kennedy mastered the power of symbol in the politics of civil rights. The slow moral commitment to the cause he showed, however, helped exacerbate a rising tide of frustration and disillusionment that could not be stemmed by the legislative achievements of LBJ. Kennedy's popular appeal increased in potency following his death and this has shaped perceptions of civil rights and the presidency in the 1960s. Many of my own students, before studying the issues in any depth, regularly assert that JFK was a great champion of African-American rights. When asked to explain where this view comes from they vaguely allude to the subconsciously absorbed representations of popular culture – a testament to the success of the politics of symbolism that characterised Kennedy's civil rights policy. This chapter seeks to examine the attitudes, aims and policies of Kennedy in relation to the struggle for black equality and briefly explore the impact this had on the Johnson administration and the civil rights movement of the 1960s.

Historians were quick to question the achievements of Kennedy's presidency in a revisionism which initially flourished in the 1970s. Critics argued that Kennedy was too conscious of the problems posed by the southern Democrats and was too timid in his support for civil rights legislation. He offered limited moral leadership on the civil rights issue.[4] Jim Heath tackled the image of JFK as a heroic supporter of black freedom by stating, 'Kennedy was not the gigantic figure in civil rights that some of his admirers claimed.'[5] Recognition of the limited tangible achievements of the Kennedy administration in the legislative arena is important. We must, however, attempt to understand the President's relationship with black America in a broader sense if we are to fully grasp his impact on the modern civil rights movement and the presidency of Johnson.

John F. Kennedy was born into a wealthy middle-class family and had little if any experience of the problems which afflicted both working-class blacks and whites. He did not visit any of the deep southern states before he was forty and he had little interest in or understanding of white southern society. In his younger years he was stationed in Charleston, South Carolina, for a four-month period at the naval shipyards, but his private correspondence reveals no interest in racial matters. The experience had little impact on his attitudes towards civil rights. Indeed even into adulthood Kennedy was not exposed to blatant acts of racism. He had no black friends and his closest black acquaintance was his valet, George Taylor.[6] JFK did not share some of the bigotry of the Boston Irish Catholic community he grew up in and he was not a racist. Such was Kennedy's ignorance of black America, however, that his brother, Robert, hired Harris Wofford, a white southern liberal whose friends included Martin Luther King, to advise the Kennedy presidential campaign in 1959.[7]

Although he was not acquainted with the deep problems of African-Americans, JFK's roll call history on civil rights issues in the House was as good as that of any other northern congressman. He supported fair-employment legislation, abolition of the poll tax and launched a one-man campaign against southern committee chairmen who opposed Home Rule for Washington DC.[8] Kennedy was motivated by a realisation that racial discrimination and impediments to legislation aimed at improving the economic life of black citizens was an embarrassment in the propaganda war with the Soviet Union. As president,

Kennedy realised that pursuing victory in the Cold War entailed eliciting support from black and white Americans.[9] It was from this common sense reading of the racial problems facing mid-century America that Kennedy's early pro-civil rights voting record emerged. He believed that foreign affairs were absolutely crucial to the nation's future and he devoted much of his energies in preparing for the 1952 Senate campaign learning about the issues.[10]

JFK was not committed to the struggle for black equality for moral or liberal reasons. Referring to the liberals of the Democratic Party, Kennedy remarked he was 'not comfortable with those people'. 'His was a non-ideological, bread-and-butter liberalism.'[11] During his first term in the Senate Kennedy told a reporter that he was not a liberal, but in fact 'a realist'.[12] This political realism also led him to use the civil rights issue for political gain. During his 1952 Senate election campaign against Henry Cabot Lodge Jnr, Kennedy chose to highlight the differences between the civil rights voting record of himself and his opponent. He aggressively courted the black vote in original and imaginative ways. He organised 'Kennedy teas' in black districts where members of the public could come and meet the candidate, he fed the black press details of pro-civil rights positions and drew visible black advisers into his inner circle. This approach was, however, the harbinger of a policy of symbolism which belied at best a superficial understanding of the racial problems in American society.[13]

Kennedy proved a shifting figure on the civil rights issue who could win impressive black electoral support whilst simultaneously drawing the ire of liberals. A former Massachusetts mayor said of him in 1960, 'there's something about Jack — and I don't know quite what it is — that makes people want to believe in him. Conservatives and liberals both tell you that he's with them.'[14] Kennedy was criticised by liberals when he failed to record a vote of censure against McCarthy and he drew further condemnation when he voted to support a jury trial amendment which weakened the 1957 Civil Rights Act. Kennedy was caught in the cross-fire of the diverging Democratic Party and had to move skilfully in the late 1950s to build a national consensus which would allow him to win the presidential nomination in 1960. His vote on the jury trial amendment won him friends in the South, whilst the hiring of a black secretary and appropriation of some of the moderate demands of the NAACP in his 1958 Senatorial election campaign, allowed him to increase his share of the black vote. Kennedy chose careful legislative programmes like anti-bombing legislation, which allowed him to gain black approval and further strengthen ties with key southern leaders.[15]

Kennedy was, at times, a cynical politician and his engagement with the civil rights issue was shaped heavily by his desire to present himself as the national consensus figure that could hold the Democratic Party together. In his 1960 presidential campaign the Kennedy team purposely crafted their message depending on the audience. Kennedy was careful not to offend southern opinion and his Texas-born running mate, Lyndon Johnson, was the dominant campaign presence in the South. The Kennedy team used the black press to disseminate a more pro-civil rights message than that presented in the mainstream media and which was not picked up by white voters. Kennedy offered symbolic messages that he was the candidate who favoured progress in civil rights. This was never more the case than when he telephoned Coretta Scott King to offer his sympathy and help after her husband was imprisoned in 1960. Pamphlets were distributed in black neighbourhoods which compared Kennedy's compassion with Nixon's studied distance from the issue.[16]

In 1960 Kennedy managed to build a national consensus robust enough to take him into the White House – just. His victory margin was decidedly slim and he relied significantly on the black vote. This vote reflected increased black allegiance to the Democratic Party since the New Deal but was also significantly built on Kennedy's symbolic association with the issue of civil rights in the eyes of African-Americans. The president-elect was not morally committed to sweeping racial change, however. The dynamic between the civil rights movement and the Kennedy administration for the thousand days of his White House was thus defined before he took office. JFK was destined to disappoint because his success in cultivating black support was built largely on the cosmetic.[17] Kennedy had overcome the political problems surrounding his religion to become the first Catholic president. His religious commitment offered hope that he would vigorously struggle for racial equality. He did not, however, have a deep moral commitment to the issue. Civil rights leaders would have to force the President's hand if he was to support tangible reform. The dynamic of expectation exceeding action impacted on the Johnson presidency and would eventually contribute to the unravelling of the civil rights consensus – a consensus for steady, meaningful progress that could have been exploited early in the Kennedy presidency. Opinion polls in 1961 showed 76 per cent of southerners thought desegregation was inevitable and only 19 per cent were against blacks being treated fairly in employment and housing.[18]

Strong presidential leadership could have affected significant change. JFK, however, set the pace of change at slow, at times agonisingly slow, from his very first days in office. With such a slim mandate Kennedy believed he needed to move cautiously and thought that the shape of Congress would make it very difficult to pass legislation. He shied away from political fights on civil rights. Certainly the administration's record on congressional approval of legislation turned out to be poor. Of the President's legislative requests, 48.4 per cent were approved in 1961, 44.6 per cent in 1962 and 27.2 per cent in 1963.[19] Kennedy, however, was naturally cautious and had long been intimidated by the southern bloc – a group he had sought hard not to offend in his run to the presidency. JFK over-emphasised the problems on Capitol Hill and chose to view the glass as half empty rather than half full. A more aggressive and focussed campaign for civil rights legislation from the very beginning could have borne fruit but Kennedy was temperamentally averse to such a strategy.[20]

Some historians have chosen to shift the focus away from the problems of a potential battle with Congress and point to the fact that Kennedy had never promised sweeping civil rights legislation during the campaign. John Hart was correct when he pointed to the fact that Kennedy's civil rights stance was moderate and that towards the end of the campaign he had indicated that it was through executive action that civil rights issues could be tackled. It is indeed unfair to judge the President against something he did not indicate he was going to do – push for sweeping legislation.[21] Nevertheless, there was an expectation among many of his supporters that he would place significant reforms before Congress. This is the crucial point: Kennedy raised expectations of something more tangible because of his consistent cultivation of the black vote through symbolic gestures – the expectation exceeded his commitment. The New Frontier actively recruited blacks for federal jobs, administration officials boycotted racially exclusive clubs and Kennedy even ordered the integration of the White House kindergarten. The President did not, however, take bold strikes at discrimination with the pen of executive action, something which he had actually promised during the campaign. In a protest called 'ink for Jack', frustrated black activists sent tens of thousands of pens to the White House as part of an attempt to encourage Kennedy to sign executive orders.[22]

The President's response to civil rights was largely reactive and this was heavily shaped by his thinking on international affairs. 'The Cold War was the key to unlocking the Kennedy administration's concerns about racism' both at home and abroad.[23] JFK engaged in a domestic policy which sought to diffuse the potential embarrassment caused by racial incidents. Racial violence, southern repression and the use of federal troops provided problems for the White House which led to 'legitimacy-threatening world attention'.[24] During the freedom rides and the battle to integrate the University of Mississippi, Kennedy was acutely aware of the international ramifications of events and their use for Soviet propaganda purposes. Kennedy viewed the freedom riders as 'a pain in the ass', and throughout this and other confrontations he put little pressure on the FBI to protect civil rights workers – he was more concerned with spying on them.[25] Nevertheless, the freedom rides marked the beginning of a series of civil rights demonstrations which convinced activists that this was the way to put pressure on the administration to change its policy.[26] They saw that Kennedy's embarrassment over such incidents could be utilised to encourage him to act. The March on Washington was conceived as a demonstration to put pressure on the government to push ahead with and pass the civil rights legislation tabled in 1963.

Kennedy's caution and vacillation on the issue of civil rights was characterised by Martin Luther King as 'schizophrenic'.[27] In his relations with the emerging nations of the Third World, Kennedy offered symbolic gestures and rhetoric to indicate sympathy for their racial struggle in order to counteract Soviet overtures for their allegiance. This same anticommunism, however, motivated his support for NATO allies against anti-colonial insurgency. In relation to South Africa, the Kennedy White House took a 'rhetorically tough stand against apartheid', without jeopardising the positive aspects of its relationship with the nation.[28] This policy was mirrored in domestic affairs where Kennedy used symbolism to associate himself with the struggle for black equality whilst seeking not to provoke the disapproval of white southerners.

This tightrope policy precluded a firm legislative commitment until 1963. During the Albany demonstrations in the summer of 1962 Kennedy had begun to realise the potential threat of the civil rights struggle to damage the domestic fabric of the nation as opposed to simply exposing a Cold War liability. Furthermore, the problems in Birmingham strengthened this belief: the administration viewed the violence in the city and worried the situation could spiral out of control.[29] In June 1963 the President addressed the nation, stating 'we face a moral crisis as a country and as a people … it is time to act in Congress'.[30] There was broad support for civil rights legislation and, had Kennedy lived, it would have passed. It had taken the President over two years, though, to reach a place where he could fully embrace a moral commitment to civil rights. Kennedy's symbolic support of the black struggle for equality was successful politically in the sense that the overwhelming majority of African-Americans supported him. JFK 'had made it unfashionable to be racist'.[31] Nevertheless, his cautious approach to executive and legislative action had contributed to a more desperate and urgent demand for freedom which provided the centrifugal energy for the eventual collapse of the non-violent civil rights movement.

Lyndon Johnson understood the need for more assertive moral leadership on civil rights before Kennedy's assassination but after the fateful day in Dallas he was increasingly unable to stem the tide of unrest caused by its delay.

In the first two years of the Kennedy administration Johnson followed the lead of the President and remained cautious on the civil rights issue. He did not actively engage in Senate debates on the filibuster rule, and the gains of the Committee on Equal Employment Opportunities which he headed were meagre.[32] In June 1963, however, Johnson spoke with White House aide Ted Sorensen about the administration's civil rights stance. In a lengthy telephone conversation Johnson spelled out exactly what he believed Kennedy had to do on the issue of civil rights. Johnson was annoyed that he had not been consulted on Kennedy's civil rights bill, arguing he had only heard about it by reading the *New York Times*. The Vice President asserted that a more skilful approach to congressional problems was needed. More importantly, Johnson argued that Kennedy needed to go to the South and explain directly that he, as Commander-in-Chief, had to order black people into battle and they needed to be treated equally in America. Johnson believed a strong personal commitment to legislative change would ensure a 'man is put in the position almost where he's a bigot to be against the President'.[33]

The Vice President had signalled his own moral commitment to racial change when speaking at Gettysburg in May 1963. Johnson argued, 'the Negro today asks justice. We do not answer him – and we do not answer those who lie beneath this soil ... the time for waiting is gone.' Johnson had travelled a political and personal journey in which he had increasingly developed a moral commitment to civil rights. It was this commitment that motivated his full-throated call for the passage of civil rights legislation following Kennedy's assassination.[34] His progress towards such a position, however, was difficult. The Texan stood at the other side of the Democratic interparty struggle from JFK. A southerner viewed with suspicion by northern liberals to Kennedy's north-eastern intellectual observed with caution by southerners. Following the advice of his mentor, leader of the southern caucus Richard Russell, Johnson 'went along to get along' and voted against the civil rights legislation that reached the Senate floor in the 1950s.[35] LBJ was an ambitious politician and he was not about to commit political suicide by standing against the southern bloc. He also voted against some measures on principle: he thought it wrong to alter the Senate filibuster rules and he disagreed with Truman's approach to civil rights legislation.

His closeness to the southern caucus made many liberals averse to Johnson. Even after the passage of major civil rights legislation in 1964 they were relatively unimpressed. Johnson himself commented, 'I got their goddamn legislation passed for them, but they gave me no credit.'[36] LBJ operated in the shadow of JFK and this coloured reaction to his civil rights record. Unlike his presidential predecessor, however, Johnson grew up with the experiences of ethnic minorities around him and formed an early and enduring personal commitment to their problems. Delivering the presidential address to the Southern Historical Association in 1978, Professor Frantz spoke about his research on Johnson's response to the issue of civil rights. 'I started out to watch [him] turn 180 degrees as he progressed down the road toward national importance. Along the way I discovered he was moving in a remarkably straight line, a generally progressive line.'[37]

From his formative years teaching Hispanic children in Cotulla, Texas, Johnson developed a genuine concern for minority groups. Although he subscribed to the traditional racial mores of the region, as a committed New Dealer Johnson initiated several schemes as director of the Texas branch of the National Youth Administration. He made important efforts to improve the opportunities of jobless black youths.[38] Despite its limitations, the 1957 Civil Rights Act, the first major piece of legislation on the issue since Reconstruction, would not have been passed without Johnson's considerable skills in the Senate. Johnson's vision for America increasingly came to embrace racial equality. His commitment to change was sincere and he moved 'farther and faster on the road to change than Kennedy had or probably would have'.[39] When he gave his speech before Congress supporting passage of Voting Rights legislation in 1965, Johnson used the words of the civil rights anthem, 'We shall overcome'. Watching on television in Birmingham, Martin Luther King wept tears of joy.[40]

Johnson's leadership on the civil rights issue was, however, importantly affected by the legacy of the Kennedy White House. Kennedy's vacillation on the issue and his slow moral commitment to legislative change had caused frustration among civil rights leaders. King believed that, had Kennedy lived, 'there would have been continual delays and attempts to evade [strong civil rights legislation] at every

167

point, and water it down at every point'.[41] His symbolic gestures offered false hope of more concrete change and this led to a dynamic in which the movement's leadership used mass demonstrations to put pressure on the administration. The Birmingham demonstrations of 1963 had raised the spectre of widespread domestic discord and undoubtedly influenced Kennedy's policies. King continued to use the tactics learned under JFK's presidency when Johnson was in the Oval Office. He called for a march in Selma to 'arouse the federal government', and the violence that erupted was played out on television, which moved Johnson to call for passage of voting rights legislation.[42]

Johnson was aware of his own place in history and his desire to pass defining civil rights legislation was not devoid of politics. His policy towards civil rights was also informed by the Kennedy years. Johnson was determined to ensure that the White House offered the clear voice of leadership on the struggle for equality. He continually urged established civil rights leaders to keep activism under control. Fearing violent repercussions in the South, Johnson followed Kennedy in failing to champion serious efforts at school desegregation.[43] The White House attempted to force a moratorium on mass marches and demonstrations after the passage of the 1964 Civil Rights Act and helped to craft the message of black leaders after meetings with the President.[44] Increasingly, however, Johnson was unable to carry civil rights leaders with him. In the days after the passage of the Voting Rights Act, racial violence erupted in Watts, Los Angeles. The enduring problems of black poverty and social breakdown, problems which several administrations helped to exacerbate through inaction, began to emerge front and centre as the mainstream civil rights movement unravelled.[45]

This process was subtly and intricately linked to the war in Vietnam. 'Like an acid eating at the vitals of America, the war destroyed the strong consensus on foreign policy ... and both directly and indirectly aggravated the country's domestic troubles.'[46] The moral consensus that Johnson had mobilised to ensure the passage of landmark civil rights legislation had affirmed a war in South East Asia to defeat the forces of Communist tyranny. Nevertheless, Johnson's 'Great Society' was forced into full retreat when civil rights leaders began to speak out against the war in Vietnam. Violence in the ghettos, black power rhetoric and the anti-war message of King showed that the fight against communism in Vietnam and the struggle for social justice had diverged from elements of a shared vision to diametrically opposed objectives.[47] As racial riots increasingly afflicted America, Johnson felt despair and disappointment that blacks were repaying his firm commitment to their struggle with violence and disorder.[48] Liberals criticised the war in Vietnam, conservatives argued the President had moved too fast on the civil rights issue and the shadow of Kennedy continued to stretch onto the national stage. In 1969 a factory worker in Texas lamented the social turmoil and the untimely death of Kennedy: 'he would have done some good if they would of gave him some time and hadn't killed him'.[49]

The power of symbolism which Kennedy utilised created an enduring image of a president whose personal commitment to equality offered great hope for the nation. That same politics of representation ensured a tragic vision of Johnson's America, engulfed by urban and international violence. Yet part of the explanation for the explosion of urban black America can be found in frustrations at the slow progress of real racial change under Kennedy. The groundswell for change in black America was a force which could not be realistically controlled by the White House but Kennedy's politics of symbolism raised hopes that when dashed increased the volume of the calls for change.

18

MARTIN, MALCOLM AND
BLACK AMERICA

James Cone wrote that 'if Americans of all races intend to create a just
and peaceful future, then they must listen to both Martin and Malcolm'.[1]
Martin Luther King and Malcolm X were the most influential black
leaders of the last century. Traditional narratives of their work as civil
rights activists portray the men as great ideological opposites. King's
dream of racial integration in the United States, to be achieved through
redemptive love, is juxtaposed with Malcolm's hatred of white America and the fiery rhetoric of this archetypal angry young black man.
Although significantly different in their outlook, largely because of
their contradictory backgrounds, the two men did share common
ground. Malcolm moved closer to Martin in his embrace of human rights
in the year before his assassination in 1965 and King thought more
deeply about those in the ghetto, whose struggles Malcolm voiced,
before he too was gunned down.

The purpose of this chapter is to reflect on the ideas and legacy of
these two men, and to link them to problems facing black Americans at the beginning of the twenty-first century. Neither Martin's
'dream' nor Malcolm's 'nightmare' fully describes the experience of
African-Americans in the contemporary United States. Since the
1960s progress for some has been offset by worsening problems for
others. Popular images of Martin and Malcolm, however, have been
shaped in order to reduce the potency of their messages of change.
Malcolm is portrayed as the angry and violent face of Black Power,
whilst his increasing embrace of human rights for all is ignored.
Martin is sanitised as a moderate, a welcomed antithesis to Malcolm's
anger, and his meaning is dominated by the rhetoric of hope expressed
in his famous 'I have a Dream' oration. Their legacies have been
shaped in such a way as to neutralise the call for sweeping social
changes that both were voicing before they were killed. Crucially, the
economically and socially deprived black Americans who these men

170

increasingly championed remain an unhealed scar on the nation's landscape.

Although they were both born into Baptist families, Malcolm and Martin experienced radically different childhoods. In his autobiography Martin recalled that the Church had always been a 'second home' for him. His parents taught him that as a Christian he should love white people even though he did not have to accept racial oppression.[2] Malcolm's father was an active member of Marcus Garvey's Universal Negro Improvement Association and attracted the attention of white supremacists. The family home was burned to the ground and when Malcolm was six years old his father was murdered. Wracked by grief and unable to cope with the strain of supporting her family, his mother was committed to a psychiatric hospital.[3] The broken home of Malcolm's childhood was, therefore, far from the relatively affluent and comfortable family life that King enjoyed.

Their experience of education also differed sharply. King attended Morehouse College and Crozer Theological Seminary where his reading of the social gospel theorist Walter Rauschenbusch further convinced him of the need for the Church to concern itself with social problems. In his 1960 essay 'Pilgrimage to Non-violence', King also writes of the great influence of Gandhi's philosophy of non-violence and the power of love.[4] Malcolm was a promising student, a bright and articulate young man. In his autobiography, however, he tells of being expelled from his Junior High School in Lansing, Michigan, after placing a drawing pin on the seat of his white teacher. Malcolm was sent to a reform school, where he was educated alongside mainly white classmates. Disillusioned by life at the reform school after his English teacher told him that his race made his ambition of becoming a lawyer impractical, Malcolm wrote to his half-sister in Boston and asked to go and live with her in 1941.[5]

Working as a porter on the Boston to New York route he became a petty criminal with the nickname of 'Detroit Red'. Malcolm was arrested for burglary in 1945 and sentenced to seven years in prison. The length of his sentence was no doubt influenced by the fact that one of his accomplices was also his white mistress.[6] Malcolm's education continued, however, as a fellow prisoner encouraged him to take advantage of the prison library and the various correspondence courses on offer. Then his brother Reginald wrote to him with the news not to eat pork or smoke and he would show him how to get out of prison. So started Malcolm's journey to membership of the Nation of Islam.[7] In 1952, as King was studying in his second year at Boston University, Malcolm was released from prison on parole and began living the lifestyle of a black Muslim. Shortly after arriving in Detroit to live with his brother Wilfred, he met the leader of the Nation of Islam, Elijah Muhammad, who renamed him Malcolm X.[8]

As we will later consider the way Martin and Malcolm's legacies have been shaped by others, it is worth pausing to acknowledge how the two men constructed their own image with respect to their formative years. Keith Miller has dissected the ways in which King crafted a philosophical persona in order to appeal to white liberals. In 'Pilgrimage to Non-violence' much of his analysis of Rauschenbusch is taken from the work of the preacher Harry Emerson Fosdick. Miller argues that King wanted to convince white readers of 'Pilgrimage' that a fight for civil rights could be justified after careful study of Euro-American philosophy. Much of his worldview sprang from the traditions of the black church and the teachings of his father but King did not want to be perceived as just another black preacher railing against segregation.[9] In his autobiographical writing Malcolm too sought to reconstruct a specific image. For example, he was not expelled from Junior High in Lansing but in fact completed the seventh grade. He also omits the conversations he had with the Ku Klux Klan in 1961 about the possibility of giving financial aid to Elijah Muhammad to help him and his followers obtain land for a separate black community. Malcolm crafted a narrative 'of his escape from functional illiteracy, his exodus from mental and social slavery, and his conversion to true belief'.[10]

That both men were so keen to present a careful version of their story was testament to their position as the most prominent black leaders of the 1960s. Martin's careful acknowledgement of white philosophy and Malcolm's account of black struggle and self-discovery are also reflective of their contrasting messages. A year before Martin was to begin his rise to national prominence in Montgomery, Alabama, Malcolm was appointed the head of Temple Number Seven in New York. From 1953 to 1959 Malcolm was largely unknown in white America, speaking to black audiences across the country about the 'white devil' that held them in a grip of social, economic and psychological oppression.[11] Malcolm identified with the disillusioned masses of the ghetto and spoke to their needs. As Elijah Muhammad's principal evangelist, Malcolm attacked the integrationist philosophy of Martin in the early 1960s. He stated 'white people follow King ... white people subsidize King ... the masses of black people don't support King'.[12]

Malcolm told his audiences, 'the white man is our first and main enemy. Our second enemy are the Uncle Toms, such as Martin Luther

King and his turn the other cheek method.' He referred to Martin as a 'traitor', a 'chump' and the 'Reverend Dr. Chickenwing'.[13] King chose not to engage in verbal sparring with Malcolm and the Nation of Islam for fear that coverage of their message would dissuade sympathetic whites from supporting the civil rights movement. He did criticise their views after Southern Christian Leadership Conference executive director, Wyatt Walker, nearly got into a fist fight with Malcolm X during a televised debate in 1963. Such criticism further increased Nation of Islam antipathy towards him and he was pelted with eggs as he arrived to speak at a church in Harlem.[14] King stayed true to his message of non-violence and sought to help southern blacks fight the racial segregation that denied them access to the promises of America.

The speeches of Martin and Malcolm reveal the contradictions in their ideological conceptions of the black struggle. In 1961 King told students at Lincoln University, 'America is essentially a dream, a dream as yet unfulfilled. It is a dream of a land where all men of all races, of all nationalities and all creeds can live together as brothers.'[15] Malcolm raged, 'No I'm not an American, I'm one of the 22 million black people who are the victims of Americanisation ... I don't see any American dream; I see an American nightmare.'[16] Martin called on blacks to love white people in the way Jesus had instructed man to 'love your enemies'. He argued that love could be a powerful force, 'love is understanding, redemptive, creative, good will for all men'.[17] Malcolm retorted, 'I don't think we should run around trying to love somebody who doesn't love us.'[18] King argued that the destiny of the black population was tied up with the destiny of America. He promised, 'we're going to win our freedom because both the sacred heritage of our nation and the eternal will of the almighty God are embodied in our echoing demands ... We shall overcome'.[19] Malcolm asserted, 'revolutions are never waged singing "we shall overcome". Revolutions are based on bloodshed. Revolutions are never compromising.'[20]

Martin believed that by remaining non-violent and through the redemptive suffering of shedding their own blood blacks would eventually be free. Malcolm called for 'reciprocal bleeding' for whites and blacks and justified the use of armed self-defence as part of any means necessary to be employed in the freedom struggle.[21] Both men saw the great evil of racism in American society but chose different philosophies in order to combat it. These philosophies were significantly shaped by their backgrounds but also by the socio-political climate in which they operated. King sought to expose the brutality of the Jim Crow system by campaigning to destroy legal segregation. Malcolm, however, faced the realities of the northern ghetto in which economic injustice and de facto segregation trapped African-Americans. King's belief in the American dream led him on a path towards integration. Malcolm, though, believed in black nationalism and the liberation of his race through self-discovery, arguing, 'the black man has to be shown how to free himself'.[22]

This clear dichotomy provides the dominant popular narrative of the lives of Martin and Malcolm. It overlooks, however, the tentative convergence of the two men's thoughts in the final years of their lives. Following the assassination of President Kennedy in 1963, Malcolm ignored an order by Elijah Muhammad, which prohibited Nation of Islam ministers from commenting, and was suspended from the movement for ninety days. The suspension was a manifestation of the growing divide between Malcolm and the Nation of Islam. Elijah Muhammad saw the organisation in strictly religious terms whereas Malcolm saw the Nation as the solution to the social, economic and political problems of black America.[23] As Malcolm moved away from the shadow of Muhammad he was also moving closer to the mainstream civil rights movement. His changing outlook was heavily influenced by his journey through Africa and the Middle East in 1964. On the pilgrimage to Mecca Malcolm saw white and black Muslims worshipping together. Referring to the whites he saw, Malcolm observed, 'there was a difference between them and the white ones over here'.[24] Malcolm's mind was opened to the possibility of working with white people in a way it had not been before.

Although his outlook and strategy remained significantly different from that of King, Malcolm realised that his black Muslim image alienated him from the vast majority of Christian blacks and from other civil rights leaders. In 1964 he formed the Organisation of Afro-American Unity and called for cooperation among all black leaders and for common approaches to the problems of American racism.[25] Malcolm told young Mississippians who were on a trip to New York in late 1964 that he was not against white people.[26] He signalled his willingness to work with those who were genuinely interested in helping black people achieve freedom. When in January 1965 a reporter asked Malcolm whether he still believed in separation of whites and blacks and was against inter-racial marriages, Malcolm replied, 'I believe in recognising every human being as a human being – neither white, black, brown or red ... when you are dealing with humanity as a family there's no question of integration or intermarriage.'[27]

In the year before his assassination Malcolm engaged with the mainstream civil rights movement, supporting a school boycott in Brooklyn and meeting with groups of clergymen and members of the

Student Non-violent Coordinating Committee who were attracted by his ideas on Black Nationalism. 'When Malcolm became an independent leader, his inspiration was derived more from Martin than Muhammad, as he sought to build an organisation that could include a range of blacks with different political and religious orientations.'[28] Just as he was beginning to explore different paths in the freedom struggle, Malcolm was killed by members of the Nation of Islam in February 1965. When asked to comment on the death, King lamented the fact that it had come at a time when Malcolm was re-evaluating his ideas and moving closer to working with white people. The assassination also came at a time when King was facing up to the continued problems in the black community, problems which could not simply be solved by civil and voting rights legislation.[29] The racial violence in Watts, Los Angeles, in the summer of 1965 and the problems he faced trying to combat the de facto segregation of Chicago in 1966 forced King to rethink the meaning of black freedom and the strategy needed to achieve it.

Malcolm had spoken of the poor housing, poor schooling and poor jobs that plagued the African-American community and Martin began to address these issues more fully. In 1967 King spoke of America needing to be 'born again'. He asserted that the movement for freedom 'must address itself to the question of restructuring the whole of American society'.[30] Martin, unlike Malcolm, supported a coalition of the poor and dispossessed across racial lines. Speaking of the poor people's campaign, which he planned to lead to Washington in the summer of 1968, King argued, 'we are coming to demand that the government address itself to the problem of poverty'.[31] King's middle-class background meant he did not instinctively identify with the black masses in the ghetto as Malcolm did, but in his final years he saw that the economic degradation of the working class was a massive problem for black America. In 1968 King spoke of the disparity of opportunity for young black and white men in America and the 'social dynamite' that this situation created.[32] It was this dynamite which had fired the angry rhetoric of Malcolm.

When King began to criticise the Vietnam War and American imperialism in his later years he was moving in a more radical direction and broke with established black leaders. Rather than expressing an 'invested patriotism' which had faith that one day black tenacity and non-violent struggle would be rewarded with full equality, King articulated an 'iconoclastic patriotism'. He showed devotion to the nation by fundamentally challenging American racism in all its forms.[33] Following King's assassination in April 1968, race riots erupted across urban America. This reaction to Martin's death served to highlight the great problems of racial injustice which were central to the black ghetto. This ghetto was given voice by Malcolm X who lived and then articulated the problems of race which could not be solved by the civil rights legislation of the mid-1960s. The shaping of Martin's legacy in the popular imagination, however, distanced him from the radical messages of his later years when he began to address the problem of poverty and economic inequality in America. The divide between Martin and Malcolm, a divide deeply shaped by their differing class and family backgrounds, was widened in the process of remembering them. By ignoring the important threads which did join them, popular history increasingly neutralised their radical messages. As a consequence, twenty-first-century black America remains crucially divided between the middle classes who can embrace Martin's 'dream' and those trapped in the ghetto living Malcolm's 'nightmare'.

King's example and the message he brought to the South had an undoubted impact. In the decades that have passed since his death the white South has gradually shifted away from the racism of its past. Governor George Wallace, identified by King as one of the most vicious racists of the region, appeared at black churches and hired blacks for his staff in the 1980s. Presidents Carter and Clinton, both from the South, appointed more blacks to positions in the federal government than any of their predecessors.[34] Nevertheless, a commitment to remove the clearly visible elements of America's racial past is not a commitment to deal with the structural racism deeply embedded in US society. Young black ghetto residents remained 'invisible' to the Clinton administration.[35] Indeed presidential praise for King has often sought to reduce the potency of his message. The 1983 bill which introduced the Martin Luther King national holiday came in a decade in which federal civil rights programmes were not significantly advanced. Reagan repeatedly used King's own words and his memory in order to make the case that individual action was now required to fulfil the 'dream' that King had spoken of. Although King indicated approval of affirmative action initiatives when he talked about 'balancing the equation' of whites and blacks in 1964, Reagan argued that King was against such legislation. Reagan saw no need for federal action: 'he talked about civil rights as an issue that King had successfully resolved in the past and argued that individual efforts were needed for any additional progress'.[36]

It was not only Reagan and white conservatives who objected to affirmative action for African-Americans. Black conservatives who spoke with the voice of the middle class, which had reaped the rewards of affirmative action in the area of college admission and promotion in the business world, called for an end to such legislation. They argued that these programmes were no longer needed and ran contrary to King's dream of a colour-blind America. The conservatives recognised that affirmative action had not helped the black poor, but still opposed even race-neutral federal supports for those in the ghetto, instead preaching a message of self-reliance and individual responsibility.[37] King's image was shaped in such a way as to divorce him from the truly radical message of his later years, when he challenged America to face up to the problems of the poor and dispossessed of all races. As one historian argued, King has been made into a 'non-abrasive hero whose recorded speeches can be used as inspirational resources for rocking our memories to sleep'.[38]

The non-abrasive image of King is solidified by the way he is presented in history textbooks and the comparisons drawn between him and Malcolm X. Echoing their presentation by the media of the time, Martin and Malcolm are represented as opposite ends of a moderate and radical spectrum. Certainly King's courting of white liberals, most especially in the period 1955 to 1965, required him to keep his distance from Malcolm. Nevertheless, many textbooks fail to deal with the changes in Martin's aims after 1965 and most gloss over his call for economic change and his opposition to the Vietnam War. Discussion of the thin threads which began to join Martin and Malcolm in their later years is virtually non-existent.[39] Whilst King's moderate image has made him a hero figure for both white and black Americans, Malcolm's appeal is largely restricted to the latter. His rhetoric and life story make him a natural hero for the young black men of the ghetto. The influence of Malcolm's image on rap music comes from his articulation of a black rage which is still felt by a generation of young African-Americans trapped in social and economic inequality.[40]

Central to Malcolm's appeal to this generation is his rejection of the non-violent integrationist vision which dominates the popular legacy of Martin. Nevertheless, by isolating Malcolm from Martin and vice versa, a divided approach to the struggle for equality is reinforced and with it the divide between the black middle class and the ghetto. The growth of this black middle class since the 1960s is one of the most dramatic examples pointed to by those who argue for significant progress for African-Americans since the 1960s. The census of 2000 revealed that the top 20 per cent of black households had higher incomes than 62 per cent of white households, and the top 40 per cent higher than the bottom 41 per cent of white households. The major factors underlying the rise of the black middle class have been increased educational achievement and advancement up the occupational and income ladder.[41] The occupational gap between whites and blacks had closed significantly by 2000. White Americans were still more likely to hold managerial positions but the difference was less dramatic than in the mid-twentieth century.[42] The picture is not one of unqualified progress, however. Although the number of blacks receiving a bachelor's degree increased steadily from 1970 to 2002, among 25- to 29-year-olds twice as many whites received degrees as blacks. The racial differential is greater for younger cohorts, which suggests a worsening education gap.[43]

The growth of the middle class has been simultaneous with worsening conditions for a black underclass in which black males have been particularly marginalised. The number of young black men not participating in the labour force increased in the second half of the twentieth century. Many of these men have been incarcerated; between 1990 and 2000 the number of 26- to 30-year-olds in prison increased by one-third. At the dawn of the twenty-first century 49 per cent of prisoners nationwide were black, but only 13 per cent of the overall population was African-American.[44] The Sentencing Project of 2005 found sentencing disparities, with blacks convicted of the same crimes as whites more likely to be incarcerated.[45] One in four African-Americans continue to live in poverty. The black poor experience 'hypersegregated' neighbourhoods in which more than 40 per cent of the residents exist below the poverty line.[46] African-Americans trapped in these inner-city communities are those who Malcolm championed but his historical image is dominated by his radicalism, advocacy of violence and separatist religious ideals. They are also those whose plight Martin began to embrace, a reality which has been forgotten as part of the construction of his moderate and whitewashed popular legacy.

African-American political opinion and participation have been shaped in the post-civil rights era by the divide between the 'haves' and 'have nots' in the black community. The number of African-Americans who now hold office as representatives of mainstream political parties would have been unthinkable before the civil rights movement. Black electoral success has been offset, however, by income inequality and social distress. When considering political participation, the negative impact of the persistence of poverty has been far more significant than the positive gains from political empowerment.[47] Martin's and Malcolm's call to address the needs of the black poor have not been heeded. Scholars of the persistent inequality faced by African-Americans have argued that policies which bring individual social mobility but ignore the processes which reproduce inequality are inadequate. 'They are supply-side solutions to demand-side problems.'[48] One of the demand-side problems in the black community is the need for better education and job prospects for young men. As King himself recognised in 1968, 'it isn't just a lack of work; it's also a lack of meaningful work'.[49]

The new black inequality that emerged in the last decade of the twentieth century leaves black America divided. Race remained a crucial force in American life but it worked in new ways to sift black people through screens which advanced some and left others behind.[50] These subtle developments could not have been foreseen by Malcolm or Martin. Nor could they have predicated the competition between different minority groups for federal funding following the widespread immigration which resulted from legislation in the 1960s. In Martin's poor people's campaign and Malcolm's increased willingness to work with groups outside of the black community, however, lay the roots of strategies that could have been adapted to meet these elements of the struggle for equality. By highlighting the differences at the expense of the similarities between the two men, by focussing solely on Martin the moderate and Malcolm the radical, popular memory has contributed to the growing division in black America. Different class backgrounds they undoubtedly embodied, different philosophies they unquestionably practised, but both men agreed that food, decent housing and quality health care were fundamental human rights, rights which many Americans still do not enjoy.[51] If history is to be a study of the past with the aim of improving the present and the future, then a more comprehensive and complex understanding of Martin's and Malcolm's legacy is needed.

19

AMERICAN NATIONAL MISSION AND GLOBAL CONFLICT IN THE TWENTIETH CENTURY

During the Vietnam War a leader of the Students for a Democratic Society (SDS) lamented that the America they believed in had 'broken their American heart'.[1] Images of the skin of Vietnamese children being seared by napalm dropped from US planes contradicted the fundamental principles upon which the nation was built. The conception of America was then, as well as before and after, tied to its place in relation to the rest of the world. A sense of special mission was linked to the foundation myth of the nation. As one historian has explained this myth asserted, 'God put America in a position of supremacy because its long-term purpose was to influence other nations to emulate it.'[2] The role of the United States in global conflict has, therefore, played a crucial role in deepening American national identity. Whether by distancing itself from the corruptions and violence of the Old World or by intervening to ensure the preservation of freedom and democracy, American foreign policy was intrinsically connected to America's sense of itself. The space available in this chapter precludes an attempt to survey American foreign policy in any detail – such an effort would require a singularly devoted and weighty volume. The focus here is on how American identity, national myth and sense of mission impacted on US involvement in three major twentieth-century conflicts: the First and Second World Wars and Vietnam. Some of the themes explored below will be picked up in the chapter on America and the 'war on terror' in the post 9/11 world.

In his farewell address of 1796, President Washington warned his fellow Americans to avoid permanent alliances with other nations and to steer clear of foreign entanglements. In 1823 President Monroe expressed a policy which was later to be coined the 'Monroe Doctrine'. This nationalistic statement established two separate hemispheres, the New World and the Old World. Monroe asserted that the United States would not accept any further attempts at colonisation by the

European powers in the New World. He also assured these powers that the US would not interfere in their internal affairs or in their existing interests in the Americas. These statements established what many see as the traditionally isolationist position of American foreign policy. Nevertheless, this isolationist perspective was directly shaped by the circumstances in which the United States found itself in the nineteenth century. There was a desire to stay away from European wars and entangling alliances in order to protect the fledgling Republic. A nation struggling with the kind of internal tensions that would eventually lead to civil war was not in a position to engage forcefully on the international stage.

The basic ideals of America's founding myth, that it was an exceptional nation, 'the last best hope of earth' as Lincoln stated, remained constant throughout the nineteenth and twentieth centuries. As the US became an increasingly important player on the global stage, however, a debate developed over how the nation's mission should be implemented. A sense of isolationism provided an increasingly weak echo of nineteenth-century conceptions because the nature of American power in the world changed in the twentieth century. Loren Baritz wrote that 'a whisper runs through [American] history that the people of the world really want to be like us, regardless of what they or their political leaders say'.[3] Twentieth-century debate was largely based around how much, if any, diplomatic and military force the United States should use to influence or break the hold of undesirable regimes and their leaders. Whichever path was chosen, 'in the American mind their ultimate goals have been substantially identical: to create the necessary conditions in the outside world for the achievement of America's national purpose'.[4]

This discussion assumes that ideas are crucial determinants in the direction of American foreign policy. Diplomatic historians have often rejected the study of ideology as the intrusion of intellectual history into their field. Carefully studying archival materials in search of an understanding of the policy process, they have focussed on 'geopolitics' and 'containment' and 'international realities'.[5] Leftist scholars have criticised the assertion that American foreign affairs were driven by idealism. They argue that pretensions to the promotion of democracy simply served as a rhetorical camouflage for the advance of economic interests. The doctrine of realism asserts that American policy should have been guided by the concerns of realpolitik and the nation's strategic interests.[6] Realists view the concept of ideologically driven foreign policy as naive. Focussing on sound realist concepts like national interest is seen to be more sophisticated and historically sound. These concepts are themselves, however, guided by ideas. Ideological considerations must be part of deciding what constitutes the national interest – otherwise it would exist in a vacuum.[7]

This dichotomy between idealism and realism is false because the two forces are clearly linked in the operation of foreign policy. The founders of the nation themselves would not have recognised such a distinction but instead conceived of *principle* and *prudence* as complementary considerations in policy formation. Underlying principles guide decisions but these decisions are also affected by prudent judgement based on the specific context of events.[8] These events impact on the American national interest. The pursuit of prosperity and access to foreign markets, the defence and promotion of democracy and the maintenance of national security were viewed by policy makers as interconnected elements of American interests.[9] Scholars who focus on national interest and security as an interpretive framework are able to synthesise the approaches of historians who see diplomatic history anchored to the exercise of power in the international system and those who see domestic forces as the principal engine of policy. In this way they can chart the interaction between national values and international threats.[10] Any approach to US foreign policy must acknowledge the influence of both idealism and pragmatism and it must also seek to link geopolitical developments with the concerns of domestic policy. The place of ideas is again important here because policy makers must decide which values and threats to respond to and in doing so must apply certain principles and ideology to each.

The role of America in world affairs in the twentieth century revolved around a series of great debates. These debates not only concerned how American power should be used abroad but also what the implications of this would be at home.[11] The rest of this chapter will focus on three of these debates, starting with American entry into the First World War and the struggle over whether to enter the League of Nations. In discussing America's entry into each conflict we will briefly explore the role of ideals and national interest. It is fitting that we begin with the foreign policy principles of Woodrow Wilson because his concept of liberal internationalism played such a key role in stimulating debate concerning America's role in the world. Wilson linked national security to the liberal notions of economic openness, democracy and multilateral organisations.[12]

Wilson's commitment to a plan for a new world order with America playing a key role in the international community did not emerge as soon as war broke out in Europe in 1914. The President declared American neutrality in the European conflict. With a large German-American minority among a moderately Anglophilic population, Wilson argued neutrality was necessary to stop any conflict between different factions inside the nation. More importantly, economic factors were a key consideration. The US was moving towards a depression in 1914 but the economy began to turn around when American industry became the most prominent supplier of the European powers, mostly exporting to the allies.[13] The policy of neutrality was driven by an impulse of caution. The influence of nineteenth-century foreign policy principles was therefore an important context to events. Nevertheless, as the conflict progressed, Wilson's reforming zeal became more apparent as he sought to redesign the international system in line with American values.[14]

The policy of neutrality proved difficult as tensions between the British and the Americans mounted in the first six months of the war. British blockades stopped American ships from docking at neutral ports that were deemed too close to Germany. In May 1915 relations with the British were given a boost when a German submarine sank the luxury liner *Lusitania*. Wilson calmed the country by arguing he would not make any hasty decisions based on the passions of the people following the sinking. The President said that America was too proud to fight. Wilson's 1916 election slogan 'he kept us out of war' was a vague message designed to reassure the population, which was still overwhelmingly antiwar in its sentiment.[15] But Wilson became convinced that war was unavoidable in 1917. The British produced a decoded message – the Zimmerman telegram – from the German foreign ministry to its representative in Mexico proposing an alliance against the US and then the German navy sank three American merchantmen.

Wilson's rhetoric changed. He had used moral justifications for America staying out of the war before 1917 but now saw entry into the war in moral terms. Germany was viewed as the personification of an affront by autocracy to the principles of democracy.[16] Wilson was driven by liberal idealism but his approach to the crisis was also shaped by the pragmatic concerns of national interest. This serves to highlight the inadequacy of a simple idealism–realism dichotomy. The sinking of US ships and the threat to trade, and the more immediate geographical danger of military confrontation with Mexico, prompted action. We can also see in the President's actions and ideas a strong sense of American mission, as well as a continued desire to avoid European entanglements. The US did not become a member of the Allied coalition but aligned itself with the Allied and Associated Powers; it was the only 'associated power', emphasising America's exceptionalism. In the policy of neutrality between 1914 and 1917 and in his call for a new international order, a community of power, Wilson was following the traditional impulse to stay out of entanglements with European nations and he rejected the traditional balance of power doctrine.[17]

It was in January 1918 that Wilson spelled out his fourteen-point plan for future world peace. Wilson's concept of global stability was based on national self-determination, democracy and political pluralism, economic freedom and openness and commitment to a League of Nations which was to enforce civilised conduct between nations and protect peace. He also believed that it was essential that America played a crucial role in shaping this new order.[18] When submitting the Treaty of Versailles to the Senate in 1919, Wilson's message was heavily loaded with the idealism of the American founding myth. The President urged ratification of the Treaty and the League of Nations by arguing, 'we can only go forward, with lifted eyes and freshened spirit, to follow the vision. It was of this that we dreamed at our birth. America shall in truth show the way.'[19]

The political fight over ratification of the Treaty of Versailles and the setting up of the League of Nations saw the President asking his nation to engage in global affairs on an unprecedented scale. Wilson faced huge difficulties during the political struggle that ensued. The powers of the League to enforce peace, for example, infringed on Congressional prerogatives and US sovereignty. Led by Henry Cabot Lodge, Republican senators were critical of the terms Wilson had negotiated at the post-war Paris Peace Conference.[20] A deadlock between President and Senate emerged as Wilson refused to sign the amended version of the peace treaty that the Republicans presented, and the senators therefore refused to vote for entrance to the League of Nations. An entry into some form of League was approved of by the majority of Americans but the scheme was rejected when the Senate fell short of the two-thirds majority required for ratification.[21]

Traditional historical accounts of the struggle over the League of Nations have accepted Wilson's own frameworks, which viewed him as the liberal internationalist and Lodge and his allies as reactionary isolationists. Nevertheless, this interpretation fails to fully acknowledge Wilson's aims: his conception of the League combined both multilateralism and traditional American unilateralism. Even through his ideal of the League, Wilson sought to defend America from foreign entanglements. The President attempted to convince the Senate that there was a distinction between moral and legal commitment under Article 10 of the League covenant, which dealt with the obligation to prevent aggression and maintain peace. Wilson argued that the League would guarantee peace but that the US would retain total freedom in deciding its involvement in peacekeeping actions. He tried to frame the League as consistent with American unilateralism.[22]

This interpretation of the fight over the League not only forces us to re-examine Wilsonian ideals but also highlights the overly simplistic interventionism–isolationism conception of twentieth-century US foreign policy. Despite Wilson's failure after the First World War, his legacy had a massive influence on America's role in war and peace for the rest of the twentieth century.[23] The dominant message of Wilsonian liberalism was that he would 'save America by saving the world'. Many of his countrymen, however, believed 'they would save America and let the world fend for itself'.[24] America's reactions to international relations between the wars revealed a 'deep bifurcation in the American mind' about the nation's proper role in world affairs.[25] This debate was not simply about isolationism versus interventionism. The changed nature of American influence in the world meant that the issues were more complex. The more pertinent question was how America should influence the rest of the world. Wilson's idealism and its practical outworking clearly show this.

It is apparent, nonetheless, that a broadly 'isolationist' feeling was strong in the US during the 1920s and 1930s. Restrictive immigration quotas reflected a desire to protect America from the Old World. The Senate passed a number of Neutrality Acts in the mid-1930s which were designed to shackle President Franklin D. Roosevelt and keep the US out of European wars. FDR worked hard to persuade Congress not to pass the Ludlow Amendment, which would have established a system in which Congress would not be able to declare war without a national referendum.[26] The difficulty with the policy of diplomatic neutrality though, when faced with Japanese aggression and German fascism, was the issue of morality. The American foundation myth, that the nation should be a shining light for the rest of the world, meant that there was a growing recognition that Hitler had to be stopped. Debate between the America First campaign and the Committee to Defend America by Aiding the Allies revolved around how this should be done.[27]

The level of this public debate about America's entry into the conflict was restricted by the policies of the Roosevelt administration and the President's own refusal to commit himself to a definite course of action. He campaigned for the 1940 election promising that he would keep the US out of the European war and, even as he agreed the cash-and-carry legislation to allow Britain and France to buy American-manufactured munitions, FDR did not commit himself publicly to a clear policy. The President was not prepared, however, to allow an anti-intervention sentiment to gain the type of strength in American public opinion which would restrict his later actions. The administration shied away from the kind of pro-war propaganda directed during the First World War by George Creel and the Committee on Public Information. Nevertheless debate was restricted and public opinion consciously shaped. The administration worked in concert with the media to produce a steady stream of public education which presented a picture of preparedness and calm. Roosevelt believed the issues of war and peace were too serious an issue for public debate and projected a view that the nation could meet the challenge posed by Hitler in whatever form that may take.[28]

The Lend-Lease Agreement of February 1941 clearly displayed that America was supporting the Allies in moral and practical ways. Public opinion remained predominantly non-interventionist, however. Before Pearl Harbor only a small minority of Americans told pollsters that the US should enter the conflict without a direct attack on their territory, though there was increasing support for measures to help defeat the Axis powers which stopped short of direct military involvement.[29] America was simply not ready in 1940–41 to be a major player in international affairs. US leaders were not sure what the nation's role should be.[30] The debate over this role is crucial. American idealism and national interest were interlocking forces in the search for an appropriate response to the war in Europe and tensions in the Pacific. Roosevelt's policy of gradualism which slowly moved the nation closer to military intervention was shaped by these forces. FDR increasingly maintained that helping the British was also a safeguard to American security. It was, however, the build-up of economic and diplomatic pressure on Japan which led to Pearl Harbor and US entry into the war. Geopolitical concerns over rising Japanese power and the consequent threat to an open market in China drove a foreign policy which backed Tokyo into a corner, escape from which they thought only possible through aggression.[31]

There were weak echoes of the nineteenth-century isolationist impulse in the response of Wilson and Roosevelt respectively to American involvement in the First and Second World Wars. Nevertheless, a sense of American mission in the world provided an overwhelming ideological framework which suggested the US should act. The major debate was over the form and the extent of this action. American involvement in the Second World War and the massive economic and military commitment required to defeat the Axis powers had a significant impact on US attitudes to foreign affairs. The economic wasteland of post-war Europe, the massive build up of American military power, and the rising threat of communism effected a change in outlook. Wilson's assertion that America should lead the world away from the old balance of power approach to European power politics was clearly repudiated by the establishment of NATO after the Second World War.

The international dynamics created by the Cold War provided the geopolitical climate which drew America into a conflict in Vietnam. US policy makers saw South East Asia as a key battleground against the forces of communism and from the end of the Second World War through the Nixon presidency successive administrations sought to bolster anti-communist forces in Vietnam. Escalation of the number of American forces in South Vietnam was conditioned to a large extent by the strategic conception of US leaders. An all-out American attack on communist North Vietnam would provoke intervention by the Chinese in the same way that had been the case during the Korean War. This would lead to calls for the use of nuclear weapons. The scenario of an escalating nuclear confrontation was far worse than the kind of protracted, material and morale-sapping limited war which unfolded in Vietnam.[32]

A realist interpretation of American involvement in Vietnam focusses on the Cold War dynamic and on the sense of national interest and security which was tied up in preserving South Vietnam. Nevertheless, ideology was a constant influence. As the war dragged on the US was increasingly defending American credibility. It had said it would protect Saigon and so it had to in order to show the rest of the Free World that confidence in America was not misplaced.[33] The American foundation myth and its outworking was a constant element of the dialogue between those who wanted to stay the course and those who wanted to pull out. In John F. Kennedy's celebrated inaugural address could be heard the echoes of Wilsonian liberalism. He asserted, 'we shall pay any price, bear any burden, meet any hardship, support any friend, oppose any foe to assure the survival and the success of liberty'.[34] For President Johnson a sense of Christian mission worked alongside strategic concerns. The decision to go into Vietnam and stay so long cannot be divorced from a sense of American mission that was rooted deep in the nation's history. Johnson's words showed that he looked to the American foundation myth when justifying the moral authority of the US to act on the international stage.[35]

The protracted nature of the war in Vietnam provided a serious challenge to those who favoured significant military intervention as the outworking of America's foundation myth. Vietnam challenged the American foundation myth and showed American leaders that they could not remake the world in the image of the United States.[36] Daniel Bell wrote, in 1975, of an end to American exceptionalism. 'The American Century', he contended, 'lasted scarcely 30 years. It foundered on the shoals of Vietnam.'[37] American failure in Vietnam questioned its legitimacy as a world power but it also raised doubts about the morality of the nation. Concerns were raised too about the legitimacy of an activist state, not because it failed to protect the nation but because it failed to embody the ideals that were used to justify its existence.[38] As the voice of the anti-war movement grew louder across the nation, America's sense of identity was contested by competing forces who adopted differing perspectives on how to operationalise the foundation myth. Those who believed that America should withdraw from the conflict and stand as an example of freedom rather than act as its instrument, used America's sense of mission to call for an end to involvement in Vietnam. A particularly pertinent anti-war slogan asked the rhetorical question 'would napalm convert you to democracy?'[39]

Much has been made of the role of the media in shaping public attitudes towards the war in Vietnam. The first televised conflict in American history had the effect of bringing suffering into people's living rooms and asking questions about the legitimacy of the nation's conduct. Certainly after the Tet Offensive of 1968 public opinion had some constraint over government policy and the media became less deferential and more adversarial towards officials and their policies as the war progressed. Nevertheless, the role of the media in turning opinion against the war has been exaggerated. The correlation is not as strong as President Johnson and others suggested. Very limited coverage of the war involved scenes of heavy fighting and reporters were clear in asserting that Tet was not a victory for the Vietcong. More than anything the TV news showed the conflict in Vietnam for what it was, a confusing and incoherent war of attrition. It was this which contributed to the war weariness of the American people.[40]

As an introduction to the study of the legacy of the War, one historian has argued, 'Vietnam is an invitation only to amnesia – a hard and numb scar we prefer not to notice.'[41] The American experience in Vietnam severely shook the nation's foundation myth but it did not destroy it. The myth was not monolithic; it could be expressed in different ways. There were clear polar opposites provided by those who wished America to stay out of foreign entanglements like Vietnam and those who favoured a more forceful use of American military and diplomatic power. Nevertheless, it was the many shades of difference in between that provided the framework for America's response to global conflicts in the twentieth century. Major debate surrounded how the American mission should operate and how much and what type of influence should be utilised. The belief that the United States vacillated between simple isolationism and interventionism is inconsistent with the nature of America's place in the world in the twentieth century.

The fact that the American foundation myth and its outworking is not one-dimensional allowed it to survive the challenge of Vietnam.[42] That defeat, and its manner, has had an unmistakable impact on American foreign policy decisions to the present day. America's sense of mission, rooted in its foundation myth, has not, however, faded. The US response to the 9/11 attacks and the struggle in Iraq continue to show the importance of foreign affairs as part of the construction of national identity. These terrorist attacks have also had a significant impact on civil liberties and the limits of American citizenship. These issues will be explored in the next chapter.

20

AMERICAN IDENTITY AND THE 'WAR ON TERROR'

There is a sense that the terrorist attacks on the United States on 11 September 2001 provided a paradigm shift in the psyche of the nation, a feeling that nothing would be the same again. The horrifying events of that day and the subsequent responses of the Bush administration have provided some significant changes in the direction of foreign policy in the post-Cold War world. This must not disguise, however, the reality of great continuities with the past. Indeed the administration itself constructed the meaning of the 'war on terror' by referring to historical precedents and invoking the collective memory of previous conflicts.[1] In a paradoxical discourse of selective remembrance, American policy was linked to memories of the past whilst simultaneously being justified as a response to an unprecedented and uniquely dangerous conflict.

In the previous chapter we noted that the American foundation myth and sense of mission were able to survive the national trauma of the Vietnam War. The terrorist attacks of 9/11 stimulated calls for America to play a directly interventionist role in world affairs in order to preserve and outwork that mission. President Bush embraced a vision of American exceptionalism which promised to use US power to rid the world of evil and tyranny. In his 2002 State of the Union Address he argued, 'Americans are a free people who know that freedom is the right of every person and the future of every nation. The liberty we prize is not America's gift to the world, it is God's gift to humanity.'[2] In the rhetoric and policy of the administration there was a strong sense of idealism. As with previous responses to global conflicts, however, this has been accompanied by the competing and complementary concept of national interest. Neo-conservative policy makers seek to promote democracy and freedom but often as a secondary concern to the pragmatic primacy of national security.

Attempts by the government to explain the war on terror relied on straightforward conceptual frameworks and historical precedents which in turn promoted a simplistic clash of civilisations interpretation.[3] An uncritical and prescriptive patriotism was mobilised in support of the war on terror, a war which rapidly expanded in its geographical and strategic scope between 9/11 and the invasion of Iraq. As discussed previously, America's sense of itself has long been connected to its relationship with the rest of the world. What makes the war on terror so important in this respect is the great paradox it presents. In seeking to promote democracy and freedom in the face of organised terror, the Bush administration compromised those very principles both at home and abroad. The restriction of civil liberties and the emergence of a prescriptive patriotic spirit appeared as consequences of the 9/11 attacks and presented questions which struck at the very heart of US national identity. This prescriptive patriotism was accompanied by pernicious racial assumptions which impacted on the construction of American citizenship.

The nature of the attacks on the Twin Towers had a massive impact on the minds of Americans. There was nothing new in the technology utilised by the attackers but they used aeroplanes as destructive weapons against civilian targets in an unprecedented way. Twenty-four-hour news channels brought the horrific scenes of the passenger jets smashing into the World Trade Center, and its collapse into apoc-alyptic clouds of dust, to homes across the world. There was a clear sense that this was something new and terrifying. The concept of an epoch-defining change as a result of September 11th was an irresistible narrative in popular culture in the period following the terrorist attacks. There was an all-embracing sense that the world had crossed a line into a new and dangerous age. Undoubtedly the events of 9/11 presented the US with significant foreign policy problems which asked new and difficult questions of the American polity. One historian explained that the attacks 'forced a reconsideration, not only of where we are as a nation and where we may be going, but also of where we've been, even of who we are'.[4] The concept of American power was dra-matically challenged by the death and destruction that could be achieved by a new 'amoeba-like foe' which could not be tackled using conventional American military strength.[5]

The Bush administration's efforts to shape the historical memory of the events of 9/11 in order to support its foreign and domestic poli-cies, focussed on presenting the Al Qaeda attacks as examples of a significant discontinuity between the past and the future. The dangers of this for American nationalism and the preservation of civil liberties and Constitutional principles will be explored later in this chapter. Let us first turn to a discussion of how much America's place in the world has changed since that September morning. In the immediate after-math of the terrorist attacks Bush spoke of a 'different kind of war that requires a different type of approach and a different type of mentality'. Vice President Cheney argued that the war may never end, 'at least not in our lifetime'.[6] The administration sought to present the war on terror as a great departure in US foreign policy. A nationalist consensus was promoted which repressed the tangled reality of American involvement in the Middle East over the previous half a century. The war was framed within another grand narrative of good versus evil, of civilisation versus barbarism. America had fought fascism and communism and now it was to face Islamic fundamentalism and state-sponsored terror.[7]

The attacks on the World Trade Center certainly signalled a new challenge for American foreign policy and that policy has responded by moving in new directions; however, there was considerable continuity between America's place in the world before and after 9/11. In the period after the end of the Cold War there was great discussion of the increasing power of globalisation and the blurring of the boundaries between the domestic and the international. American policy makers saw this as a good thing because people and capital could move more freely and enhance US prosperity. The hijackers, though, revealed the largely unconsidered alternative. The new globalisation and freedom of movement could be turned against America with devastating consequences.[8] The nebulous and elusive nature of the nation's new enemy contributed to the Bush administration's attempt to present the war on terror as a great clash of civilisations. The enemy had to be identified in clear and simple terms partly because it was so very difficult to identify with clarity.

The effort to confront a patent evil was partly a result of the absence of a great unifying force driving US foreign policy in the period after the fall of the Berlin Wall and the collapse of the Soviet Union. There was no central organising principle to bind American diplomatic strategy together in the post-Cold War world. George Bush Senior referred to a 'New World Order' but had no real policy to go with it. Bill Clinton pursued policies which could broadly be classified as 'democracy promotion' but his application of this philosophy was inconsistent.[9] American policy too often proclaimed principles without supporting them with concrete policy and this led to disillusionment abroad. The US was more interested in the rights of Kosovars than it was in the plight of Chechens or Tibetans.[10] The old vague concept of democracy promotion was replaced by a war against terror and the 'axis of evil' which sponsored the terrorists. This sense of change was in large part a consequence of the lack of a grand narrative to explain US foreign policy in the post-Cold War era. The inconsistency between ideals and actions continued after the war on terror was initiated, however. The Bush administration spoke of the need for freedom and democracy but it overlooked the human rights abuses of countries like Pakistan in return for its help in the fight against the terrorists. In seeking the support of Russia, the US was forced to tacitly accept Chechens as terrorists rather than an oppressed people.

In the previous chapter we noted that American acceptance of a balance of power conception of world affairs and willingness to participate in multilateral organisations only emerged after the Second World War. The dominant experience of American foreign policy has viewed the nation as an indispensable power. During the First World War, Wilson committed the US to the 'Allied and Associated powers'. America was the only associated power. In the post-Cold War period American involvement with NATO and the UN still revealed that the country's leaders expected a degree of freedom in their military actions. During the Gulf War the Americans clearly led the allied coalition despite the politically motivated and cosmetic appearance of a dual command system with the Saudis. During the Balkans crisis there was friction between America and her NATO allies about military command and the use of air power. This tendency to want a free hand is a clearly identified trend in the history of American military involvement in international affairs.[11] It was a reflection of continuity then that the Bush administration, despite a brief effort at multilateralism in the period immediately after 9/11, pursued an increasingly unilateral approach to the war on terror. In Bush's 'coalition of the willing', the US was very much the senior partner and had freedom of action in military operations.

President Bush embraced a heightened form of US exceptionalism in his approach to the war on terror. The idea that America is somehow exceptional and has a mission to show the world the merits of freedom and democracy has a long history in the American past and was discussed in the previous chapter. This sense of exceptionalism has promoted a unilateral approach to foreign affairs. The adoption of this approach by the Bush administration was not simply a reaction to the events of 9/11. Indeed early in his presidency Bush signalled a move towards unilateralism or even isolationism with the rejection of the Kyoto treaty and the decision to pull out of the ABM treaty.[12] After the terrorist attacks of September 11th Bush moved closer to a pure form of American exceptionalism which was fused with strong Christian ideals and rhetoric. Just as Wilson had exhibited the idea of

American exceptionalism with his fourteen points to lead the world to peace and freedom, and just as American leaders in the 1960s believed it was America's mission to save South East Asia from the threat of communism, so the Bush administration believed the US could bring democracy to Iraq. Writing in 2006 Robert Patman argued, 'in the space of five years since 9/11 a new sense of exclusive American exceptionalism has manifested itself ... in the struggle against terrorism'.[13] This sense of mission and its impact on American foreign policy was not a new phenomenon which emerged after September 11th though, it was an intensification of existing ideology.

Although the Bush administration sought to present the 9/11 attacks as a watershed moment which had changed the global landscape dramatically and ushered in a new era of warfare, significant allusions were made to previous American conflicts. Failing to look closely at the consequences of US presence in the Arab world, the administration instead focussed on a simple good versus evil explanation of the war on terror. Language and policies were adapted from the Cold War years. The Soviet regime and her allies were replaced as the evil other by Islamic terrorists and the states that harboured and supported them. Bush's categorisation of the enemy as the 'axis of evil' brought together the memory of the Axis powers of the Second World War and Reagan's description of the Soviet Union as the 'Evil Empire'.[14] The administration also made repeated use of analogies between the 9/11 attacks and the Japanese strike against Pearl Harbor. America was the innocent victim of a horrific assault which had aroused the nation to anger. The geopolitical complexities of the build-up to December 1941 were ignored as were introspective questions about the path to September 2001.[15]

The Bush administration sought superficial analogies with US foreign policy challenges of the past in order to frame the war on terror in familiar terms of American good versus an evil other. It ignored the more complex reality of continuities with the past, however, in order to justify policies in the face of a new and terrifying enemy. The US was familiar with terrorism as a tactic before September 11th – what changed was the fact that the American people's sense of invulnerability was shattered.[16] The presumption of a clear and appropriate response to the terrorist attacks of 9/11 required a selective amnesia in regard to America's previous response to terrorism. The Bush administration pursued a unilateral approach of direct strike against the enemy. The most significant American encounter with terrorism in the late twentieth century was the Iran hostage crisis of 1979–80. In this case a direct military effort to free the hostages failed and only through negotiation were they finally released. The sheer horror of the 9/11 attacks provided a significantly new element to American encounters with terrorism but to assert there was no relevant past connected to the war on terrorism was wrong. The Bush administration helped to promote a 'layered discourse of refusal and remembrance' in which only partial aspects of America's thirty-year encounter with terrorism in the Middle East were highlighted. This facilitated the dominant message from the administration that a totally new war had just begun.[17]

In 2003 the war on terror expanded to a new front when the US invaded Iraq. Saddam Hussein's regime was said to be linked to Al Qaeda and it was alleged he had weapons of mass destruction which could be used against America and her allies. Nevertheless, the Bush administration's policy towards Iraq shows significant continuity with the past and US involvement there has forced uncomfortable comparisons with the painful memory of Vietnam. The sanctions imposed on Iraq after the end of the Gulf War were designed to stop the Hussein regime from threatening Iraq's neighbours. These sanctions crippled the economy of the country, caused thousands of deaths and retarded the development of a professional and educated class. This was a war by other means. Bush continued the sanctions and weapons inspections during the first year of his presidency.[18] The tyranny of Hussein's regime and the evil he was responsible for are not to be forgotten but American policy towards Iraq has led to the loss of many Iraqi lives. Bush used the 9/11 attacks and the war on terror as a pretext to remove the Baath party leadership once and for all. When the President went on television on 17 March 2003 to tell Saddam Hussein that he had 48 hours to leave Iraq or face a US attack we witnessed a radical departure in US foreign policy. But the subsequent war was not a conflict which had been sparked by the 9/11 attacks. It was the continuance of a decade-long struggle against Saddam Hussein's regime.

As the US occupation of Iraq continued, so the number of dead American servicemen grew. Those who believed that America was in danger of being trapped in a war it could not win began to make comparisons with the failures of the Vietnam conflict. Given the great national trauma that accompanied that conflict, it is not surprising that the Bush administration sought to deflect attention from comparisons between Iraq and Vietnam. In November 2006, Secretary of State Condoleezza Rice argued that historical parallels between the two conflicts were 'neither helpful nor right'. The main evidence used to support this view centred on the ethnic nature of the problems in

Iraq compared with the ideological struggles dominant during the Vietnam War. Detailed scholarly attention, however, has revealed similarities between the two US engagements, which are overlooked by simplistic conceptions of the nature of the respective conflicts.[19]

The attempts of the Bush administration to present the war on terror as a radical departure from the past ignore the significant threads of continuity which tie America's place in the world before and after the 9/11 attacks. This conception of a new war has, however, enabled the US to pursue unilateral interventionist policies with more confidence than it would have without the events of September 11th. Let us now turn to the impact these policies had on patriotism, citizenship and civil liberties.

In the period immediately after the terrorist attacks of 9/11 there was an outpouring of nationalist spirit in America. This was most visually striking in the hanging of flags. The stars and stripes was the ubiquitous symbol of national solidarity. The national trauma of September 11th evoked a shared sense of American identity. The display of flags represented a spontaneous expression of collective defiance in the face of the terrorist threat. The Bush administration, however, presided over the development of a more prescriptive form of patriotism. In October 2001 America's schoolchildren were urged to take part in mass recitation of the Pledge of Allegiance. The House of Representatives unanimously voted in favour of the display of signs proclaiming 'God Bless America' in public schools. Many of these signs and symbols of patriotism had been contested in the period after the Civil War but the Bush administration championed a forced and prescriptive nationalist spirit.[20] The rhetoric coming out of the White House was characterised by hysteria and militarism and alternative views were stifled. Politicians, journalists, academics and entertainers were attacked for criticising the nation's leadership. When Senator Tom Daschle raised questions about the military campaign, Trent Lott asked pointedly, 'how dare Senator Daschle criticise President Bush while we are fighting our war on terrorism?'[21]

As the war on terror progressed there was an increasingly ascendant 'appropriate patriotism' which suggested it was unpatriotic and inappropriate to question the policies of the government.[22] The Bush administration promoted a politics of fear which provided the public with a constant stream of rhetoric and images designed to foster a perpetual state of emergency. This atmosphere was used to justify unilateral policies abroad and constitutionally dubious measures at home.[23] The word 'homeland' was increasingly used to describe the nation after 9/11. American national identity has always been linked to geography, the movement of the frontier, and the vibrancy of the New World has usually been contrasted with the fixed 'homeland' of the Old World. National identity has been seen as dynamic and mobile but the use of the word 'homeland' to describe America suggested something which is rooted and fixed. Homeland has nativist and exclusionary connotations which restricts what it is to be American. It sees anything outside the nation's boundaries as a threat and suggests a danger posed by diversity.[24]

Indeed the fear and hysteria constructed by the Bush administration and the increasingly prescriptive patriotic spirit had profound consequences for American attitudes towards ethnic minorities. In one of many anecdotal examples, a Federal Express driver working in a Middle Eastern neighbourhood in Brooklyn told a reporter that whenever he delivered to a property with a high Arab population he would tell the landlord who would then call the FBI to get the residents checked out.[25] Detailed empirical research by political scientists has revealed a strong connection between ethnocentrism and support for the war on terror.[26] It is difficult to ascertain the exact extent to which 9/11 and the administration's responses changed people's opinions of ethnic minorities but they certainly heightened latent xenophobia and racial prejudice. A Gallup poll in the year after September 11th found that one-third of the American public thought that Arab-Americans should be interned in the way 12,000 Japanese-Americans had been during the Second World War. Racial profiling led to those of Arab appearance being thrown off aeroplanes and being subjected to racial violence. Many of these individuals were legal citizens of the US but they were considered as others on account of their racial identity.[27]

This rise of prescriptive patriotism and racially restrictive concepts of citizenship was portentous for both the moral and democratic health of the United States. The Bush administration increasingly exploited the climate of fear to restrict civil liberties at home and so compromised the legitimacy of fighting a war against terror in the name of freedom and democracy. In the days after September 11th historian Eric Foner warned that the American public should not allow the conditions of war to restrict their liberties. He argued that civil liberties were not gifts from the government which could be given and taken at will but were instead the fruits of long years of struggle.[28] The Bush administration did, however, move swiftly to restrict civil rights in the name of national security. Within two months of the 9/11 attacks the government passed the Patriot Act which expanded federal power to protect the nation against terrorism. The Act was so named in order to wrap constitutionally dubious policy in the flag of nationalism. The law permitted the detention of immigrants suspected of terrorism and expanded the powers of the security services to access e-mails and other private records, use wiretapping surveillance and prosecute hundreds of people detained on immigration violations. The expanded wiretap authority allowed for a circumvention of the Fourth Amendment's probable cause requirement and allowed the government to listen in on citizens' private conversations.[29] In February 2006 a number of scholars of constitutional law wrote an open letter to Congress criticising the Bush administration's domestic wiretapping programme. They argued that surveillance of individuals without just cause or plausible legal authority violated the law.[30] The month before the letter appeared, former Vice President Gore asserted that Bush should face impeachment hearings because of the unconstitutionality of the domestic wiretapping programme.[31]

Just as the Bush administration drew criticism because of its restriction of civil rights at home, so it has been condemned over its use of the lawless penal colony that is Guantanamo Bay. The detainees there are not classified as prisoners of war and so are not protected by the Geneva Convention, nor are they protected by the US Constitution. Instead they exist in a state of legal limbo with no recourse to due process or constitutionally sanctioned justice. This site of American power, untouched by international or domestic law, is accompanied by institutions inside the US where immigrants are detained indefinitely.[32] This reality strikes at the very heart of American civil liberties. A nation with a strong sense of its own exceptional character and mission invites a huge credibility gap when it so blatantly contradicts its own national creed.

American foreign policy decisions since 9/11 have provided further mixed messages on the nature of American commitments to freedom and democracy around the globe. In the Middle East the US accepted the justifications of many Arab governments who increased anti-democratic measures in the name of fighting terrorism. The impact of US pressure for pro-democracy forces in the region has been ambiguous. Policies demanding reform in nations like Syria and Libya were accompanied by security objectives; once these objectives had been achieved then pro-democracy programmes were abandoned. Neo-conservative policy makers have shown themselves willing to forcefully promote democracy only where vital US national security interests are threatened.[33] The Bush administration's commitment to stay the course in Iraq was motivated as much by the potential national security implications of withdrawal as it was by a desire to bring democracy to the Iraqi people. At the time of writing the efforts to remake Iraq reveal much about America's leaders, whilst the extent to which they benefit the Iraqis remains unclear.

As was the case with American involvement in twentieth-century conflicts, engagement with the war on terror asks as many questions of America itself as it does of its allies and enemies. Ignoring the complexities of US foreign policy in the post-Cold War world, the Bush administration sought to present the war on terror as a radical departure with the past. The calls to fight a new war in a new way have seen the administration restrict civil liberties and foster a prescriptive patriotism, so undermining American credibility. With military forces mired in Afghanistan and Iraq, and much of the international community troubled by examples of unilateral American policy, the precise role of the United States in the global future remains unclear. If, however, the US is to help grow the fruits of democracy in hitherto barren areas of the world it must lead by example. America must fully embrace a pluralistic, open and reflexive nationalism which extends the benefits of citizenship to men and women of all races and creeds that live within its shores.

NOTES

Introduction

1 G. Gerstle, *American Crucible: Race and Nation in the Twentieth Century*, Princeton: Princeton University Press, 2001, p.4.

1 Nation in embryo

1 T. H. Breen, 'Creative Adaptations: Peoples and Cultures', in J. P. Greene and J. R. Pole (eds) *Colonial British America: Essays in the New History of the Early Modern Era*, Baltimore: Johns Hopkins University Press, 1991, p.197.
2 M. Zuckerman, 'Regionalism', in D. Vickers (ed.) *A Companion to Colonial America*, London: Blackwell, 2003, p.321.
3 G. B. Nash, 'Social Development', in Greene and Pole, *Colonial British America*, pp.235–6.
4 D. J. Boorstin, *The Americans: The Colonial Experience*, New York: Vintage Books, 1958, p.4.
5 J. Butler, *Becoming America: The Revolution before 1776*, Cambridge: Harvard University Press, 2000, p.10.
6 Nash, 'Social Development', pp.237–8.
7 R. Hofstadter, *America at 1750: A Social Portrait*, New York: Alfred A. Knopf, 1974, p.146; R. S. Dunn, 'Servants and Slaves: The Recruitment and Employment of Labour', in Greene and Pole, *Colonial British America*, p.183.
8 Butler, *Becoming America*, p.10.
9 Hofstadter, *America at 1750*, pp.150–51.
10 J. E. McWilliams, 'Beyond Declension: Economic Adaptation and the Pursuit of Export Markets in the Massachusetts Bay Region, 1630–1700', in R. Olwell and A. Tully (eds) *Cultures and Identities in Colonial British America*, Baltimore: Johns Hopkins University Press, 2006, pp.121–4.
11 Dunn, 'Servants and Slaves', p.183.
12 Zuckerman, 'Regionalism', in Vickers, *A Companion to Colonial America*, pp.327–8.
13 Nash, 'Social Development', p.239.
14 Hofstadter, *America at 1750*, pp.154–6.
15 Dunn, 'Servants and Slaves', p.182; G. B. Nash, *The Unknown American Revolution*, London: Penguin Books, 2005, p.32.
16 Dunn, 'Servants and Slaves', p.171; Butler, *Becoming America*, pp.29–32.

17 D. D. Hall, 'Religion and Society', in Greene and Pole, *Colonial British America*, pp.328–9.
18 Boorstin, *The Americans*, pp.34–5, 60–62.
19 Nash, 'Social Development', p.242.
20 Hofstadter, *America at 1750*, p.89; Butler, *Becoming America*, p.37.
21 Butler, *Becoming America*, pp.37–9.
22 E. S. Morgan, *American Slavery, American Freedom*, New York: Norton, 1975, pp.304–8.
23 R. S. Dunn, 'Review of E. S. Morgan's *American Slavery, American Freedom*', *William and Mary Quarterly*, 1976, pp.669–72.
24 Breen, 'Creative Adaptations: Peoples and Cultures', in Greene and Pole, *Colonial British America*, p.211.
25 Hofstadter, *America at 1750*, p.166.
26 P. D. Morgan, 'African-Americans', in Vickers, *A Companion to Colonial America*, p.149.
27 Dunn, 'Servants and Slaves', pp.175–6; Hofstadter, *America at 1750*, pp.167–9.
28 Boorstin, *The Americans*, p.84.
29 Boorstin, *The Americans*, pp.90–95; Hofstadter, *America at 1750*, pp.170–72.
30 Zuckerman, 'Regionalism', in Vickers, *A Companion to Colonial America*, p.329.
31 J. H. Merrell, 'Indian History During the English Colonial Era', in Vickers (ed.) *A Companion to Colonial America*, pp.119–20; Butler, *Becoming America*, pp.13–15.
32 Merrell, 'Indian History During the English Colonial Era', pp.130–31.
33 D. K. Richter, 'Native Americans, the Plan of 1764, and a British Empire that Never Was', in Olwell and Tully, *Cultures and Identities in Colonial British America*, pp.290–92.
34 Butler, *Becoming America*, p.32.
35 J. Smolenski, 'Becoming Americans: Revisiting Identity and Assimilation in the Colonial Period', *Reviews in American History*, 2005, vol.33, pp.34–7.
36 Butler, *Becoming America*, p.22.
37 Breen, 'Creative Adaptations: Peoples and Cultures', p.217.
38 Morgan, 'African-Americans', p.144.
39 Breen, 'Creative Adaptations: Peoples and Cultures', p.203.
40 Morgan, *American Slavery, American Freedom*, pp.332–6.
41 D. C. Littlefield, 'Almost an Englishman: Eighteenth-Century Anglo-African Identities', in Olwell and Tully, *Cultures and Identities in Colonial British America*, pp.72, 92–4.
42 E. Countryman, 'Large Questions in a Very Large Place', in Vickers, *A Companion to Colonial America*, p.538.
43 Breen, 'Creative Adaptations: Peoples and Cultures', p.222.
44 T. H. Breen, 'An Empire of Goods: The Anglicisation of Colonial America, 1690–1776', *Journal of British Studies*, 1986, vol.25, p.487.
45 Smolenski, 'Becoming Americans', p.37.
46 T. H. Breen, 'Ideology and Nationalism on the Eve of the American Revolution: Revisions Once More in Need of Revising', *Journal of American History*, 1997, vol.84, p.33.
47 M. J. Rozbicki, 'Cultural Development of the Colonies', in J. P. Greene and J. R. Pole (eds) *A Companion to the American Revolution*, London: Blackwell, 2004, pp.80–81.

2 Reasons for revolt

1 E. S. Morgan, *The Birth of the Republic, 1763–1789*, Chicago: University of Chicago Press, 1992, p.66.

2 T. Draper, *A Struggle for Power: The American Revolution*, London: Little, Brown, 1996, pp.195–6.
3 G. S. Wood, *The American Revolution*, London: Phoenix Paperback, 2005, p.26.
4 Draper, *A Struggle for Power*, p.226.
5 Morgan, *The Birth of the Republic*, pp.34–6.
6 G. B. Nash, *The Unknown American Revolution*, London: Penguin Books, 2005, p.89.
7 Draper, *A Struggle for Power*, p.357.
8 Morgan, *The Birth of the Republic*, p.47.
9 Wood, *The American Revolution*, p.33.
10 M. Jensen, 'The American People and the American Revolution', *Journal of American History*, 1970, vol.57, p.21.
11 Wood, *The American Revolution*, pp.35–6.
12 Morgan, *The Birth of the Republic*, pp.59–60, 64–5.
13 Draper, *A Struggle for Power*, p.428.
14 Morgan, *The Birth of the Republic*, pp.68–71.
15 B. Bailyn, *The Ideological Origins of the American Revolution*, Cambridge: Harvard University Press, 1992, p.95.
16 G. S. Wood, 'Rhetoric and Reality in the American Revolution', *William and Mary Quarterly*, 1966, vol.23, p.24.
17 G. S. Wood, *The Creation of the American Republic, 1776–1787*, New York: Norton & Company, 1972, p.10.
18 Bailyn, *The Ideological Origins of the American Revolution*, p.95.
19 Wood, *The Creation of the American Republic*, p.49.
20 For explanations of the Progressive interpretations see C. A. Beard, *An Economic Interpretation of the Constitution*, New York: Macmillan, 1946, and A. M. Schlesinger, *Prelude to Independence: The Newspaper War on Britain, 1764–1776*, New York: Alfred A. Knopf, 1958.
21 Morgan, *The Birth of the Republic*, pp.50–51.
22 J. J. Ellis, *His Excellency: George Washington*, New York: Vintage Books, 2005, p.52.
23 Nash, *The Unknown American Revolution*, p.185.
24 R. Beeman, 'Deference, Republicanism, and the Emergence of Popular Politics in Eighteenth-Century America', *William and Mary Quarterly*, 1992, vol.49, p.410.
25 Morgan, *The Birth of the Republic*, p.51.
26 Wood, 'Rhetoric and Reality', p.26.
27 J. Appleby, 'The Social Origins of American Revolutionary Ideology', *Journal of American History*, 1978, vol.64, p.958.
28 Morgan, *The Birth of the Republic*, pp.73–4.
29 I. Kramnick (ed.) *Thomas Paine: Common Sense*, London: Penguin Books, 1986, pp.54–5.
30 G. B. Nash, 'The Transformation of Urban Politics 1700–1764', in S. N. Katz (ed.) *Colonial America*, New York: McGraw-Hill, 1993, p.550.
31 J. Butler, *Becoming America: The Revolution Before 1776*, Cambridge: Harvard University Press, 2000, p.130.
32 M. Jensen, 'The American People and the American Revolution', *Journal of American History*, 1970, vol.57, pp.21–3.
33 Nash, *The Unknown American Revolution*, p.147.
34 M. J. Rozbicki, 'Between Private and Public Spheres: Liberty as Cultural Property in Eighteenth Century British America', in R. Olwell and A. Tully (eds) *Cultures and Identities in Colonial British America*, Baltimore: Johns Hopkins University Press, 2006, p.297.

35 Rozbicki, 'Between Private and Public Spheres', p.302.
36 T. H. Breen, 'Ideology and Nationalism on the Eve of the American Revolution: Revisions Once More in Need of Revising', *Journal of American History*, 1997, vol. 84, pp.33–5.
37 Rozbicki, 'Between Private and Public Spheres', pp.309–12.
38 Wood, 'Rhetoric and Reality', p.30; Nash, *The Unknown American Revolution*, p.194.
39 E. Countryman, 'Social Protest 1765–76', in J. P. Greene and J. R. Pole (eds) *A Companion to the American Revolution*, London: Blackwell, 2004, pp.189–91.
40 T. H. Breen, *The Marketplace of Revolution: How Consumer Politics Shaped American Independence*, Oxford: Oxford University Press, 2004, p.xv; Butler, *Becoming America*, p.235.
41 Breen, *The Marketplace of Revolution*, p.299.
42 Ibid., p.305.
43 Nash, *The Unknown American Revolution*, p.150.
44 Breen, *The Marketplace of Revolution*, p.xviii.
45 J. P. Greene, 'Identity and Independence', in Greene and Pole, *A Companion to the American Revolution*, pp.232–4.

3 The Constitution

1 J. M. Murrin, 'Roof Without Walls: The Dilemma of American National Identity', in R. Beeman, S. Botein and E. C. Carter (eds) *Beyond Confederation: Origins of the Constitution and American National Identity*, Chapel Hill: University of North Carolina Press, 1987, p.347.
2 G. S. Wood, *The American Revolution*, London: Phoenix Paperback, 2005, p.70.
3 E. S. Morgan, *The Birth of the Republic 1763–1789*, Chicago: University of Chicago Press, 1992, p.121.
4 G. S. Wood, *The Creation of the American Republic, 1776–1787*, New York: Norton & Company, 1972, pp.393–5.
5 J. N. Rakove, *Original Meanings: Politics and Ideas in the Making of the Constitution*, New York: Vintage Books, 1996, pp.24–6.
6 M. D. Kaplanoff, 'Confederation: Movement for a Stronger Union', in J. P. Greene and J. R. Pole (eds) *A Companion to the American Revolution*, London: Blackwell, 2004, pp.466–7.
7 R. D. Brown, 'Shay's Rebellion and the Ratification of the Federal Constitution in Massachusetts', in Beeman *et al.*, *Beyond Confederation*.
8 P. S. Onuf, 'Reflections on the Founding: Constitutional Historiography in Bicentennial Perspective', *William and Mary Quarterly*, 1989, vol.46, p.346.
9 M. D. Kaplanoff, 'The Federal Convention and the Constitution', in Greene and Pole, *A Companion to the American Revolution*, pp.471–3.
10 J. H. Hutson, 'Riddles of the Federal Constitutional Convention', *William and Mary Quarterly*, 1987, vol.44, pp.420–23.
11 J. N. Rakove, 'The Great Compromise: Ideas, Interests, and the Politics of Constitution Making', *William and Mary Quarterly*, 1987, vol.44, p.427.
12 Publius (Madison) 'Federalist 54', in I. Kramnick (ed.) *The Federalist Papers*, London: Penguin Books, 1987, p.335.
13 P. Finkelman, 'Slavery and the Constitutional Convention: Making a Covenant with Death', in Beeman *et al.*, *Beyond Confederation*, pp.194–7.
14 Morgan, *The Birth of the Republic 1763–1789*, p.141.

15 Rakove, *Original Meanings*, pp.86–8.
16 Finkelman, 'Slavery and the Constitutional Convention', pp.224–5.
17 Kaplanoff, 'The Federal Convention and the Constitution', p.475.
18 K. Morgan, 'Slavery and the Debate over Ratification of the United States Constitution', *Slavery and Abolition*, 2001, vol.22, p.60.
19 M. Dry, 'The Debate over the Ratification of the Constitution', in Greene and Pole, *A Companion to the American Revolution*, p.485.
20 Publius (Madison) 'Federalist 10', in Kramnick, *The Federalist Papers*, p.125.
21 Dry, 'The Debate over the Ratification of the Constitution', p.492.
22 Wood, *The Creation of the American Republic*, p.520.
23 D. R. McCoy, *The Last of the Fathers: James Madison and the Republican Legacy*, Cambridge: Cambridge University Press, 1991, p.61.
24 G. S. Wood, 'Interests and Disinterestedness in the Making of the Constitution', in Beeman *et al.*, *Beyond Confederation*, p.81.
25 See C. A. Beard, *An Economic Interpretation of the Constitution of the United States*, New York: Macmillan, 1946.
26 Wood, 'Interests and Disinterestedness', p.109.
27 Wood, *The Creation of the American Republic*, p.513.
28 Ibid., p.562.
29 J. Appleby, 'The Social Origins of American Revolutionary Ideology', *Journal of American History*, 1978, vol.64.
30 M. M. Edling, *A Revolution in Favor of Government: Origins of the U.S. Constitution and the Making of the American State*, Oxford: Oxford University Press, 2003, p.39.
31 S. Cornell, 'Aristocracy Assailed: The Ideology of Backcountry Anti-Federalism', *Journal of American History*, 1990, vol.76, p.1168.
32 Wood, 'Interests and Disinterestedness', p.93.
33 Cornell, 'Aristocracy Assailed', p.1168.
34 M. J. Rozbicki, 'Between Private and Public Spheres: Liberty as Cultural Property in Eighteenth Century British America', in R. Olwell and A. Tully (eds) *Cultures and Identities in Colonial British America*, Baltimore: Johns Hopkins University Press, 2006, p.315.
35 Edling, *A Revolution in Favor of Government*, p.45.
36 Ibid., p.100.
37 R. E. Ellis, 'The Persistence of Anti-Federalism after 1789', in Beeman *et al.*, *Beyond Confederation*, p.299.
38 Dry, 'The Debate over the Ratification of the Constitution', p.493.
39 Wood, 'Interests and Disinterestedness', p.102.
40 Murrin, 'Roof Without Walls', pp.346–7.

4 Flawed heroes

1 J. J. Ellis, *His Excellency: George Washington*, New York: Vintage Books, 2005, p.162.
2 P. D. Morgan and M. L. Nicholls, 'Slave Flight: Mount Vernon, Virginia and the Wider Atlantic World', in T. Harvey and G. O'Brien (eds) *George Washington's South*, Gainesville: University Press of Florida, 2005, p.202. Judge escaped to New Hampshire and Washington ordered her to be put on a ship back to Virginia, but she married a free mulatto and settled down in New Hampshire.
3 T. Jefferson, *Notes on the State of Virginia*, London: Penguin Books, 1999, pp.150–51.
4 P. Finkelman, *Slavery and the Founders: Race and Liberty in the Age of Jefferson*, New York: M. E. Sharpe, 2nd edn, 2001, p.170.

5 K. Morgan, 'George Washington and the Problem of Slavery', *Journal of American Studies*, 2000, vol.34, p.290.

6 Ellis, *His Excellency*, p.263.

7 Finkelman, *Slavery and the Founders*, pp.130–31. Ellis argues that Jefferson was concerned with the humanity of his slave workers and would not sell them without their consent if it broke up families. It would seem he was less concerned about this than Washington, however.

8 Jefferson, *Notes on the State of Virginia*, p.146.

9 H. Wiencek, *An Imperfect God: George Washington, His Slaves and the Creation of America*, London: Macmillan, 2004, pp.44–5; D. Twohig, 'That Species of Property: Washington's Role in the Controversy over Slavery', in D. Higginbotham (ed.) *George Washington Reconsidered*, Charlottesville: University of Virginia Press, 2001, p.116; Ellis, *His Excellency*, p.46.

10 Ellis, *His Excellency*, p.259.

11 Wiencek, *Imperfect God*, p.188.

12 P. D. Morgan, 'To Get Quit of Negroes: George Washington and Slavery', *Journal of American Studies*, 2005, vol.39, pp.412–13.

13 Ellis, *His Excellency*, p.47.

14 Morgan and Nicholls, 'Slave Flight: Mount Vernon, Virginia, and the Wider Atlantic World', in Harvey and O'Brien, *George Washington's South*, pp.197–9.

15 Morgan, 'George Washington and the Problem of Slavery', p.289.

16 Morgan, 'To Get Quit of Negroes', pp.414–16.

17 Morgan, 'George Washington and the Problem of Slavery', p.291; S. Schama, *Rough Crossings: Britain, the Slaves and the American Revolution*, London: BBC Books, 2005, pp.148–9.

18 Morgan, 'George Washington and the Problem of Slavery', pp.291–3; Morgan, 'To Get Quit of Negroes', pp.418–19.

19 Morgan, 'George Washington and the Problem of Slavery', p.299.

20 Twohig, 'That Species of Property', p.122.

21 Finkelman, *Slavery and the Founders*, p.116.

22 Morgan, 'To Get Quit of Negroes', p.428.

23 Twohig, 'That Species of Property', p.126.

24 Morgan, 'To Get Quit of Negroes', p.425.

25 D. Malone, *Jefferson and His Time*, 6 vols, Boston: Little, Brown, 1948–81; M. D. Peterson, *The Jefferson Image in the American Mind*, New York: Oxford University Press, 1960.

26 J. J. Ellis, *American Sphinx: The Character of Thomas Jefferson*, New York: Alfred A. Knopf, 1997.

27 A. Gordon-Reed, 'The Memories of a Few Negroes Rescuing America's Future at Monticello', in J. E. Lewis and P. S. Onuf (eds) *Sally Hemings and Thomas Jefferson: History, Memory and Civic Culture*, Charlottesville: University Press of Virginia, 1999, p.238.

28 Finkelman, *Slavery and the Founders*, pp.142–4.

29 W. Cohen, 'Thomas Jefferson and the Problem of Slavery', *Journal of American History*, 1969, vol.56, pp.506–7.

30 P. S. Onuf, 'To Declare them a Free and Independent People: Race, Slavery and National Identity in Jefferson's Thought', *Journal of the Early Republic*, 1998, vol.18, pp.12–18.

31 Finkelman, *Slavery and the Founders*, pp.144–5; Jefferson, *Notes on the State of Virginia*, pp.144–5; Cohen, 'Thomas Jefferson and the Problem of Slavery', p.508.

32 Finkelman, *Slavery and the Founders*, p.147.

33 Ibid., p.148: Cohen, 'Thomas Jefferson and the Problem of Slavery', p.511.

34 R. G. Kennedy, *Mr. Jefferson's Lost Cause: Land, Farmers, Slavery, and the Louisiana Purchase*, Oxford: Oxford University Press, 2003, pp.249–50.

35 G. Wills, *Negro President: Jefferson and the Slave Power*, Boston: Houghton Mifflin, 2005, pp.5–9. Jefferson secured election as President in 1800 as a direct consequence of the three-fifths rule and its impact on representation in the House.

36 B. Bailyn, 'Jefferson and the Ambiguities of Freedom', *Proceedings of the American Philosophical Society*, 1993, vol.137, p.506.

37 Jefferson, *Notes on the State of Virginia*, pp.146–51.

38 Ibid., p.145.

39 Cohen, 'Thomas Jefferson and the Problem of Slavery', pp.519–20; J. Sidbury, 'Saint Dominigue in Virginia: Ideology, Local Meanings, and Resistance to Slavery, 1790–1800', *Journal of Southern History*, 1997, vol.63, pp.537–8.

40 Jefferson, *Notes on the State of Virginia*, p.151.

41 Bailyn, 'Jefferson and the Ambiguities of Freedom', p.20.

42 Some have speculated that Washington fathered a slave child by the name of West Ford, but the evidence is far from conclusive and is considerably less likely than the Jefferson–Hemings relationship. See Wiencek, *Imperfect God*, pp.289–310.

43 J. J. Ellis, 'Jefferson: Post DNA', *William and Mary Quarterly*, 2000, vol.57, p.125.

44 Ellis, 'Jefferson: Post DNA', p.132. Philip Morgan shows that inter-racial sex was part of the world of eighteenth-century Chesapeake but it was usually not open. Jefferson was not alone in keeping his affair secret. P. D. Morgan, 'Interracial Sex in the Chesapeake and the British Atlantic World, c. 1700–1820', in Lewis and Onuf, *Sally Hemings and Thomas Jefferson*, pp.75–8.

45 A. Burstein, 'Jefferson's Rationalizations', *William and Mary Quarterly*, 2000, vol.57.

46 P. S. Onuf, 'Every Generation is an Independent Nation: Colonization, Miscegenation, and the Fate of Jefferson's Children', *William and Mary Quarterly*, 2000, vol.57.

47 Ibid.', p.168.

48 Ellis, 'Jefferson: Post DNA', p.127.

49 Cohen, 'Thomas Jefferson and the Problem of Slavery', p.519; E. M. Halliday, *Understanding Thomas Jefferson*, New York: HarperCollins, 2001, pp.159–60.

50 See Finkelman, *Slavery and the Founders*, p.135.

51 Ellis, 'Jefferson: Post DNA', p.138.

52 A. Gordon-Reed, 'Engaging Jefferson: Blacks and the Founding Fathers', *William and Mary Quarterly*, 2000, vol.57 p.173.

5 Ignoring Washington's warning

1 J. J. Ellis, 'Farewell: Washington's Wisdom at the End', in D. Higginbotham (ed.) *George Washington Reconsidered*, Charlottesville: University of Virginia Press, 2001, p.220.

2 M. W. Kruman, 'The Second American Party System and the Transformation of Revolutionary Republicanism', *Journal of the Early Republic*, 1992, vol.12, p.510.

3 R. P. Formisano, 'Political Character, Antipartyism and the Second Party System', *American Quarterly*, 1969, vol.21, p.686.

4 M. F. Holt, *The Political Crisis of the 1850s*, New York: Norton, 1983, p.37.

5 Kruman, 'The Second American Party System', p.510.

6 P. Goodman, 'The First American Party System', in W. N. Chambers and W. D. Burnham (eds) *The American Party Systems: Stages of Political Development*, New York: Oxford University Press, 2nd edn, 1975, p.84.

7 Kruman, 'The Second American Party System', p.514.

8 Formisano, 'Political Character', p.707.

9 J. Appleby, *Inheriting the Revolution: The First Generation of Americans*, Massachusetts: Harvard University Press, 2000, p.27.

10 M. Lienesch, 'Thomas Jefferson and the Democratic Experience', in P. S. Onuf (ed.) *Jeffersonian Legacies*, Charlottesville: University of Virginia Press, 1993, pp.326–7.

11 Ibid., p.329.

12 R. P. McCormick, 'Political Development and the Second Party System', in Chambers and Burnham, *The American Party Systems*, p.95.

13 D. Ratcliffe, 'The State of the Union, 1776–1860', in S.-M. Grant and B. Holden Reid (eds) *The American Civil War*, London: Longman, 2000, pp.10–11.

14 Holt, *The Political Crisis of the 1850s*, p.7.

15 Goodman, 'The First American Party System', p.64.

16 Appleby, *Inheriting the Revolution*, p.55.

17 J. H. Baker, 'The Ceremonies of Politics: Nineteenth-Century Rituals of National Affirmation', in W. J. Cooper, Jnr, M. F. Holt and J. McCardell (eds) *A Master's Due: Essays in Honor of David Herbert Donald*, Baton Rouge: Louisiana State University Press, 1985, p.166.

18 D. Brown, 'Jeffersonian Ideology and the Second Party System', *Historian*, 1999, vol.62.

19 Baker, 'The Ceremonies of Politics', p.178.

20 Appleby, *Inheriting the Revolution*, p.27.

21 Goodman, 'The First American Party System', pp.87–9.

22 A. I. P. Smith, *No Party Now: Politics in the Civil War North*, Oxford: Oxford University Press, 2006, p.25.

23 McCormick, 'Political Development and the Second Party System', pp.102–3.

24 Holt, *The Political Crisis of the 1850s*, p.7.

25 B. Holden Reid, *The Origins of the American Civil War*, London: Longman, 1996, pp.37–8.

26 McCormick, 'Political Development and the Second Party System'; Holt, *The Political Crisis of the 1850s*; E. Foner, *Politics and Ideology of the Age of the Civil War*, New York: Oxford University Press, 1980.

27 McCormick, 'Political Development and the Second Party System', pp.111–12; Holt, *The Political Crisis of the 1850s*, pp.28–9.

28 McCormick, 'Political Development and the Second Party System', pp.96–101.

29 Ibid., p.112.

30 Holt, *The Political Crisis of the 1850s*, p.23.

31 M. F. Holt, 'The Election of 1840, Voter Mobilisation, and the Emergence of the Second Party System', in Cooper *et al.* (eds) *A Master's Due*, pp.53–8.

32 S. C. Fox, 'The Bank Wars, the Idea of "Party", and the Division of the Electorate in Jacksonian Ohio', *Ohio History*, 1979, vol.88, pp.267–74.

33 Kruman, 'The Second American Party System', pp.536–7.

34 Holt, *The Political Crisis of the 1850s*, p.238.

35 McCormick, 'Political Development and the Second Party System', pp.111–12.

36 M. F. Holt, *The Fate of their Nation: Politicians, Slavery Extension and the Coming of the Civil War*, New York: Hill & Wang, 2004, pp.43–4.

37 J. L. Sundquist, *Dynamics of the Party System: Alignment and Realignment of Political Parties in the United States*, Washington DC: The Brookings Institution, 1983, p.63.
38 Sundquist, *Dynamics of the Party System*, pp.72–3.
39 Foner, *Politics and Ideology*, p.35.
40 McCormick, 'Political Development and the Second Party System', p.113.
41 G. W. Wolff, 'Party and Section: The Senate and the Kansas–Nebraska Bill', in R. P. Swierenga (ed.) *Beyond the Civil War Synthesis*, Connecticut: Greenwood Press, 1975.
42 Foner, *Politics and Ideology*, p.45.
43 W. E. Gienapp, 'The Crisis of American Democracy: The Political System and the Coming of the Civil War', in G. S. Boritt (ed.) *Why the Civil War Came*, New York: Oxford University Press, 1996, p.96.
44 Holt, *The Political Crisis of the 1850s*, p.10.
45 Ibid., pp.136–7.
46 Holt, *The Fate of their Nation*, pp.99–101.
47 Holt, *Political Crisis of the 1850s*, pp.120–25; Gienapp, 'The Crisis of American Democracy', pp.110–12.
48 Fox, 'The Bank Wars', p.237.

6 Slavery and the causes of the American Civil War

1 Lincoln to Stephens, 22 December 1860, in P. Parish (ed.) *Abraham Lincoln: Speeches and Letters*, London: Everyman, 1993, p.154.
2 W. E. Gienapp, 'The Crisis of American Democracy: The Political System and the Coming of the Civil War', in G. S. Boritt (ed.) *Why the Civil War Came*, New York: Oxford University Press, 1996, p.82.
3 E. L. Ayers, *What Caused the Civil War: Reflections on the South and Southern History*, New York: Norton, 2005, pp.131–2, 144.
4 C. and M. Beard, *The Rise of American Civilization*, New York: Macmillan, 1927; E. Foner, 'The Causes of the American Civil War: Recent Interpretations and New Directions', in R. P. Swierenga (ed.) *Beyond the Civil War Synthesis*, Connecticut: Greenwood Press, 1975, pp.19–21.
5 J. G. Randall, 'A Blundering Generation', in K. M. Stampp (ed.) *The Causes of the Civil War*, New York: Simon & Schuster, 1991.
6 K. M. Stampp, *The Imperilled Union*, New York: Oxford University Press, 1980, pp.200–203. For another example of this approach see A. Craven, 'Coming of the War between the States: An Interpretation', *Journal of Southern History*, 1936, vol.2.
7 For examples of this trend see E. Foner, *Free Soil, Free Labour, Free Men: The Ideology of the Republican Party before the Civil War*, New York: Oxford University Press, 1970; J. M. McPherson, *Abraham Lincoln and the Second American Revolution*, New York: Oxford University Press, 1991.
8 Stampp, *The Imperilled Union*, p.245.
9 J. H. Silbey, 'The Civil War Synthesis in American Political History', in Swierenga, *Beyond the Civil War Synthesis*. For an example of this new political history see M. F. Holt, *The Political Crisis of the 1850s*, New York: Norton, 1983.
10 Ayers, *What Caused the Civil War*, pp.132–3.
11 P. Finkelman, *Slavery and the Founders: Race and Liberty in the Age of Jefferson*, New York: M. E. Sharpe, 2nd edn, 2001, p.36.

12 J. J. Ellis, 'Farewell: Washington's Wisdom at the End', in D. Higginbotham (ed.) *George Washington Reconsidered*, Charlottesville: University of Virginia Press, 2001, p.240.

13 D. R. McCoy, *The Last of the Fathers: James Madison and the Republican Legacy*, Cambridge: Cambridge University Press, 1991, pp.272–3.

14 B. Holden Reid, *The Origins of the American Civil War*, London: Longman, 1996, pp.68, 92, 99.

15 B. Levine, *Half Slave and Half Free: The Roots of the Civil War*, New York: Hill & Wang, p.14.

16 G. Wills, *Negro President: Jefferson and the Slave Power*, Boston: Houghton Mifflin, 2005, pp.5–9.

17 E. Foner, *Politics and Ideology of the Age of the Civil War*, New York: Oxford University Press, 1980, p.36.

18 S.-M. Grant, *North over South: Northern Nationalism and American Identity in the Antebellum Era*, Kansas: University Press of Kansas, 2000, pp.135–7.

19 S.-M. Grant, 'Representative Mann: Horace Mann, the Republican Experiment and the South', *Journal of American Studies*, 1998, vol.32, pp.113–15.

20 E. Foner, *Free Soil, Free Labour, Free Men*, p.50.

21 J. B. Stewart, 'The Aims and Impact of Garrisonian Abolitionism', in Swierenga, *Beyond the Civil War Synthesis*.

22 L. Gara, 'Slavery and the Slave Power: A Crucial Distinction', in Swierenga, *Beyond the Civil War Synthesis*.

23 G. Wills, *Negro President*, pp.2–6.

24 S.-M. Grant, *North over South*, p.150.

25 C. Eaton, *The Growth of Southern Civilisation, 1790–1860*, London: Harper, 1961, pp.295–300.

26 J. P. Daly, *When Slavery was Called Freedom: Evangelicalism, Proslavery, and the Causes of the Civil War*, Kentucky: University Press of Kentucky, 2002, pp.132–4.

27 B. Holden Reid, *The Origins of the American Civil War*, p.86.

28 Ayers, *What Caused the Civil War*, p.142.

29 D. Ratcliffe, 'The State of the Union, 1776–1860', in S.-M. Grant and B. Holden Reid (eds) *The American Civil War*, London: Longman, 2000, pp.30–31.

30 Stampp, *The Imperilled Union*, p.36.

31 Gienapp, 'The Crisis of American Democracy', pp.84–7.

32 Holt, *The Political Crisis of the 1850s*, pp.61–6.

33 The Compromise of 1850 consisted of several political deals designed to solve the sectional crisis sparked by debates over whether land annexed from Mexico should be slave or free.

34 M. F. Holt, 'The Politics of Impatience: The Origins of Know-Nothingism', *Journal of American History*, 1973, vol.60, pp.315–20.

35 Foner, *Politics and Ideology*, p.35.

36 S. Wilentz, *The Rise of American Democracy: Jefferson to Lincoln*, New York: Norton, 2005, p.787.

37 Holt, *The Political Crisis of the 1850s*, pp.193–6; W. E. Gienapp, 'The Crime Against Sumner: The Caning of Charles Sumner and the Rise of the Republican Party', *Civil War History*, 1979, vol.25.

38 Ayers, *What Caused the Civil War*, p.141.

39 S. A. Channing, *Crisis of Fear: Secession and South Carolina*, New York: Simon & Schuster, 1970, p.291.

40 J. Davis, 'The Indispensable Slaves', in Stampp, *The Causes of the Civil War*, p.155.

41 C. B. Dew, *Apostles of Disunion: Southern Secession Commissioners and the Causes of the Civil War*, Charlottesville: University of Virginia Press, 2001.

42 Channing, *Crisis of Fear*, p.286.

43 Ayers, *What Caused the Civil War*, pp.135–6.

44 Holt, *The Political Crisis of the 1850s*, pp.253–7.

45 J. C. Inscoe, *Mountain Masters: Slavery and the Sectional Crisis in Western North Carolina*, Tennessee: University of Tennessee Press, 1996, p.231.

46 W. W. Freehling, 'The Divided South, Democracy's Limitations, and the Causes of the Peculiarly North American Civil War', in Boritt, *Why the Civil War Came*, pp.167–71.

47 B. Collins, 'Southern Secession in 1860–61', in Grant and Holden Reid (eds) *The American Civil War*, p.61.

48 Holden Reid, *The Origins of the American Civil War*, pp.180–86.

49 Ibid., pp.188–91.

50 M. W. Summers, 'Freedom and Law Must Die Ere They Sever: The North and the Coming of the Civil War', in Boritt, *Why the Civil War Came*, p.180.

51 Lincoln's Peoria Speech, 16 October 1854, in P. Parish (ed.) *Abraham Lincoln: Speeches and Letters*, London: Everyman, 1993, p.58.

7 Southern and Confederate nationalism

1 J. M. McPherson, 'Was Blood Thicker than Water? Ethnic and Civic Nationalism in the American Civil War', *Proceedings of the American Philosophical Society*, 1999, vol.43, p.102.

2 C. Adams, *When in the Course of Human Events: Arguing the Case for Secession*, New York: Rowman & Littlefield, 2000, p.224.

3 D. G. Faust, *The Creation of Confederate Nationalism: Ideology and Identity in the Civil War South*, Baton Rouge: Louisiana State University Press, 1988, p.3.

4 G. W. Gallagher, *The Confederate War: How Popular Will, Nationalism, and Military Strategy Could Not Stave Off Defeat*, Cambridge: Harvard University Press, 1999, p.172.

5 McPherson, 'Was Blood Thicker than Water?', p.103.

6 B. Anderson, *Imagined Communities: Reflections on the Origins and Spread of Nationalism*, London: Verso, 1991, p.47.

7 C. Eaton, *The Growth of Southern Civilisation, 1790–1860*, London: Harper, 1961, pp.295–300.

8 J. McCardell, *The Idea of a Southern Nation: Southern Nationalists and Southern Nationalism, 1830–1860*, New York: Norton, 1979, pp.175–6.

9 P. F. Paskoff and D. J. Wilson (eds) *The Cause of the South: Selections from De Bow's Review, 1846–67*, Baton Rouge: Louisiana State University Press, 1982.

10 S.-M. Grant, *North Over South: Northern Nationalism and American Identity in the Antebellum Era*, Lawrence: University Press of Kansas, 2000, pp.94–5.

11 E. L. Ayers, *What Caused the Civil War: Reflections on the South and Southern History*, New York: Norton, 2005, p.52.

12 Ibid., p.55.

13 W. J. Cash, *The Mind of the South*, London: Penguin Books, 1973, p.92.

14 Anderson, *Imagined Communities*, pp.6–7.

15 Eaton, *The Growth of Southern Civilisation, 1790–1860*, pp.68–9.

16 McCardell, *The Idea of a Southern Nation*, p.81.

17 S.-M. Grant, *The War for a Nation*, New York: Routledge, 2006, p.35.

18 D. M. Potter, *The South and the Sectional Conflict*, Baton Rouge: Louisiana State University Press, 1968, p.53.

19 E. Foner, *Free Soil, Free Labour, Free Men: The Ideology of the Republican Party before the Civil War*, New York: Oxford University Press, 1970, p.46.

20 S.-M. Grant, *North over South*, p.59.

21 Potter, *The South and the Sectional Conflict*, p.66.

22 Anderson, *Imagined Communities*, p.64.

23 McCardell, *The Idea of a Southern Nation*, pp.61–5.

24 B. Collins, 'Southern Secession in 1860–61', in S.-M. Grant and B. Holden Reid (eds) *The American Civil War*, London: Longman, 2000, pp.60–62.

25 W. W. Freehling, 'The Divided South, Democracy's Limitations, and the Causes of the Peculiarly North American Civil War', in G. Boritt (ed.) *Why the Civil War Came*, New York: Oxford University Press, 1996, p.170.

26 E. H. Walther, 'Fire-Eaters and the Riddle of Southern Nationalism', *Southern Studies*, 1992, vol.3, pp.68–72.

27 M. P. Johnson, *Toward a Patriarchal Republic: The Secession of Georgia*, Baton Rouge: Louisiana State University Press, 1977, pp.37–45, 176–8.

28 Eaton, *The Growth of Southern Civilisation, 1790–1860*, pp.321–4.

29 Faust, *Confederate Nationalism*, p.21.

30 A. S. Rubin, *A Shattered Nation: The Rise and Fall of the Confederacy, 1861–1868*, Chapel Hill: University of North Carolina Press, 2005, p.86.

31 Grant, *War for a Nation*, pp.190–91.

32 Gallagher, *The Confederate War*, pp.28–9.

33 Rubin, *A Shattered Nation*, pp.54–8.

34 Gallagher, *The Confederate War*, p.77.

35 Faust, *The Creation of Confederate Nationalism*, pp.26–9.

36 M. Crawford, 'Jefferson Davis and the Confederacy', in Grant and Holden Reid, *The American Civil War*, pp.110–11.

37 Gallagher, *The Confederate War*, pp.64–5, 90–96.

38 Faust, *The Creation of Confederate Nationalism*, p.16.

39 Ibid., pp.62–9.

40 Ibid., p.84.

41 Rubin, *A Shattered Nation*, pp.105–11.

42 G. M. Foster, *Ghosts of the Confederacy: Defeat, the Lost Cause and the Emergence of the New South, 1865–1913*, New York, Oxford University Press, 1987, p.196.

43 Rubin, *A Shattered Nation*, p.246.

44 Gallagher, *The Confederate War*, p.70.

8 Lincoln and liberty

1 A. M. Schlesinger, Jnr, 'War and the Constitution: Abraham Lincoln and Franklin D. Roosevelt', in G. S. Boritt (ed.) *Lincoln the War President*, New York: Oxford University Press, 1992, pp.166–72.

2 C. Bradley, D. Cole, W. Dellinger, R. Dworkin, R. Epstein, P. B. Heymann *et al.*, 'On NSA Spying: A Letter to Congress', *New York Review of Books*, Feb. 2006, vol.53.

3 J. M. McPherson, *Abraham Lincoln and the Second American Revolution*, New York: Oxford University Press, 1991, p.63.

4 Abraham Lincoln, Annual Message to Congress, 1 December 1862, in P. J. Parish (ed.) *Abraham Lincoln: Speeches and Letters*, London: Everyman, 1993, p.233.

5 P. Lucie, 'Individual Rights and Constitutional Powers: The Impact of the Civil War', in S.-M. Grant and B. Holden Reid (eds) *The American Civil War*, London: Longman, 2000, p.314.

6 G. M. Fredrickson, *The Inner Civil War: Northern Intellectuals and the Crisis of the Union*, Chicago: University of Illinois Press, 1993, pp.58–9.

7 Lincoln, First Inaugural Address, 4 March 1861, in Parish, *Abraham Lincoln*, p.166.

8 C. N. Degler, 'One Among Many: The United States and National Unification', in Boritt (ed.) *Lincoln the War President*, pp.106–9.

9 T. J. DiLorenzo, *The Real Lincoln: A New Look at Abraham Lincoln, His Agenda, and an Unnecessary War*, New York: Three Rivers Press, 2003. In seeking to expose the 'myths' about Lincoln, DiLorenzo's work provides a character assassination of extreme proportions. Much of Lincoln's words are taken out of context or selected from a speech to prove a certain point which is actually contradicted by Lincoln elsewhere in the same speech or text.

10 M. E. Neely, Jnr, *The Fate of Liberty: Abraham Lincoln and Civil Liberties*, New York: Oxford University Press, 1991, p.198.

11 Schlesinger, Jnr, 'War and the Constitution', pp.155–6.

12 Lincoln, Message to Congress in Special Session, 4 July 1861, in Parish, *Abraham Lincoln*, p.177.

13 J. M. McPherson, *Battle Cry of Freedom*, London: Penguin Books, 1990, p. 435; D. H. Donald, 'Abraham Lincoln and Jefferson Davis as Commanders in Chief', in G. S. Boritt (ed.) *The Lincoln Enigma: The Changing Faces of an American Icon*, Oxford: Oxford University Press, 2001, p.84.

14 Neely, Jnr, *The Fate of Liberty*, p.53.

15 Ibid., pp.54–5.

16 Ibid., pp.68–72; R. J. Carwardine, *Lincoln*, Harlow: Pearson Education, 2003, p.253.

17 Lincoln, Letter to Erastus Corning, 12 June 1863, in Parish, *Abraham Lincoln*, p.247.

18 Ibid., p.249.

19 Neely, Jnr, *The Fate of Liberty*, pp.65–7; Carwardine, *Lincoln*, pp.254–5.

20 F. L. Klement, *Dark Lanterns: Secret Political Societies, Conspiracies, and Treason Trials in the Civil War*, Baton Rouge: Louisiana State University Press, 1984, pp.149–50.

21 Neely, Jnr, *The Fate of Liberty*, pp.61, 137.

22 H. M. Hyman, *A More Perfect Union: The Impact of the Civil War and Reconstruction on the Constitution*, Boston: Houghton Mifflin, 1975, pp.256–9.

23 Lincoln, Memorandum on the President's duty if not re-elected, 23 August 1864, in Parish, *Abraham Lincoln*, p.279.

24 A. I. P. Smith, *No Party Now: Politics in the Civil War North*, Oxford: Oxford University Press, 2006, pp.66, 161.

25 S. B. Oates, *With Malice Towards None: A Life of Abraham Lincoln*, New York: HarperCollins, 1994, p.357.

26 I. Bernstein, *The New York City Draft Riots*, New York: Oxford University Press, 1990, pp.26–30.

27 A. C. Guelzo, 'Defending Emancipation: Abraham Lincoln and the Conkling Letter, 1863', *Civil War History*, 2002, vol.48, p.317.

28 Carwardine, *Lincoln*, p.204.

29 Lincoln, To a Delegation of Border State Congressmen, 12 July 1862, in Parish, *Abraham Lincoln*, p.209.

30 G. S. Boritt, 'Did he Dream of a Lily-white America? The Voyage to Lincolnia', in Boritt, *The Lincoln Enigma*, pp.7–11.
31 Lincoln, Letter to Horace Greeley, 22 August 1862, in Parish, *Abraham Lincoln*, p.215.
32 H. L. Trefousse, *Lincoln's Decision for Emancipation*, Philadelphia: Lippincott, 1975, pp.46–50.
33 Guelzo, 'Defending Emancipation', p.330.
34 D. B. Davis, 'The Emancipation Moment', in Boritt, *Lincoln the War President*, pp.86–8; Guelzo, 'Defending Emancipation', p.331.
35 M. E. Neely, Jnr, *The Last Best Hope of Earth*, Cambridge: Harvard University Press, 1993, pp.113–15.
36 Frederickson, *The Inner Civil War*, pp.123–5.
37 E. Foner, *Forever Free*, New York: Vintage Books, 2005, p.50.
38 Carwardine, *Lincoln*, p.238.
39 D. L. Wilson, *Lincoln's Sword*, New York: Alfred A. Knopf, 2007, pp.204, 206–7.
40 Lincoln, Letter to James Conkling, 26 August 1863, in Parish, *Abraham Lincoln*, p.261.
41 Boritt, 'Did he Dream of a Lily-white America?', p.14.
42 Carwardine, *Lincoln*, pp.237–8.
43 G. Wills, *Lincoln at Gettysburg: The Words that Remade America*, New York: Simon & Schuster, 1992, pp.144–8.
44 Lincoln, Second Inaugural Address, 4 March 1865, in Parish, *Abraham Lincoln*, p.289.
45 Lincoln, Address at Sanitary Fair, 18 April 1864, in Parish, *Abraham Lincoln*, p.277.
46 J. M. McPherson, *Abraham Lincoln and the Second American Revolution*, New York: Oxford University Press, 1991, pp.62–4.
47 H. Belz, 'Review Essay: Lincoln Liberty and Executive Power', *Pennsylvania History*, 1992, vol.59, pp.56–9.
48 Carwardine, *Lincoln*, p.296.
49 P. S. Paludan, 'Emancipating the Republic: Lincoln and the Means and Ends of Antislavery', in J. M. McPherson, *We Cannot Escape History: Lincoln and the Last Best Hope of Earth*, Chicago: University of Illinois Press, 1995, p.58.
50 Lucie, 'Individual Rights and Constitutional Powers', pp.322–4.

9 Reconstruction

1 E. Foner, *Reconstruction: America's Unfinished Revolution*, New York: Harper & Row, 1989, p.xxv.
2 E. L. Ayers, *What Caused the Civil War: Reflections on the South and Southern History*, New York: Norton, 2005, p.148.
3 P. R. Muller, 'Look Back without Anger: A Reappraisal of William A. Dunning', *Journal of American History*, 1974, vol.61, p.333.
4 Ibid., pp.334–7.
5 W. E. B. DuBois, 'Black Reconstruction', in K. M. Stampp and L. F. Litwack (eds) *Reconstruction: An Anthology of Revisionist Writings*, Baton Rouge: Louisiana State University Press, 1969.
6 See, for example, K. M. Stampp, *The Era of Reconstruction, 1865–1877*, New York: Alfred A. Knopf, 1965.
7 Foner, *Reconstruction*, p.xxi. For a view on the conservatism of Republicans in their constitutional outlook see H. M. Hyman, *A More Perfect Union: The Impact of the Civil War and Reconstruction on the Constitution*, Boston: Houghton Mifflin, 1975.

8 See, for example, L. F. Litwack, *Been in the Storm So Long: The Aftermath of Slavery*, New York: Random House, 1979; E. Foner, *Forever Free: The Story of Emancipation and Reconstruction*, New York: Random House, 2005.

9 H. Tulloch, *The Debate on the American Civil War*, Manchester: Manchester University Press, 1999, p.235.

10 T. J. Pressly, 'Racial Attitudes, Scholarship, and Reconstruction: A Review Essay', *Journal of Southern History*, 1966, vol.32.

11 Litwack, *Been in the Storm So Long*, p.224.

12 Foner, *Reconstruction*, pp.66–7.

13 Hyman, *A More Perfect Union*, p.420.

14 Foner, 'The Meaning of Freedom in the Age of Emancipation', *Journal of American History*, 1994, vol.81, p.454.

15 J. M. McPherson, 'The Ballot and Land for the Freedmen, 1861–65', in Stampp and Litwack, *Reconstruction*, pp.136–9; R. O. Curry, 'The Abolitionists and Reconstruction: A Critical Appraisal', *Journal of Southern History*, 1968, vol.34, pp.530–35.

16 Litwack, *Been in the Storm So Long*, pp.382–6.

17 Foner, *Forever Free*, pp.76–7.

18 Foner, *Reconstruction*, pp.244–5.

19 Ibid., p.257.

20 Foner, *Forever Free*, p.117.

21 H. Belz, 'The Constitution and Reconstruction', in E. Anderson and A. A. Moss (eds) *The Facts of Reconstruction: Essays in Honour of John Hope Franklin*, Baton Rouge: Louisiana State University Press, 1991, p.210.

22 H. Cox Richardson, *The Death of Reconstruction*, Cambridge: Harvard University Press, 2001, p.43.

23 Belz, 'The Constitution and Reconstruction', p.206.

24 P. Finkelman, 'Rehearsals for Reconstruction: Antebellum Origins of the Fourteenth Amendment', in Anderson and Moss, *The Facts of Reconstruction*, pp.23–7.

25 Belz, 'The Constitution and Reconstruction', p.212.

26 Foner, *Reconstruction*, p.342.

27 M. Perman, 'Counter Reconstruction: The Role of Violence in Southern Redemption', in Anderson and Moss, *The Facts of Reconstruction*, p.134.

28 Foner, *Forever Free*, p.129.

29 DuBois, 'Black Reconstruction', pp.447, 459.

30 V. L. Wharton, 'The Negro and Politics, 1870–75', in Stampp and Litwack, *Reconstruction*, pp.361, 366–9.

31 J. Williamson, 'The Meaning of Freedom', in Stampp and Litwack, *Reconstruction*, pp.209–10; Foner, *Forever Free*, p.90.

32 Litwack, *Been in the Storm So Long*, pp.451, 461, 471.

33 R. C. Morris, 'Educational Reconstruction', in Anderson and Moss (eds) *The Facts of Reconstruction*, pp. 144, 164–6.

34 Foner, *Forever Free*, p.89.

35 B.T. Washington, *Up From Slavery*, in *Three Negro Classics*, New York: HarperCollins, 1999, p.45.

36 E. Foner, 'The Meaning of Freedom in the Age of Emancipation', *Journal of American History*, 1994, vol.81, p.452.

37 DuBois, 'Black Reconstruction', p.433.

38 Foner, *Reconstruction*, p.236.

39 J. M. McPherson, 'The Ballot and Land for the Freedmen, 1861–65', in Stampp and Litwack, *Reconstruction*, pp.154–5.

40 Richardson, *The Death of Reconstruction*, p.126; Foner, *Reconstruction*, p.237.

41 Curry, 'The Abolitionists and Reconstruction', p.240.

42 H. N. Rabinowitz, 'Segregation and Reconstruction', in E. Anderson and A. Moss, *The Facts of Reconstruction*, pp.90–93.

43 Foner, *Forever Free*, p.89.

44 L. and J. Cox, 'Negro Suffrage and Republican Politics: The Problem of Motivation in Reconstruction Historiography', in Stampp and Litwack, *Reconstruction*, pp.159, 172.

45 Richardson, *The Death of Reconstruction*, pp.75–7.

46 Foner, *Reconstruction*, p.446.

47 Foner, *Forever Free*, pp.178–80.

48 Richardson, *The Death of Reconstruction*, pp.140–43.

49 Hyman, *A More Perfect Union*, pp.338–40; Foner, *Reconstruction*, pp.556–7.

50 Rabinowitz, 'Segregation and Reconstruction', in E. Anderson and A. Moss, *The Facts of Reconstruction*, pp.96–7.

51 A. L. Robinson, 'Beyond the Realm of Social Consensus: New Meanings of Reconstruction for American History', *Journal of American History*, 1981, vol.68, pp.295–7; Richardson, *The Death of Reconstruction*, pp.57, 133.

52 Richardson, *The Death of Reconstruction*, pp.82, 224.

53 C. Vann Woodward, *The Burden of Southern History*, Baton Rouge: Louisiana State University Press, 1993, p.84.

54 Foner, *Forever Free*, p.78.

10 Civil War memory and American national identity

1 J. Cullen, *The Civil War in Popular Culture: A Reusable Past*, Washington: Smithsonian Books, 1995, pp.9–15; S.-M. Grant, 'From Union to Nation? The Civil War and the Development of American Nationalism', in S.-M. Grant and B. Holden Reid (eds) *The American Civil War*, London: Longman, 2000, p.334.

2 Abraham Lincoln, First Inaugural Address, 4 March 1861, in P. J. Parish (ed.) *Abraham Lincoln: Speeches and Letters*, London: Everyman, 1993, p.169.

3 Abraham Lincoln, The Gettysburg Address, 19 November 1863, in Parish (ed.) *Abraham Lincoln*, p.267.

4 D. W. Blight, *Race and Reunion: The Civil War in American Memory*, Cambridge: Harvard University Press, 2001, p.9.

5 A. Fahs, 'The Feminised Civil War: Gender, Northern Popular Literature, and the Memory of the War, 1861–1900', *Journal of American History*, 1999, vol.4, p.1493.

6 M. J. Grow, 'The Shadow of the Civil War: A Historiography of Civil War Memory', *American Nineteenth Century History*, 2003, vol.4, p.96.

7 D. W. Blight, 'Decoration Days: The Origins of Memorial Day in North and South', in A. Fahs and J. Waugh (eds) *The Memory of the Civil War in American Culture*, Chapel Hill: University of North Carolina Press, 2004, p.94; J. R. Neff, *Honouring the Civil War Dead: Commemoration and the Problem of Reconciliation*, Lawrence: University Press of Kansas, 2005, p.20.

8 C. E. O'Leary, *To Die For: The Paradox of American Patriotism*, Princeton: Princeton University Press, 1999, p.6.

9 M. Lawson, *Patriot Fires: Forging a New American Nationalism in the Civil War North*, Lawrence: University Press of Kansas, 2002, pp.13, 181.

10 Blight, *Race and Reunion*, p.16.

11 W. A. Blair, *Cities of the Dead: Contesting the Memory of the Civil War in the South, 1865–1914*, Chapel Hill: University of North Carolina Press, p.23.

12 O'Leary, *To Die For*, p.114.
13 Neff, *Honouring the Civil War Dead*, p.76.
14 Blair, *Cities of the Dead*, p.37.
15 Blight, *Race and Reunion*, p.57.
16 D. W. Blight, 'For Something beyond the Battlefield: Frederick Douglass and the Struggle for the Memory of the Civil War', *Journal of American History*, 1989, vol.75, p.1175.
17 Blight, *Race and Reunion*, p.139.
18 N. Silber, *The Romance of Reunion: Northerners and the South 1865–1900*, Chapel Hill: University of North Carolina Press, 1993, p.65.
19 Blight, 'Decoration Days', p.113.
20 G. LaFantasie, 'Joshua Chamberlain and the American Dream', in G. S. Boritt (ed.) *The Gettysburg Nobody Knows*, Oxford: Oxford University Press, 1997, p.36.
21 J. Pettegrew, 'The Soldier's Faith: Turn of the Century Memory of the Civil War and the Emergence of Modern American Nationalism', *Journal of Contemporary History*, 1996, vol.31, pp.63–5.
22 O'Leary, *To Die For*, pp.50–51.
23 Blight, *Race and Reunion*, pp.174–5.
24 O'Leary, *To Die For*, pp.68–9.
25 A. Fahs, 'The Feminized Civil War: Gender, Northern Popular Literature, and the Memory of the War, 1861–1900', *Journal of American History*, 1999, vol.85, pp.1467–76.
26 A. S. Rubin, *A Shattered Nation: The Rise and Fall of the Confederacy, 1861–1868*, Chapel Hill: University of North Carolina Press, 2005, pp.52–6.
27 Blair, *Cities of the Dead*, p.97.
28 Silber, *The Romance of Reunion*, pp.37–8.
29 O'Leary, *To Die For*, pp.75, 99.
30 Fahs, 'The Feminized Civil War', p.1487.
31 Silber, *The Romance of Reunion*, p.175.
32 Neff, *Honouring the Civil War Dead*, p.42.
33 Blair, *Cities of the Dead*, pp.174–9.
34 Neff, *Honouring the Civil War Dead*, pp.112–21.
35 Ibid., p.136.
36 G. W. Gallagher, 'Shaping Public Memory of the Civil War: Robert E. Lee, Jubal A. Early, and Douglas Southall Freeman', in Fahs and Waugh, *The Memory of the Civil War*, pp.42–4.
37 J. M. McPherson, 'Long-Legged Yankee Lies: The Southern Textbook Crusade', in Fahs and Waugh, *The Memory of the Civil War*, p.70.
38 G. M. Foster, *Ghosts of the Confederacy: Defeat, the Lost Cause and the Emergence of the New South, 1865–1913*, New York: Oxford University Press, 1987, p.195.
39 Blair, *Cities of the Dead*, p.50.
40 Blight, *Race and Reunion*, pp.51–3.
41 Neff, *Honouring the Civil War Dead*, p.182.
42 Blight, *Race and Reunion*, p.291.
43 Silber, *The Romance of Reunion*, pp.134–7.
44 Blight, *Race and Reunion*, p.11.
45 O'Leary, *To Die For*, pp.205–7.
46 J. Wiener, 'Civil War, Cold War, Civil Rights: The Civil War Centennial in Context, 1960–65', in Fahs and Waugh, *The Memory of the Civil War*, pp.243–53.

11 Introducing Jim Crow

1 G. E. Hale, *Making Whiteness: The Culture of Segregation in the South, 1890–1940*, New York: Vintage Books, 1999, p.47.
2 Jim Crow was the name of a song and dance written by Thomas Rice in 1832. The term Jim Crow was used as an adjective and applied to black people from the late 1830s.
3 C. Vann Woodward, *The Strange Career of Jim Crow*, Oxford: Oxford University Press, comm. edn, 2002.
4 C. Vann Woodward, 'Strange Career Critics: Long May They Persevere', *Journal of American History*, 1988, vol.75, p.857.
5 Woodward, 'Strange Career Critics', p.860.
6 Woodward, *The Strange Career of Jim Crow*, pp.44–5.
7 Ibid., pp.45–7.
8 Ibid., pp.55–7.
9 J. Dailey, 'The Limits of Liberalism in the New South: The Politics of Race, Sex, and Patronage in Virginia, 1879–83', in J. Dailey, G. E. Gilmore and B. Simon (eds) *Jumpin' Jim Crow: Southern Politics from Civil War to Civil Rights*, Princeton: Princeton University Press, 2000, pp.90–91.
10 Woodward, *The Strange Career of Jim Crow*, p.61.
11 S. Hackney, *From Populism to Progressivism in Alabama*, Princeton: Princeton University Press, 1969, p.37.
12 Woodward, *The Strange Career of Jim Crow*, pp.18–27.
13 Ibid., pp.36–9.
14 B. J. Fields, 'Origins of the New South and the Negro Question', *Journal of Southern History*, 2001, vol.67, p.820.
15 H. N. Rabinowitz, 'More Than the Woodward Thesis: Assessing the Strange Career of Jim Crow', *Journal of American History*, 1988, vol.75, p.847.
16 G. B. Tindall, *South Carolina Negroes*, Columbia: University of South Carolina Press, 1952, pp.300–301.
17 J. Williamson, *After Slavery: The Negro in South Carolina during Reconstruction, 1861–1877*, New Hampshire: University Press of New England, 1990, p.298.
18 J. Oldfield, 'State Politics, Railroads, and Civil Rights in South Carolina, 1883–89', *American Nineteenth Century History*, 2004, vol.5, pp.78, 88.
19 R. A. Fischer, *The Segregation Struggle in Louisiana 1862–1877*, Urbana: University of Illinois Press, 1974, pp.138–43.
20 Woodward, *The Strange Career of Jim Crow*, p.34.
21 A. K. Sandoval-Strausz, 'Travellers, Strangers and Jim Crow: Law, Public Accommodations, and Civil Rights in America', *Law and History Review*, 2005, vol. 23, p.33.
22 Woodward, 'Strange Career Critics', p.861.
23 H. N. Rabinowitz, 'From Exclusion to Segregation: Southern Race Relations, 1865–90', *Journal of American History*, 1976, vol.63, pp.325–30.
24 H. N. Rabinowitz, *Race Relations in the Urban South: 1865–1890*, Athens: University of Georgia Press, 1996, p.331.
25 G. E. Gilmore, *Gender and Jim Crow: Women and the Politics of White Supremacy in North Carolina*, Chapel Hill: University of North Carolina Press, 1996, p.2.
26 Dailey, 'The Limits of Liberalism in the New South', p.90.
27 Hackney, *From Populism to Progressivism in Alabama*, p.40.
28 Woodward, *The Strange Career of Jim Crow*, pp.76–80.

29 C. Vann Woodward, *American Counterpoint*, Boston: Little, Brown and Co., 1971, pp.243–4.
30 Oldfield, 'State Politics, Railroads, and Civil Rights', p.83.
31 Gilmore, *Gender and Jim Crow*, pp.29, 107–8.
32 J. Williamson, *A Rage For Order: Black–White Relations in the American South Since Emancipation*, New York: Oxford University Press, 1986, pp.88–90.
33 Hale, *Making Whiteness*, p.21.
34 G. M. Frederickson, *The Black Image in the White Mind*, New York: Harper & Row, 1971, pp.261–5; T. F. Gossett, *Race: The History of an Idea in America*, Oxford: Oxford University Press, 1997, pp.270–72.
35 Dailey, 'The Limits of Liberalism in the New South', pp.99–103.
36 Gilmore, *Gender and Jim Crow*, pp.67–71.
37 Williamson, *A Rage for Order*, pp.90–94.
38 Gossett, *Race*, p.271.
39 Gilmore, *Gender and Jim Crow*, p.91.
40 W. Fitzhugh Brundage (ed.) *Under Sentence of Death: Lynching in the South*, Chapel Hill: University of North Carolina Press, 1997, p.4.
41 Williamson, *A Rage for Order*, p.123.
42 Ibid., p.119.
43 Fischer, *The Segregation Struggle*, pp.151–2.
44 Oldfield, 'State Politics, Railroads, and Civil Rights', p.88.
45 G. Gerstle, *American Crucible: Race and Nation in the Twentieth Century*, Princeton: Princeton University Press, 2001, pp.59–64.
46 W. Fitzhugh Brundage, 'White Women and the Politics of Historical Memory in the New South, 1880–1920', in Dailey *et al.* (eds) *Jumpin' Jim Crow*, pp.126–7
47 Hale, *Making Whiteness*, p.44.
48 J. C. Cobb, *The Brown Decision, Jim Crow and Southern Identity*, Athens: University of Georgia Press, 2005, p.26.
49 Hale, *Making Whiteness*, pp.124–5.

12 Prejudice and paternalism

1 M. A. Elliott, 'Indian Patriots on Last Stand Hill', *American Quarterly*, 2006, p.988.
2 L. Sadosky, 'Great Expectations, Great Disappointments: American Indians and the Emergence of Modern American Culture', *Reviews in American History*, 2005, vol.33, p.387.
3 Elliott, 'Indian Patriots on Last Stand Hill', p.1009.
4 F. E. Hoxie, *The Campaign to Assimilate the Indians, 1880–1920,* Lincoln: University of Nebraska Press, 2001, p.3.
5 D. Brown, *Bury My Heart at Wounded Knee: An Indian History of the American West*, London: Vintage, 1991, p.273.
6 C. Bolt, *American Indian Policy and American Reform: Case Studies of the Campaign to Assimilate the American Indians*, London: Allen & Unwin, 1987, p.81.
7 F. P. Prucha, *American Indian Treaties: The History of a Political Anomaly*, Berkeley: University of California Press, 1997, pp.310–12.
8 Prucha, *American Indian Treaties*, p.335.
9 F.P. Prucha, *The Great Father: The United States Government and the American Indians*, Lincoln: University of Nebraska Press, 1986, p.223.
10 Bolt, *American Indian Policy*, p.90.
11 Hoxie, *The Campaign to Assimilate the Indians*, p.15.

12 Prucha, *The Great Father*, p.199.
13 T. Holm, *The Great Confusion in Indian Affairs: Native Americans and Whites in the Progressive Era*, Austin: University of Texas Press, 2005, p.17.
14 Hoxie, *The Campaign to Assimilate the Indians*, p.2.
15 Holm, *The Great Confusion in Indian Affairs*, p.6.
16 Holm, Ibid., pp.8–10.
17 Prucha, *The Great Father*, p.209.
18 Hoxie, *The Campaign to Assimilate the Indians*, pp.33–6.
19 Bolt, *American Indian Policy*, p.99.
20 D. J. Murray, *Modern Indians*, Durham: British Association for American Studies, 1982, pp.10–11.
21 Hoxie, *The Campaign to Assimilate the Indians*, p.79; Holm, *The Great Confusion in Indian Affairs*, p.13.
22 Prucha, *The Great Father*, p.227.
23 Holm, *The Great Confusion in Indian Affairs*, pp.24–6, 41–5.
24 S. Senier, 'Allotment Protest and Tribal Discourse: Reading Wynema's Successes and Shortcomings', *The American Indian Quarterly*, 2000, vol.24, p.426. On Indian resistance to assimilation see also F. E. Hoxie, *Talking Back to Civilization: Indian Voices From the Progressive Era*, Boston: Bedford Books, 2001.
25 Prucha, *The Great Father*, pp. 236–9, 281–3.
26 R. A. Trennert, 'Educating Girls at Nonreservation Boarding Schools, 1878–1920', in F. M. Binder and D. M. Reimers (eds) *The Way We Lived: Essays and Documents in American Social History, 1865–Present*, Massachusetts: D.C. Heath, 1996, pp.56–7.
27 K. T. Lomawaima and T. L. McCarty, *To Remain an Indian: Lessons in Democracy from a Century of Native American Education*, New York: Teachers College Press, 2006, p.50; Prucha, *The Great Father*, p.285.
28 Lomawaima and McCarty, *To Remain an Indian*, p.51.
29 Prucha, *The Great Father*, pp. 263–7.
30 H. E. Fritz, 'The Last Hurrah of Christian Humanitarian Indian Reform: The Board of Indian Commissioners, 1909–18', *Western Historical Quarterly*, 1985, vol.16.
31 Holm, *The Great Confusion in Indian Affairs*, p.162.
32 Hoxie, *The Campaign to Assimilate the Indians*, p.113.
33 Prucha, *American Indian Treaties*, p.356.
34 Holm, *The Great Confusion in Indian Affairs*, pp.165–6.
35 Bolt, *American Indian Policy*, p.100.
36 Hoxie, *The Campaign to Assimilate the Indians*, p.111.
37 Holm, *The Great Confusion in Indian Affairs*, p.152.
38 F. E. Hoxie, 'Exploring a Cultural Borderland: Native American Journeys of Discovery in the Early Twentieth Century', *Journal of American History*, 1992, vol.79, p.981.
39 Lomawaima and McCarty, *To Remain an Indian*, p.53.
40 Hoxie, *The Campaign to Assimilate the Indians*, p.241.
41 Sadosky, 'Great Expectations, Great Disappointments', p.394.
42 Holm, *The Great Confusion in Indian Affairs*, pp.146–7.
43 Bolt, *American Indian Policy*, p.107; Holm, *The Great Confusion in Indian Affairs*, p.179.
44 Hoxie, *The Campaign to Assimilate the Indians*, p.242.
45 Prucha, *The Great Father*, p. 321.
46 G. D. Taylor, *The New Deal and American Indian Tribalism*, University of Nebraska Press, 1980, pp. 145–50.
47 Hoxie, *The Campaign to Assimilate the Indians*, p.236.

48 Prucha, *The Great Father*, p.402.
49 *Herald Tribune*, 8 December 2006.

13 American identity and the American West

1 A. Fabian, 'History for the Masses: Commercializing the Western Past', in W. Cronon, G. Miles and J. Gatlin (eds) *Under an Open Sky: Rethinking America's Western Past*, New York: Norton, 1992, p.227.
2 F. J. Turner, 'The Significance of the Frontier in American History', *Annual Report of the American Historical Association*, 1893, p.227.
3 A. G. Bogue, 'Frederick Jackson Turner Reconsidered', *The History Teacher*, 1994, vol.27, pp.199–203.
4 J. M. Faragher, 'The Frontier Trail: Rethinking Turner and Reimagining the American West', *American Historical Review*, 1993, vol.98, p.117.
5 Bogue, 'Frederick Jackson Turner Reconsidered', p.207.
6 R. A. Billington, *Westward Expansion*, New York: Macmillan, 1960, p.3.
7 Ibid., p.745.
8 M. Walsh, *The American West: Visions and Revisions*, Cambridge: Cambridge University Press, 2005, pp.3–6.
9 P. N. Limerick, *The Legacy of Conquest: The Unbroken Past of the American West*, New York: Norton, 1987, p.27.
10 D. Worster, *Under Western Skies: Nature and History in the American West*, Oxford: Oxford University Press, 1992, pp.28–32.
11 Ibid., p.237.
12 R. White, 'Animals and Enterprise', in C. A. Milner II, C. A. O'Connor and M. A. Sandweiss (eds) *The Oxford History of the American West*, Oxford: Oxford University Press, 1994.
13 For further examples of the New Western History, see P. N. Limerick, C. A. Milner II and C. E. Rankin (eds) *Trials Toward a New Western History*, Lawrence: University Press of Kansas, 1991.
14 Worster, *Under Western Skies*, pp.231–2.
15 P. N. Limerick, 'Turnerians All: The Dream of a Helpful World in an Intelligible World', *The American Historical Review*, 1995, vol.100, p.710.
16 Faragher, 'The Frontier Trail: Rethinking Turner and Reimagining the American West', p.106; D. M. Wrobel, 'Beyond the Frontier-region Dichotomy', *Pacific Historical Review*, 1996, vol.65, p.402.
17 Limerick, *The Legacy of Conquest*, p.324.
18 Cronon *et al.*, *Under an Open Sky*.
19 Walsh, *The American West*, p.10.
20 W. Cronon, 'Kennecott Journey: The Paths Out of Town', in Cronon *et al.*, *Under an Open Sky*, p.32.
21 C. A. Milner II, 'The View from Wisdom: Four Layers of History and Regional Identity', in Cronon *et al.*, *Under an Open Sky*, p.222.
22 C. Friday, 'Where to Draw the Line? The Pacific, Place and the United States', in W. Deverell (ed.) *A Companion to the American West*, London: Blackwell, 2004, p.282.
23 M. Steiner, 'From Frontier to Region: Frederick Jackson Turner and the New Western History', *Pacific Historical Review*, 1995, vol.64, pp.481–4.
24 W. Cronon, G. Miles and J. Gitlin, 'Becoming West: Toward a New Meaning for Western History', in Cronon *et al.*, *Under an Open Sky*, p.26.
25 Wrobel, 'Beyond the Frontier-region Dichotomy', p.413.

26 Milner II, 'The View from Wisdom', p.204.
27 Limerick, *The Legacy of Conquest*, p.26.
28 Wrobel, 'Beyond the Frontier-region Dichotomy', pp.424–5.
29 D. Flamming, 'African-Americans in the Twentieth Century West', in Deverell, *A Companion to the American West*, pp.223–5.
30 R. A. Gutiérrez, 'Hispanics and Latinos', in Deverell, *A Companion to the American West*, pp.392–5.
31 J. M. Faragher, 'American, Mexican, Métis: A Community Approach to the Comparative Study of North American Frontiers', in Cronon *et al.*, *Under an Open Sky*, pp.90–109.
32 Wrobel, 'Beyond the Frontier-region Dichotomy', p.429.
33 Worster, *Under Western Skies*, p.26.
34 Limerick, *The Legacy of Conquest*, p.179.
35 M. A. Bellesiles, 'Western Violence', in Deverell, *A Companion to the American West*, p.165.
36 Walsh, *The American West*, p.42.
37 D. K. Richter, *Facing East From Indian Country: A Native History of Early America*, Cambridge: Harvard University Press, 2001, p.188.
38 D. R. Lewis, 'Native Americans in the Nineteenth Century American West', in Deverell, *A Companion to the American West*, pp.147–8.
39 G. Miles, 'To Hear an Old Voice: Rediscovering Native Americans in American History', in Cronon *et al.*, *Under an Open Sky*, pp.55–60; F. E. Hoxie, 'Thinking Like an Indian: Exploring American Indian Views of American History', *Reviews in American History*, 2001, vol.29.
40 A. De León, *Racial Frontiers: Africans, Chinese and Mexicans in Western America, 1848–1890*, Albuquerque: University of New Mexico Press, 2002, p.43; D. G. Gutiérrez, *Walls and Mirrors: Mexican Americans, Mexican Immigrants, and the Politics of Ethnicity*, Berkeley: University of California Press, 1995, p.37.
41 Gutiérrez, 'Hispanics and Latinos', pp.395–400; Gutiérrez, *Walls and Mirrors*, pp.88–92.
42 Q. Taylor, *In Search of the Racial Frontier: African-Americans in the American West, 1528–1990*, New York: Norton, 1998, p.18.
43 De León, *Racial Frontiers*, pp.35–9.
44 Taylor, *In Search of the Racial Frontier*, pp.230–36.
45 Flamming, 'African-Americans in the Twentieth Century West', pp.224–7.
46 S. Deutsch, 'Landscape of Enclaves: Race Relations in the West 1865–1990', in Cronon *et al.*, *Under an Open Sky*, p.115.
47 Flamming, 'African-Americans in the Twentieth Century West', p.225.
48 S. H. Tsai, 'Chinese Immigration 1848–82', in S. Chan *et al.* (eds) *Peoples of Colour in the American West*, Massachusetts: D. C. Heath and Co., 1994, pp.110–16; De León, *Racial Frontiers*, pp.12–13.
49 Limerick, *The Legacy of Conquest*, pp.264–8.
50 Deutsch, 'Landscape of Enclaves', p.114.
51 De León, *Racial Frontiers*, p.57.

14 Immigration and assimilation: melting pot or salad bowl?

1 M. D'Innocento and J. P. Sirefman (eds) *Immigration and Ethnicity: American Society: 'Melting Pot' or 'Salad Bowl?'* Connecticut: Greenwood Press, 1992, p.x.
2 M. M. Gordon, 'Assimilation in America: Theory and Reality', *Daedalus*, 1961, vol.90, p.266.

3 V. N. Parrillo, *Diversity in America*, California: Pine Forge Press, 1996, p.9.

4 J. Higham, 'Integrating America: The Problem of Assimilation in the Nineteenth Century', *Journal of American Ethnic History*, 1981, vol.1, pp.7–15.

5 R. Daniels, *Coming to America: A History of Immigration and Ethnicity in American Life*, New York: HarperPerennial, 1990, pp.126–8; D. R. Roediger, *The Wages of Whiteness: Race and the Making of the American Working Class*, London: Verso, 2003, pp.140–41.

6 H. Tsai, 'Chinese Immigration 1848–82', in S. Chan *et al.* (eds) *Peoples of Colour in the American West*, Massachusetts: D.C. Heath and Co., 1994.

7 Higham, 'Integrating America', p.22.

8 Daniels, *Coming to America*, pp.12, 124–5.

9 V. L. Ruiz, 'Nuestra América: Latino History as United States History', *Journal of American History*, 2006, vol.96, p.663.

10 D. G. Guitiérrez, *Walls and Mirrors: Mexican Americans, Mexican Immigrants, and the Politics of Ethnicity*, Berkeley: University of California Press, 1995, p.57.

11 E. Morawska, 'The Sociology and Historiography of Immigration', in A. Yans-McLaughlin (ed.) *Immigration Reconsidered*, New York: Oxford University Press, 1990, p.195.

12 O. Handlin, *The Uprooted*, Boston: Little, Brown, 1951.

13 Morawska, 'The Sociology and Historiography of Immigration', pp.194, 209; R. J. Vecoli, 'Contadini in Chicago: A Critique of the Uprooted', *Journal of American History*, 1964, vol.51.

14 Gordon, 'Assimilation in America', pp.272–3.

15 G. Gerstle, *American Crucible: Race and Nation in the Twentieth Century*, Princeton: Princeton University Press, 2001, p.53.

16 Parrillo, *Diversity in America*, p.7.

17 Ibid., pp.12–14; M. A. Jones, *American Immigration*, Chicago: University of Chicago Press, 1992, pp.231–9.

18 Gordon, 'Assimilation in America', pp.268–9.

19 Gerstle, *American Crucible*, pp.56, 77.

20 J. Dorinson, 'The Educational Alliance: An Institutional Study in Americanisation and Acculturation', in D'Innocento and Sirefman, *Immigration and Ethnicity*.

21 Guitiérrez, *Walls and Mirrors*, pp.88–92.

22 M. M. Gordon, *Assimilation in American Life*, New York: Oxford University Press, 1964.

23 N. Glazer and D. P. Moynihan, *Beyond the Melting Pot: The Negroes, Puerto Ricans, Jews, Italians, and Irish of New York City*, Cambridge: MIT Press, 2nd edn, 1970, pp.13–14.

24 R. Alba and V. Nee, 'Rethinking Assimilation Theory for a New Era of Immigration', *International Migration Review*, 1997, vol.31, p.838.

25 Gerstle, *American Crucible*, pp.257–61.

26 A. R. Zolberg, 'Reforming the Back Door: The Immigration Reform and Control Act of 1986 in Historical Perspective', in Yans-McLaughlin, *Immigration Reconsidered*, pp.320–21.

27 Alba and Nee, 'Rethinking Assimilation Theory', p.842.

28 M. M. Gordon, 'Toward a General Theory of Racial and Ethnic Group Relations', in N. Glazer and D. P. Moynihan (eds) *Ethnicity: Theory and Experience*, Cambridge: Harvard University Press, 1975, p.88.

29 Guitiérrez, *Walls and Mirrors*, pp.190–94.

30 D. Bell, 'Ethnicity and Social Change', in Glazer and Moynihan, *Ethnicity*, pp.169–71.

NOTES

31 H. J. Gans, 'Symbolic Ethnicity: The Future of Ethnic Groups and Cultures in America', *Racial and Ethnic Studies*, 1979, vol.2; M. C. Waters, 'The Construction of a Symbolic Ethnicity: Suburban White Ethnics in the 1980s', in D'Innocento and Sirefman, *Immigration and Ethnicity*.

32 N. Glazer, 'Is Assimilation Dead?' *The Annals of the American Academy of Political and Social Science*, 1993, vol.530, pp.131–6.

33 E. Anderson, 'Beyond the Melting Pot Reconsidered', and N. Foner, 'Beyond the Melting Pot Three Decades Later: Recent Immigrants and New York's New Ethnic Mixture', *International Migration Review*, 2000, vol.34.

34 Zolberg, 'Reforming the Back Door: The Immigration Reform and Control Act of 1986 in Historical Perspective', pp.322, 336–7.

35 Parrillo, *Diversity in America*, p.2; G. Lipsitz, *The Possessive Investment in Whiteness: How White People Profit From Identity Politics*, Philadelphia: Temple University Press, 1998, pp.47–8.

36 *The Washington Times*, 28 January 2004.

37 Parrillo, *Diversity in America*, pp.178–80; *US Census Bureau*, 2004.

38 N. Glazer, 'Multiculturalism and a New America', in J. Higham (ed.) *Civil Rights and Social Wrongs: Black–White Relations Since World War Two*, Pennsylvania: Pennsylvania State University Press, 1999, p.133.

39 N. Glazer, 'Beyond the Melting Pot, 35 Years Later', *International Migration Review*, 2007, vol.34, pp.270–74; Alba and Nee, 'Rethinking Assimilation Theory', pp.845–54.

40 R. G. Rumbaut, 'Assimilation and its Discontents: Between Rhetoric and Reality', *International Migration Review*, 1997, vol.34.

41 D. Ravitch, 'Our Pluralistic Common Culture', in Higham, *Civil Rights and Social Wrongs*, p.146.

15 Gender, race and the vote, 1865–1920

1 E. C. Stanton, 'Declaration of the Rights of Women, 1876', in L. K. Kerber and J. Sherron De Hart (eds) *Women's America: Refocusing the Past*, New York: Oxford University Press, 2000, p.259.

2 L. M. Alexander, 'The Challenge of Race: Rethinking the Position of Black Women in the Field of Women's History', *Journal of Women's History*, 2004, vol.16, pp.50–54.

3 The issue of racial identity is not one simple black and white dichotomy, and Hispanic experience is just one significant omission here. Whilst recognising this, the chapter is limited to such a discussion because of the space available here.

4 B. Aptheker, 'Directions for Scholarship', in A. D. Gordon (ed.) *African-American Women and the Vote, 1837–1965*, Amherst: University of Massachusetts Press, 1997, pp.205–206.

5 S. M. Evans, *Born for Liberty: A History of Women in America*, New York: The Free Press, 1997, p.156.

6 E. Barkley Brown, 'To Catch the Vision of Freedom: Reconstructing Southern Black Women's Political History, 1865–80', in V. L. Ruiz and E. C. DuBois (eds) *Unequal Sisters: A Multicultural Reader*, New York: Routledge, 2000, pp.129–32.

7 E. C. DuBois, 'Taking the Law into Our Own Hands: *Bradwell, Minor*, and Suffrage Militance in the 1870s', in N. A. Hewitt and S. Lebsock (eds) *Visible Women: New Essays on American Activism*, Urbana: University of Illinois Press, 1993, p.23.

8 Evans, *Born for Liberty*, pp.122–5.

223

9 Dubois, 'Taking the Law into Our Own Hands', p.33.
10 Brown, 'To Catch the Vision of Freedom', p.135.
11 M. M. Gardner, 'Working on White Womanhood: White Working Women in the San-Francisco Anti-Chinese Movement, 1877–90', *Journal of Social History*, 1999, vol.33, pp.73–6.
12 E. Barkley Brown, 'Negotiating and Transforming the Public Sphere: African-American Political Life in the Transition from Slavery to Freedom', in J. Dailey, G. E. Gilmore and B. Simon (eds) *Jumpin' Jim Crow: Southern Politics From Civil War to Civil Rights*, Princeton: Princeton University Press, 2000, p.52.
13 P. Baker, 'The Domestication of Politics: Women and American Political Society, 1780–1920', *The American Historical Review*, 1984, vol. 89, p.642.
14 S. M. Evans, 'Women's History and Political Theory', in Hewitt and Lebsock, *Visible Women*, pp.126–31.
15 K. K. Sklar, 'Florence Kelley and Women's Activism in the Progressive Era', Kerber and J. Sherron De Hart, *Women's America*, pp.314–22.
16 Baker, 'The Domestication of Politics: Women and American Political Society, 1780–1920', pp.637–8; E. C. DuBois, 'Woman Suffrage around the World: Three Phases of Suffrage Internationalism', in Ruiz and Dubois (eds) *Unequal Sisters*, pp.278–80.
17 M. Ladd-Taylor, 'Hull House Goes to Washington: Women and the Children's Bureau', in N. Frankel and N. S. Dye (eds) *Gender, Class, Race, and Reform in the Progressive Era*, Lexington: University of Kentucky Press, 1991, pp.111–13.
18 Baker, 'The Domestication of Politics', p.664.
19 M. Turner, 'Better Citizens Without the Ballot: American Anti-Suffrage Women and Their Rationale during the Progressive Era', *Journal of Women's History*, 1993, vol.5, p.42.
20 J. A. Rouse, 'Atlanta's African-American Women's Attack on Segregation, 1900–1920', in Frankel and Dye, *Gender, Class, Race, and Reform*, pp.13–19.
21 N. A. Hewitt, 'Politicising Domesticity: Anglo, Black and Latin Women in Tampa's Progressive Movements', in Frankel and Dye, *Gender, Class, Race, and Reform*, p.25.
22 C. Neverdon-Morton, 'Advancement of the Race through African-American Women's Organisations in the South, 1895–1925', in Gordon, *African-American Women and the Vote*, pp.122–3.
23 Hewitt, 'Politicising Domesticity', pp.36–8.
24 G. Gilmore, 'Forging Inter-racial Links in the Jim Crow South', in Kerber and De Hart, *Women's America*, pp.288–91.
25 K. Delegard, 'Women's Movement, 1880s–1920s', in N. A. Hewitt (ed.) *A Companion to American Women's History*, London: Blackwell, 2002, p.329.
26 Baker, 'The Domestication of Politics', p.642.
27 Evans, *Born for Liberty*, p.164.
28 E. C. DuBois, 'Working Women, Class Relations, and Suffrage Militance: Harriot Stanton Blatch and the New York Woman Suffrage Movement, 1894–1909', *Journal of American History*, 1987, vol.74, pp.46–50.
29 DuBois, 'Woman Suffrage around the World', pp.285–6.
30 E. C. DuBois, 'Harriot Stanton Blatch and the Winning of Women Suffrage', in Kerber and De Hart, *Women's America*, p.333.
31 R. Terborg-Penn, 'African-American Women and the Vote', in Gordon, *African-American Women and the Vote*, pp.18–19.
32 S. Lebsock, 'Woman Suffrage and White Supremacy: A Virginia Case Study', in Hewitt and Lebsock, *Visible Women*, pp.76–7.

33 Evans, *Born for Liberty*, pp. 166–72.
34 DuBois, 'Woman Suffrage around the World', p.287.
35 Gilmore, 'Forging Inter-racial Links', p.291.
36 Lebsock, 'Woman Suffrage and White Supremacy', pp.86–9.

16 Origins of the civil rights movement

1 W. E. B. DuBois, *Souls of Black Folk*, in *Three Negro Classics*, New York: Harper-Collins, 1999, p.386.
2 P. Sullivan, *Days of Hope: Race and Democracy in the New Deal Era*, Oxford: Oxford University Press, 1978, p.67
3 M. Marable, *Race, Reform and Rebellion: The Second American Reconstruction in Black America, 1945–1982*, London: Macmillan Press, 1984, p.66.
4 T. Branch, *Parting the Waters: America in the King Years 1954–63*, New York: Simon & Schuster, 1988, p.922.
5 A. Fairclough, *Better Day Coming: Blacks and Equality 1890–2000*, New York: Penguin Books, 2002.
6 M. Marable, *Race, Reform and Rebellion*.
7 J. Dowd Hall, 'The Long Civil Rights Movement and the Political Uses of the Past', *The Journal of American History*, 2005, vol.91, p.1234.
8 A. Meier and J. H. Bracey Jnr, 'The NAACP as a Reform Movement, 1909–65: "To Reach the Conscience of America"', *Journal of Southern History*, 1993, vol.59, p.6.
9 Fairclough. *Better Day Coming*, pp.74–6; Meier and Bracey Jnr, 'The NAACP as a Reform Movement', p.11.
10 Meier and Bracey Jnr, 'The NAACP as a Reform Movement', pp.10–11.
11 Ibid., p.13.
12 A. H. Taylor, *Travail and Triumph*, Connecticut: Greenwood Press, 1976, pp. 56–60; R. Dalfiume, 'The Forgotten Years of the Negro Revolution', *Journal of American History*, 1968, vol.55, p.100.
13 H. Sitkoff, *A New Deal for Blacks: The Emergence of Civil Rights as a National Issue*, New York: Oxford University Press, 1978, p.295.
14 J. Kirk, 'He Founded a Movement: W. H. Flowers, the CNO and the Origins of Black Activism in Arkansas', in B. Ward and A. J. Badger (eds) *The Making of Martin Luther King and the Civil Rights Movement*, Basingstoke: Macmillan, 1996, pp.29–35.
15 R. D. Kelley, *Race Rebels: Culture, Politics, and the Black Working Class*, New York: The Free Press, 1996, pp.117–20.
16 See, for example, D. L. Chappell, *A Stone of Hope: Prophetic Religion in the Death of Jim Crow*, Chapel Hill: University of North Carolina Press, 2004; A. Calhoun-Brown, 'Upon this Rock: The Black Church, Nonviolence, and the Civil Rights Movement', *Political Science and Politics*, 2000, vol.33.
17 E. D. Hoffman, 'The Genesis of the Modern Movement for Equal Rights in South Carolina', in B. Sternsher (ed.) *The Negro in Depression and War*, Chicago: Quadrangle Books, 1969, p.201.
18 S. W. Angell, *Bishop Henry McNeal Turner and African-American Religion in the South*, Knoxville: University of Tennessee Press, 1992, p.244.
19 Kelley, *Race Rebels*, p.42; R. Kelley, 'We Are Not What We Seem: Rethinking Black Working-Class Opposition in the Jim Crow South', *Journal of American History*, 1993, vol.80, p.80.
20 Taylor, *Travail and Triumph*, pp.148–50.

21 Hoffman, 'The Genesis of the Modern Movement', pp.204–5.
22 A. Meier and E. Rudwick, *Along the Colour Line: Explorations in the Black Experience*, Urbana: University of Illinois Press, 1976, pp. 315–17.
23 R. Halpern, 'Organised Labour, Black Workers and the Twentieth Century South: The Emerging Revision', in M Stokes and R. Halpern (eds) *Race and Class in the American South since 1890*, Rhode Island: Berg, 1994, pp.43–5, 66–70.
24 Kelley, 'We Are Not What We Seem: Rethinking Black Working-class Opposition in the Jim Crow South', p.86; Kelley, *Race Rebels*, pp.58–9.
25 Fairclough. *Better Day Coming*, pp.94–5.
26 A. T. Gilmore, 'The Black Southern Response to the Southern System of Race Relations: 1900 to Post World War Two', in R. Haws (ed.) *The Age of Segregation: Race Relations in the South, 1890–1945*, Jackson: University of Mississippi Press, 1978, pp.75–8.
27 See, for example, T. B. Tyson, *Radio Free Dixie: Robert F. Williams and the Roots of Black Power*, Chapel Hill: University of North Carolina Press, 1999.
28 S. A. Sandage, 'A Marble House Divided: The Lincoln Memorial, the Civil Rights Movement, and the Politics of Memory, 1939–63', *Journal of American History*, 1993, vol.80, p.143.
29 Dalfiume, 'The Forgotten Years of the Negro Revolution', pp.97–9.
30 Ibid., p.94.
31 Kelley, *Race Rebels*, pp.64–5.
32 D. C. Hine, 'Black Professionals and Race Consciousness: Origins of the Civil Rights Movement, 1890–1950', *Journal of American History*, 2003, vol.89, pp.1280–91.
33 Dalfiume, 'The Forgotten Years of the Negro Revolution', p.106.
34 D. L. Chappell, *Inside Agitators: White Southerners in the Civil Rights Movement*, Baltimore: Johns Hopkins University Press, 1994, pp.48–9.
35 Sullivan, *Days of Hope*, pp.52–3; M. Sosna, *In Search of the Silent South*, New York: Columbia University Press, 1977, pp.60–65.
36 Sullivan, *Days of Hope*, pp.65–7; J. Egerton, *Speak Now Against the Day: The Generation Before the Civil Rights Movement in the South*, Chapel Hill: University of North Carolina Press, 1994, pp.190–92.
37 Sitkoff, *A New Deal for Blacks*, p.83.
38 Gilmore, 'The Black Southern Response', p.72.
39 L. Levine, *Black Culture and Black Consciousness: Afro-American Folk Thought from Slavery to Freedom*, New York: Oxford University Press, 1977, pp.421–8.
40 Kelley, 'We Are Not What We Seem', p.77; Kelley, *Race Rebels*, pp.17–20.
41 Gilmore, 'The Black Southern Response', pp.75–7.
42 P. Gottlieb, 'Rethinking the Great Migration: A Perspective from Pittsburgh', in J. W. Trotter, Jnr (ed.), *The Great Migration in Historical Perspective*, Bloomington: Indiana University Press, 1991, pp.70–72.
43 Hall, 'The Long Civil Rights Movement', pp.1236–9.

17 Kennedy, Johnson and civil rights

1 W. Van DeBurg, *Black Camelot: African-American Culture Heroes in Their Times, 1960–1980*, Chicago: University of Chicago Press, 1997, p.13.
2 N. Bryant, *The Bystander: John F. Kennedy and the Struggle for Black Equality*, New York: Basic Books, 2006, p.275.
3 T. H. Williams, 'Huey, Lyndon, and Southern Radicalism', *The Journal of American History*, 1973, vol.60, p.290.

4 See, for example, H. Fairlie, *The Kennedy Promise: The Politics of Expectation*, New York: Doubleday, 1973; B. Miroff, *Pragmatic Illusions: The Presidential Politics of John F. Kennedy*, New York: David McKay, 1976.

5 J. F. Heath, *Decade of Disillusionment: The Kennedy and Johnson Years*, Bloomington: Indiana University Press, 1975, p.117.

6 Bryant, *The Bystander*, pp.23–5.

7 M. Stern, *Calculating Visions: Kennedy, Johnson and Civil Rights*, New Jersey: Rutgers University, 1992, p.21.

8 Bryant, *The Bystander*, pp.27–9.

9 T. Borstelmann, 'Hedging Our Bets and Buying Time: John Kennedy and Racial Revolutions in the American South and Southern Africa', *Diplomatic History*, 2000, vol.24, p.436.

10 R. Dallek, *John F. Kennedy: An Unfinished Life*, New York: Penguin Books, 2004, p.165.

11 Stern, *Calculating Visions*, p.11.

12 Dallek, *John F. Kennedy*, p.178.

13 Bryant, *The Bystander*, pp.35–42.

14 Dallek, *John F. Kennedy*, p.174.

15 Bryant, *The Bystander*, pp.93–7.

16 Ibid., pp.165–7, 184–6.

17 Ibid., p.190.

18 Ibid., pp.200–201.

19 Stern, *Calculating Visions*, p.46.

20 Bryant, *The Bystander*, pp.194–8.

21 J. Hart, 'Kennedy, Congress and Civil Rights', *Journal of American Studies*, 1979, vol.13.

22 Bryant, *The Bystander*, pp.222–6.

23 Borstelmann, 'Hedging Our Bets', p.447.

24 J. D. Skrentny, 'The Effect of the Cold War on African-American Civil Rights: America and the World Audience, 1945–68', *Theory and Society*, 1998, vol.27, p.262.

25 Borstelmann, 'Hedging Our Bets', p.442; K. O'Reilly, 'The FBI and the Civil Rights Movement during the Kennedy Years: From the Freedom Rides to Albany', *Journal of Southern History*, 1988, vol.54, p.205.

26 Stern, *Calculating Visions*, p.62.

27 Bryant, *The Bystander*, p.469.

28 Borstelmann, 'Hedging Our Bets', pp.456–9.

29 Bryant, *The Bystander*, p.328; A. Fairclough, *To Redeem the Soul of America: The Southern Christian Leadership Conference and Martin Luther King*, Athens: University of Georgia Press, 2001, p.134; M. J. Klarman, 'How Brown Changed Race Relations: The Backlash Thesis', *Journal of American History*, 1994, vol.81, pp.111–12.

30 Stern, *Calculating Visions*, p.88.

31 Bryant, *The Bystander*, p.463.

32 R. Dallek, *Flawed Giant: Lyndon Johnson and His Times 1961–1973*, Oxford: Oxford University Press, 1998, pp.30–31.

33 S. F. Lawson, 'I Got it from the *New York Times*: Lyndon Johnson and the Kennedy Civil Rights Program', *Journal of Negro History*, 1982, vol.67, p.162.

34 Williams, 'Huey, Lyndon, and Southern Radicalism', p.286.

35 Stern, *Calculating Visions*, pp.122–3.

36 Dallek, *Flawed Giant*, p.123.
37 J. B. Frantz, 'Opening a Curtain: The Metamorphosis of Lyndon B. Johnson', *Journal of Southern History*, 1979, vol.45, p.25.
38 M. Billington, 'Lyndon B. Johnson and Blacks: The Early Years', *Journal of Negro History*, 1977, vol.62, pp.17–30.
39 Williams, 'Huey, Lyndon, and Southern Radicalism', p.285.
40 Dallek, *Flawed Giant*, p.219.
41 T. Branch, *Parting the Waters: America in the King Years, 1954–63*, New York: Simon & Schuster, 1988, p.922.
42 Dallek, *Flawed Giant*, p.213.
43 D. Kotlowski, 'With All Deliberate Delay: Kennedy, Johnson, and School Desegregation', *Journal of Policy History*, 2005, vol.17.
44 B. Miroff, 'Presidential Leverage over Social Movements: The Johnson White House and Civil Rights', *Journal of Politics*, 1981, vol.43, pp.12–16.
45 Bryant, *The Bystander*, p.465.
46 Heath, *Decade of Disillusionment*, p.238.
47 R. B. Woods, 'The Politics of Idealism: Lyndon Johnson, Civil Rights and Vietnam', *Diplomatic History*, 2007, vol.31, pp.12–15.
48 Dallek, *Flawed Giant*, p.413.
49 'The Troubled America: A Special Report on the White Majority', *Newsweek*, 6 October 1969, p.23.

18 Martin, Malcolm and black America

1 J. H. Cone, *Martin and Malcolm and America: A Dream or a Nightmare*, New York: Orbis Books, 2002, p.246.
2 M. L. King, Jnr, *The Autobiography of Martin Luther King, Jr*, New York: Abacus, 2004, pp.5–8.
3 Malcolm X with A. Haley, *The Autobiography of Malcolm X*, London: Penguin, 2001, pp.79–89, 100–102.
4 M. L. King, Jnr, 'Pilgrimage to Non-violence', in J. M. Washington (ed.) *A Testament of Hope*, New York: HarperCollins, 1991, pp.35–7.
5 Malcolm X, *The Autobiography of Malcolm X*, pp.105–7, 117–20.
6 Ibid., pp.137–43; J. White, *Black Leadership in America from Booker T. Washington to Jesse Jackson*, London: Longman, 1990, p.151.
7 Malcolm X, *The Autobiography*, pp.245–9. The Nation of Islam believed that the white men were the devil whose persecution of the black race would eventually be ended. The Nation affirmed black culture and heritage and advocated greater self-knowledge for black people in America.
8 Cone, *Martin and Malcolm and America*, p.53.
9 K. D. Miller, *Voice of Deliverance: The Language of Martin Luther King, Jr. and its Sources*, Athens: University of Georgia Press, 1998, pp.56–66.
10 M. E. Dyson, *Making Malcolm: The Myth and Meaning of Malcolm X*, New York: Oxford University Press, 1995, p.135.
11 Cone, *Martin and Malcolm and America*, pp.91–4.
12 White, *Black Leadership in America*, p.153.
13 Cone, *Martin and Malcolm and America*, p.99.
14 D. J. Garrow, *Bearing the Cross*, New York: Perennial Classics, 2004, pp.275–6.
15 M. L. King, Jnr, 'The American Dream', in Washington, *A Testament of Hope*, p.208.

16 Malcolm X, 'The Ballot or the Bullet', in G. Breitman (ed.) *Malcolm X Speaks*, New York: Grove Press, 1990, p.26.
17 M. L. King, Jnr, 'Love, Law, and Civil Disobedience', in Washington, *A Testament of Hope*, p.47.
18 Malcolm X, 'After the Bombing', in Breitman, *Malcolm X Speaks*, p.177.
19 M. L. King, Jnr, 'Remaining Awake through a Great Revolution', in Washington, *A Testament of Hope*, p.277.
20 Malcolm X, 'The Black Revolution', in Breitman, *Malcolm X Speaks*, p.50.
21 Dyson, *Making Malcolm*, p.9.
22 Malcolm X, 'The Harlem "Hate Gang" Scare', in Breitman, *Malcolm X Speaks*, p.70.
23 Cone, *Martin and Malcolm and America*, pp.186–7.
24 Malcolm X, 'After the Bombing', in Breitman, *Malcolm X Speaks*, p.163.
25 Cone, *Martin and Malcolm and America*, p.193.
26 Malcolm X, 'To Mississippi Youth', in Breitman, *Malcolm X Speaks*, p.144.
27 Malcolm X, 'Last Answers and Interviews', in Breitman, *Malcolm X Speaks*, p.197.
28 Cone, *Martin and Malcolm and America*, p.200.
29 Garrow, *Bearing the Cross*, p.393.
30 M. L. King, Jnr, 'Where Do We Go From Here?' in Washington, *A Testament of Hope*, p.250.
31 M. L. King, Jnr, 'Remaining Awake Through A Great Revolution', in Washington, *A Testament of Hope*, p.274.
32 M. L. King, Jnr, 'A Testament of Hope', in Washington (ed.) *A Testament of Hope*, p.324.
33 T. C. Shaw, 'Two Warring Ideals: Double Consciousness, Dialogue, and African-American Patriotism Post-9/11', in J. Battle, M. Bennett and A. J. Lemelle (eds) *Free At Last? Black America in the Twenty-First Century*, New Brunswick: Transaction Publishers, 2006, p.33.
34 L. V. Baldwin, 'To Witness in Dixie: King, the New South, and Southern Civil Religion', in L. V. Baldwin (ed.) *The Legacy of Martin Luther King, Jr*, Notre Dame: University of Notre Dame Press, 2002, p.37.
35 Dyson, *Making Malcolm*, p.160.
36 D. M. Bostdorff and S. R. Goldzwig, 'History, Collective Memory, and the Appropriation of Martin Luther King, Jr: Reagan's Rhetorical Legacy', *Presidential Studies Quarterly*, vol.35, 2005, p.682.
37 M. L. Ondaatje, 'Counterfeit Heroes or Colour-Blind Visionaries? The Black Conservative Challenge to Affirmative Action in Modern America', *Australasian Journal of American Studies*, 2004, vol.23, pp.41–3.
38 V. G. Harding, 'Beyond Amnesia: Martin Luther King, Jr, and the Future of America', *Journal of American History*, 1987, vol.74, p.476.
39 D. P. Aldridge, 'The Limits of Master Narratives in History Textbooks: An Analysis of Representations of Martin Luther King, Jr', *Teachers College Record*, 2006, vol.108, pp.673–5.
40 Dyson, *Making Malcolm*, pp.87–96.
41 P. Attewell, D. Lavin, T. Domina and T. Levey, 'The Black Middle Class: Progress, Prospects and Puzzles', in Battle *et al.*, *Free At Last?* pp. 1–2.
42 M. B. Katz, M. J. Stern and J. J. Fader, 'The New African-American Inequality', *Journal of American History*, June 2005, pp.88–9.
43 Attewell *et al.*, 'The Black Middle Class', pp.13–14.
44 Katz *et al.*, 'The New African-American Inequality', pp.81–3.

45 J. James, 'The Mesh: Democracy and Captivity', in Battle *et al.*, *Free At Last?* p.17.

46 S. Cashin, 'Katrina: The American Dilemma Redux', in D. D. Troutt (ed.) *After the Storm*, New York: The New Press, 2006, pp.32–3.

47 F. C. Harris, V. Sinclair-Chapman and B. D. McKenzie, 'Macrodynamics of Black Political Participation in the Post Civil Rights Era', *Journal of Politics*, 2005, vol.67, pp.1156–8.

48 Katz *et al.*, 'The New African-American Inequality', p.107.

49 King, Jnr, 'A Testament of Hope', p.324.

50 Katz *et al.*, 'The New African-American Inequality', p.108.

51 Cone, *Martin and Malcolm and America*, p.297.

19 American national mission and global conflict in the twentieth century

1 R. J. Barnet, *The Rockets' Red Glare: When America Goes to War: The Presidents and the People*, New York: Simon & Schuster, 1990, p.346.

2 W. W. Cobb, Jnr, *The American Foundation Myth in Vietnam: Reigning Paradigms and Raining Bombs*, Maryland: University Press of America, 1998, p.4.

3 L. Baritz, *Backfire: A History of How American Culture Led Us into Vietnam and Made Us Fight the Way We Did*, New York: William Morrow and Company, 1985, p.30.

4 R. S. Whitcomb, *The American Approach to Foreign Affairs: An Uncertain Tradition*, Connecticut: Greenwood, 1998, p.89.

5 M. H. Hunt, 'Ideology', in M. J. Hogan and T. G. Paterson (eds) *Explaining the History of American Foreign Relations*, Cambridge: Cambridge University Press, 1996, p.200.

6 T. Smith, 'Making the World Safe for Democracy', *Diplomatic History*, 1999, vol.23, p.175.

7 Hunt, 'Ideology', pp.198–201.

8 N. Tarcov, 'Principle and Prudence in Foreign Policy: The Founder's Perspective', *Public Interest*, 1984, vol.76, p.48.

9 H. W. Brands, 'The Idea of the National Interest', *Diplomatic History*, 1999, vol.23, pp.239–40.

10 M. P. Leffler, 'National Security', in Hogan and Paterson, *Explaining the History of American Foreign Relations*, pp.202–3.

11 M. Dunne, 'US Foreign Relations in the Twentieth Century: From World Power to Global Hegemony', *International Affairs*, 2000, vol.76, p.26.

12 Smith, 'Making the World Safe for Democracy', p.178.

13 M. Small, *Democracy and Diplomacy: The Impact of Domestic Politics on U.S. Foreign Policy, 1789–1994*, Baltimore: Johns Hopkins University Press, 1996, pp.42–3.

14 M. H. Hunt, *Crises in U.S. Foreign Policy*, New Haven: Yale University Press, 1996, pp.8–9.

15 Barnet, *The Rockets' Red Glare*, pp.148–54.

16 Brands, 'The Idea of the National Interest', p.242.

17 L. E. Ambrosius, 'Woodrow Wilson, Alliances, and the League of Nations', *Journal of the Gilded Age and Progressive Era*, 2006, vol.5, pp.5–9.

18 Smith, 'Making the World Safe for Democracy', p.174.

19 Ambrosius, 'Woodrow Wilson, Alliances, and the League of Nations', p.18.

20 Hunt, *Crises in U.S. Foreign Policy*, pp.22–4.

21 Small, *Democracy and Diplomacy*, p.50.

22 Ambrosius, 'Woodrow Wilson, Alliances, and the League of Nations', pp.17–21.
23 Ibid., p.44.
24 Brands, 'The Idea of the National Interest', p.243.
25 Whitcomb, *The American Approach to Foreign Affairs*, p.99.
26 Dunne, 'US Foreign Relations in the Twentieth Century', p.34; Barnet, *The Rockets' Red Glare*, p.198.
27 Brands, 'The Idea of the National Interest', p.245.
28 R. W. Steele, 'The Great Debate: Roosevelt, the Media, and the Coming of the War, 1940–41', *Journal of American History*, 1984, vol.71.
29 Small, *Democracy and Diplomacy*, p.72.
30 Whitcomb, *The American Approach to Foreign Affairs*, p.88.
31 Hunt, *Crises in U.S. Foreign Policy*, pp.67–71.
32 R. B. Woods, 'The Politics of Idealism: Lyndon Johnson, Civil Rights, and Vietnam', *Diplomatic History*, 2007, vol.31, p.10.
33 Brands, 'The Idea of the National Interest', p.256.
34 Baritz, *Backfire*, p.42.
35 Cobb, Jnr, *The American Foundation Myth in Vietnam*, p.65.
36 L. Gardner, 'The End of Exceptionalism?' in D. Michael Shafer (ed.) *The Legacy: The Vietnam War in the American Imagination*, Boston: Beacon Press, 1990, p.28.
37 D. Bell, 'The End of American Exceptionalism', *Public Interest*, 1975, vol.41, p.204.
38 M. S. McMahon, 'The American State and the Vietnam War', in D. Farber (ed.) *The Sixties: From Memory to History*, Chapel Hill: University of North Carolina Press, 1994, p.46.
39 Cobb, Jnr, *The American Foundation Myth in Vietnam*, pp.92–9.
40 See D. C. Hallin, *The Uncensored War: The Media and Vietnam*, New York: Oxford University Press, 1986; C. J. Pach Jnr, 'And That's the Way it Was: The Vietnam War on the Network Nightly News', in Farber, *The Sixties*.
41 B. R. Barber, 'The Importance of Remembrance: The Vietnam Legacy's Challenge to American Democracy', in M. Shafer, *The Legacy: The Vietnam War in the American Imagination*, Boston: Beacon Press, 1990, p.3.
42 Cobb, Jnr, *The American Foundation Myth in Vietnam*, p.165.

20 American identity and the 'war on terror'

1 E. T. May, 'Echoes of the Cold War: The Aftermath of September 11th at Home', in M. L. Dudziak (ed.) *September 11 in History: A Watershed Moment?*, London: Duke University Press, 2003, pp.36–8.
2 R. G. Patman, 'Globalisation, the New U.S. Exceptionalism and the War on Terror', *Third World Quarterly*, 2006, vol.27, p.975.
3 M. H. Hunt, 'In the Wake of September 11th: The Clash of What?', *Journal of American History*, 2002, vol.89, pp.416–18.
4 J. L. Gaddis, 'And Now This: Lessons From the Old Era For the New One', in S. Talbott and N. Chanda (eds) *The Age of Terror: America and the World After September 11*, New York: Basic Books, 2001, p.4.
5 P. Kennedy, 'Maintaining American Power: From Injury to Recovery', in Talbott and Chanda, *The Age of Terror*, p.60.
6 M. McAlister, 'A Cultural History of the War without End', *Journal of American History*, 2002, vol.89, p.439.
7 Hunt, 'In the Wake of September 11th', pp.418–20.

8 Gaddis, 'And Now This', p.17.
9 A. Applebaum, 'The New New World Order', in W. Pleszczynski (ed.) *Our Brave New World: Essays on the Impact of September 11*, Stanford: Hoover Institution Press, 2002, pp.2–4.
10 Gaddis, 'And Now This', p.15.
11 T. A. Keaney, 'War and Terror: U.S. Perspectives and Policies', in M. Geyer (ed.) *War and Terror in Historical and Contemporary Perspective*, Washington DC: AICGS, 2003, vol.14, p.120.
12 Keaney, 'War and Terror', p.112.
13 R. G. Patman, 'Globalisation, the New U.S. Exceptionalism and the War on Terror', *Third World Quarterly*, 2006, vol.27, p.979.
14 May, 'Echoes of the Cold War', p.45.
15 D. H. Noon, 'Operation Enduring Analogy: World War Two, the War on Terror, and the Uses of Historical Memory', *Rhetoric and Public Affairs*, 2004, vol.7, pp.351–3.
16 M. B. Young, 'Ground Zero: Enduring War', in Dudziak, *September 11 in History*, p.11.
17 McAlister, 'A Cultural History of the War without End', pp.446–55.
18 N. Aruri, 'America's War Against Iraq: 1990–2002', in A. Arnove (ed.) *Iraq Under Siege: The Deadly Impact of Sanctions and War*, London: Pluto Press, 2003, pp.42–4.
19 S. N. Kalyvas and M. A. Kocher, 'Ethnic Cleavages and Irregular War: Iraq and Vietnam', *Politics & Society*, 2007, vol.34, pp.185–90.
20 C. O'Leary and T. Platt, 'Pledging Allegiance: The Revival of Prescriptive Patriotism', in P. Scraton (ed.) *Beyond September 11th*, London: Pluto Press, 2002, pp.173–5.
21 May, 'Echoes of the Cold War', p.48.
22 H. H. Koh, 'Preserving American Values: The Challenge at Home and Abroad', in Dudziak, *September 11 in History*, p.168.
23 D. Kellner, 'Bushspeak and the Politics of Lying: Presidential Rhetoric in the War on Terror', *Presidential Studies Quarterly*, 2007, vol.37, pp.626–7.
24 A. Kaplan, 'Homeland Insecurities: Transformations of Language and Space', in Dudziak, *September 11 in History*, pp.60–61.
25 Young, 'Ground Zero', p.13.
26 C. D. Ram and D. R. Kinder, 'Terror and Ethnocentrism: Foundations of American Support for the War on Terrorism', *Journal of Politics*, 2007, vol.69, p.328.
27 L. Volpp, 'The Citizen and the Terrorist', in Dudziak, *September 11 in History*, pp.155–6.
28 E. Foner, 'The Most Patriotic Act', *The Nation*, 8 October 2001.
29 May, 'Echoes of the Cold War', pp.47–9; Koh, 'Preserving American Values', p.164.
30 C. Bradley, D. Cole, W. Dellinger, R. Dworkin, R. Epstein, P. B. Heymann *et al.*, 'On NSA spying: A Letter to Congress', *New York Review of Books*, 9 February 2006, vol.2.
31 'Gore says Bush Wiretapping could be Impeachable Offence', *ABC News*, 16 January 2006.
32 Kaplan, 'Homeland Insecurities', p.67.
33 K. Dalacoura, 'U.S. Democracy Promotion in the Arab Middle East since September 11 2001: A Critique', *International Affairs*, 2005, vol.81, pp.969–72.

SELECT BIBLIOGRAPHY

The detailed references in each chapter should be used by readers who want to study particular issues in more depth, especially those to specific journal articles or essays within edited collections. The following provides a brief bibliography of the major single-volume works on each of the key periods addressed in the book.

Nation in embryo

Any study of the colonial era should start with D. J. Boorstin's *The Americans: The Colonial Experience*, which provides an excellent overview of the history of the different regions in the American colonies. R. Hofstadter's *America at 1750: A Social Portrait* gives an excellent insight into the social, economic and political shape of the colonies in the period immediately before the movement towards independence. J. P. Greene and J. R. Pole (eds), *Colonial British America: Essays in the New History of the Early Modern Era*, and D. Vickers (ed.), *A Companion to Colonial America*, both provide an excellent collection of essays on the development of the colonies. J. Butler's *Becoming America: The Revolution before 1776* explains how the colonies underwent significant changes before the Declaration of Independence.

Reasons for revolt;
The Constitution

On the American Revolution, J. P. Greene and J. R. Pole (eds), *A Companion to the American Revolution*, is an excellent summary of the most significant scholarship. Any understanding of the origins of the movement towards independence would not be complete without reading B. Bailyn, *The Ideological Origins of the American Revolution*, and G. S. Wood, *The Creation of the American Republic, 1776–1787*. E. S.

Morgan's *The Birth of the Republic, 1763–1789* is a very readable summary of the major events and issue of the American Revolution. Wood's work is also crucial to an understanding of the creation of the Constitution. R. Beeman *et al.* (eds), *Beyond Confederation: Origins of the Constitution and American National Identity*, provides an excellent collection of essays on this subject. J. N. Rakove, *Original Meanings: Politics and Ideas in the Making of the Constitution*, offers an interpretation of the Constitution's meaning which follows on from the work of Wood. M. M. Edling, *A Revolution in Favor of Government: Origins of the U.S. Constitution and the Making of the American State*, moves the debate over the origins of the Constitution into the orbit of nation-state formation.

Flawed heroes

Morgan gives us an invaluable work on the place of slavery in eighteenth-century America in *American Slavery, American Freedom*. P. Finkelman's *Slavery and the Founders: Race and Liberty in the Age of Jefferson* examines the relationship between slavery and the founding generation of American leaders. J. J. Ellis, *His Excellency: George Washington*, H. Wiencek, *An Imperfect God: George Washington, His Slaves and the Creation of America*, and J. J. Ellis, *American Sphinx: The Character of Thomas Jefferson*, are among the best biographies of the most revered of the founders.

Ignoring Washington's warning;
Slavery and the causes of the American Civil War

The essays on the antebellum period in this volume are largely focussed on the coming of the Civil War and the crisis of nationality in America in the nineteenth century. The number of scholarly works on these subjects is manifold. G. S. Boritt (ed.), *Why the Civil War Came*, and K. M. Stampp (ed.), *The Causes of the Civil War*, provide excellent starting points for a study of civil war causation. K. M. Stampp, *The Imperilled Union*, and B. Holden-Reid, *The Origins of the American Civil War*, are very good book-length examinations of the subject. M. F. Holt, *The Political Crisis of the 1850s*, E. Foner, *Politics and Ideology of the Age of the Civil War*, and S. Wilentz, *The Rise of American Democracy: Jefferson to Lincoln*, are invaluable guides to the nature of antebellum politics and explain, from differing standpoints, the role of political parties in the increasing sectionalism of antebellum America.

Southern and Confederate nationalism

The crisis of nationality faced by the American polity in the mid-nineteenth century is explored in S.-M. Grant's *North over South: Northern Nationalism and American Identity in the Antebellum Era* and D. M. Potter's *The South and the Sectional Conflict*. C. Eaton, *The Growth of Southern Civilisation, 1790–1860*, and J. McCardell, *The Idea of a Southern Nation: Southern Nationalists and Southern Nationalism, 1830–1860*, explore the extent to which the South can be viewed as a separate nation before the Civil War. On the development of the Confederate nation, D. G. Faust, *The Creation of Confederate Nationalism: Ideology and Identity in the Civil War South*, G. W. Gallagher, *The Confederate War: How Popular Will, Nationalism, and Military Strategy Could Not Stave Off Defeat*, and A. S. Rubin, *A Shattered Nation: The Rise and Fall of the Confederacy, 1861–1868*, are crucial.

Lincoln and liberty

Among the many works on Lincoln's execution of the Civil War and his role in the changing nature of liberty in America, J. M. McPherson, *Abraham Lincoln and the Second American Revolution*, G. S. Boritt (ed.), *Lincoln the War President*, M. E. Neely, Jnr, *The Fate of Liberty: Abraham Lincoln and Civil Liberties*, R. J. Carwardine, *Lincoln*, D. L. Wilson, *Lincoln's Sword*, and G. Wills, *Lincoln at Gettysburg: The Words that Remade America*, are excellent. For a concise collection of Lincoln's own words, see P. J. Parish (ed.), *Abraham Lincoln: Speeches and Letters*.

Reconstruction

Lincoln's decision to free the slaves and to support the Thirteenth Amendment provided the context for the experience of African-Americans during Reconstruction. The best starting point for any exploration of this period is E. Foner's *Reconstruction: America's Unfinished Revolution*. K. M. Stampp and L. F. Litwack (eds), *Reconstruction: An Anthology of Revisionist Writings*, provides, as the title suggest, a revisionist interpretation of Reconstruction. The constitutional impact of the period is examined in H. M. Hyman, *A More Perfect Union: The Impact of the Civil War and Reconstruction on the Constitution*, whilst the experiences of the freedmen are superbly probed in L. F. Litwack, *Been in the Storm So Long: The Aftermath of Slavery*. H. Cox Richardson, *The Death of Reconstruction*, is an excellent explanation of why the move to reconstruct the South eventually collapsed.

Civil War memory and American national identity

The failure of the nation to embrace an emancipationist legacy of the Civil War meant that the conflict played a contested role in American national identity. The seminal work on this subject is D. W. Blight's *Race and Reunion: The Civil War in American Memory*. A. Fahs and J. Waugh (eds), *The Memory of the Civil War in American Culture*, J. R. Neff, *Honouring the Civil War Dead: Commemoration and the Problem of Reconciliation*, and W. A. Blair, *Cities of the Dead: Contesting the Memory of the Civil War in the South, 1865–1914*, are valuable explorations of the place of Civil War memory in national identity. C. E. O'Leary's *To Die For: The Paradox of American Patriotism*, explains how the symbols of patriotism Americans now take for granted were disputed in the post-bellum period.

Introducing Jim Crow

The contests over the memory of the Civil War were heavily influenced by the issue of race. During and after Reconstruction African-Americans in the South faced a situation in which their citizenship was increasingly restricted. The story of the emergence of segregation in the South is told in C. Vann Woodward's *The Strange Career of Jim Crow*, still the seminal work on the issue. J. Williamson, *After Slavery: The Negro in South Carolina during Reconstruction, 1861–1877*, and R. A. Fischer, *The Segregation Struggle in Louisiana 1862–1877*, provide excellent studies of specific states. The major criticism of the Woodward thesis – a fact acknowledged by Woodward himself – is H. N. Rabinowitz's *Race Relations in the Urban South: 1865–1890*. G. E. Hale, *Making Whiteness: The Culture of Segregation in the South, 1890–1940*, is a meticulous explanation of the ways in which racial segregation was consciously constructed and J. C. Cobb, *The Brown Decision, Jim Crow and Southern Identity*, shows how segregation was viewed as a force for modernisation in the post-bellum South.

Prejudice and paternalism

As the colour line was being drawn in that region the nation's policy makers were passing legislation that had a significant impact on the place of Native Americans in the national community. F.P. Prucha, *The Great Father: The United States Government and the American Indians*, is a detailed study of government policy towards the Indians. F. E.

236

Hoxie, *The Campaign to Assimilate the Indians, 1880–1920,* explains how those policies were an attempt to force the Indian into the melting pot. T. Holm, *The Great Confusion in Indian Affairs: Native Americans and Whites in the Progressive Era*, outlines the ways in which this effort was increasingly influenced more by racism than paternalism. F. E. Hoxie, *Talking Back to Civilization: Indian Voices From the Progressive Era*, and K. T. Lomawaima and T. L. McCarty (eds), *To Remain an Indian: Lessons in Democracy From a Century of Native American Education*, show that Indians were not passive victims of US government policy.

American identity and the American West

The movement of Indians onto reservations was a crucial part of the story of the closing of the American frontier and the conquering of the West. F. J. Turner, 'The Significance of the Frontier in American History', *Annual Report of the American Historical Association*, 1893, outlines Turner's 'frontier thesis' which is the starting point for any historical investigation of the West. R. A. Billington, *Westward Expansion*, is heavily influenced by the thesis and sees the movement of the frontier as part of the different stages of societal development. P. N. Limerick, *The Legacy of Conquest: The Unbroken Past of the American West*, and D. Worster, *Under Western Skies* are crucial elucidations of the New Western History. W. Cronon, G. Miles and J. Gatlin (eds), *Under an Open Sky: Rethinking America's Western Past*, provides an excellent anthology of writings from the perspective of that very broad historical school. W. Deverell (ed.), *A Companion to the American West*, is a comprehensive collection of fresh ideas on the study of the West.

Immigration and assimilation

Turner believed that the experience of the frontier was crucial in the making of Americans. How new arrivals to the United States have been absorbed by American society is the subject of Chapter 14. M. D'Innocento and J. P. Sirefman (eds), *Immigration and Ethnicity, American Society: 'Melting Pot' or 'Salad Bowl'?*, V. N. Parrillo, *Diversity in America*, and R. Daniels, *Coming to America: A History of Immigration and Ethnicity in American Life*, provide excellent overviews of the main issues in the study of immigration and assimilation. D. G. Guitiérrez, *Walls and Mirrors: Mexican Americans, Mexican Immigrants, and the Politics of Ethnicity*, is an excellent study of Hispanic immigrants. M. M.

Gordon, *Assimilation in American Life*, and N. Glazer and D. P. Moynihan, *Beyond the Melting Pot: The Negroes, Puerto Ricans, Jews, Italians, and Irish of New York City*, are classic studies of assimilation in American society. The references in the chapter point out several journal articles which examine the 'melting pot' concept in light of developments in the late twentieth century.

Gender, race and the vote

Chapter 15 focuses on the connection between race and the campaign for female suffrage from Reconstruction through the First World War. S. M. Evans, *Born for Liberty: A History of Women in America*, and N. A. Hewitt and S. Lebsock (eds), *Visible Women: New Essays on American Activism*, are excellent works on female political activism. L. K. Kerber and J. Sherron De Hart (eds), *Women's America: Refocusing the Past*, provides an excellent overview of women's history in the United States. A. D. Gordon (ed.), *African-American Women and the Vote, 1837–1965*, V. L. Ruiz and E. C. Dubois (eds), *Unequal Sisters: A Multicultural Reader*, and N. Frankel and N. S. Dye (eds), *Gender, Class, Race, and Reform in the Progressive Era*, provide a number of essays that focus on the interconnection between race and gender in women's history.

Origins of the civil rights movement

Chapters 16 through 18 focus on different aspects of the African-American freedom struggle in the twentieth century. The literature on this topic is considerable indeed. For good overviews of the period see A. Fairclough, *Better Day Coming: Blacks and Equality, 1890–2000*, M. Marable, *Race, Reform and Rebellion: The Second American Reconstruction in Black America*, and J. White, *Black Leadership in America: From Booker T. Washington to Jesse Jackson*. On the genesis of the civil rights movement of the 1950s and 1960s, B. Ward and A. J. Badger (eds), *The Making of Martin Luther King and the Civil Rights Movement*, provides an excellent collection of essays. H. Sitkoff, *A New Deal for Blacks: The Emergence of Civil Rights as a National Issue*, shows how the civil rights agenda was given greater attention from the 1930s. Black working-class resistance, black culture and consciousness are explored in R. D. Kelley, *Race Rebels: Culture, Politics, and the Black Working Class*, and L. Levine, *Black Culture and Black Consciousness: Afro-American Folk Thought from Slavery to Freedom*.

Kennedy, Johnson and civil rights

The civil rights policies of the Kennedy and Johnson administrations are explored in J. F. Heath, *Decade of Disillusionment: The Kennedy and Johnson Years*, and M. Stern, *Calculating Visions: Kennedy, Johnson and Civil Rights*. Detailed studies of each president are provided by Robert Dallek, *Flawed Giant: Lyndon Johnson and His Times, 1961–1973*, and *John F. Kennedy: An Unfinished Life*. For an excellent study of Kennedy's approach to civil rights issues see N. Bryant, *The Bystander: John F. Kennedy and the Struggle for Black Equality*.

Martin, Malcolm and black America

The two most influential black leaders of the 1960s were Martin Luther King and Malcolm X. Both men wrote autobiographies which should be consulted as a starting point to study of their stories, M. L. King, Jnr, *The Autobiography of Martin Luther King, Jr*, and Malcolm X with A. Haley, *The Autobiography of Malcolm X*. D. J. Garrow, *Bearing the Cross*, and T. Branch, *Parting the Waters: America in the King Years, 1954–63*, are excellent single-volume biographies of King. M. E. Dyson, *Making Malcolm: The Myth and Meaning of Malcolm X*, probes the meanings and legacy of Malcolm X, whilst J. H. Cone, *Martin and Malcolm and America: A Dream or a Nightmare*, provides the best direct work of comparison of the two men. J. Battle, M. Bennett and A. Lemelle (eds), *Free At Last? Black America in the Twenty-First Century*, M. B. Katz, M. J. Stern and J. J. Fader, 'The New African-American Inequality', *Journal of American History*, June 2005, and J. L. Hochschild, *Race, Class, and the Soul of the Nation: Facing Up to the American Dream*, all explore the continued racial inequality in the years after Martin and Malcolm.

American national mission and global conflict in the twentieth century; American identity and the 'war on terror'

The final two chapters of the book focus on American foreign policy. R. J. Barnett, *The Rockets' Red Glare: When America Goes to War: The Presidents and the People*, provides a detailed explanation of the role of the President in America's decision to go to war and the shaping of public opinion. This is complemented by M. Small, *Democracy and Diplomacy: The Impact of Domestic Politics on U.S. Foreign Policy*, a concise study of the impact of foreign policy on the home front. R. S.

Whitcomb, *The American Approach to Foreign Affairs: An Uncertain Tradition*, M. J. Hogan and T. G. Paterson (eds), *Explaining the History of American Foreign Relations*, and M. H. Hunt, *Crises in U.S. Foreign Policy*, are very good introductions to the major issues associated with American foreign relations. On the U.S. war on terror since 9/11, M. L. Dudziak (ed.), *September 11 in History: A Watershed Moment?*, S. Talbott and N. Chanda (eds), *The Age of Terror: America and the World After September 11*, and W. Pleszczynski (ed.), *Our Brave New World: Essays on the Impact of September 11*, provide essay collections which open up the major issues of study.

INDEX

Abbott, Lyman 113–14
ABM treaty 193
Adams, John Quincy 22, 48, 58, 132
Adams, Sam 18
African-American women *see* black
  women
African-Americans 3–5, 139; and
  affirmative action 176–77; and Black
  Codes 85, 86, 87, 90; civil rights
  legislation during Reconstruction
  86–87, 90, 91; and civil rights
  movement *see* civil rights movement;
  colonisation schemes 41, 42, 78;
  emancipationist memory of Civil
  War 95–96, 100, 101; inequality of
  178, 179; and New Deal 158; and
  poverty 178; and prison 178; racial
  segregation of in South *see* racial
  segregation; and Reconstruction *see*
  Reconstruction; rise of middle-class
  177–78; and underclass 178; view of
  by Jefferson 41; in the West 129–30;
  see also black protest; slavery
Al Qaeda 191, 195
Alabama 90
Alabama Populists 105
Alexander, Will 158
Alien Act 33
American Civil War 3; American
  national identity and memory of *see*
  Civil War memory; Confederate
  nationalism during 68–72; critique

of South by North 56–58, 64–65;
  deaths 94; emergence of northern
  nationalism 57, 66; historiography of
  causes of 54–55; revisionist causes of
  55; slavery as cause of 54–62; and
  weaknesses in political system 58–59;
  and women 97–98
American Historical Association 122
American War of Independence 2, 3,
  16–24, 26, 37–38, 70; and
  Declaration of Independence 1, 16,
  40, 55, 80; and economic self-
  interest 20; events leading up to
  17–19; and idealism 19–20; power
  struggle between colonies and
  mother country 21
American West *see* West
American Woman Suffrage Association
  (AWSA) 144
'Americaness' 1
Anderson, Benedict 64
Anderson, Marian 156
Andrews, Sidney 85–86
Anthony, Susan B. 143
anti-federalists 30–31, 32–33, 34
Appleby, Joyce 21, 32
Arab-Americans 197
Arizona 129
Arkansas 90, 154
Arlington Cemetery 99
Articles of Confederation 25–26, 27,
  28, 41

Pearl Harbour attack 186, 194
Pennsylvania 8, 9, 12, 19
Peterson, Merrill 39
Philadelphia 8
Philadelphia Convention (1787) 25, 28–29, 39, 55
Pickering, Timothy 41, 43
Pinckney, George 29
Plains Wars 128
Pleasants, Robert 38
Plessy v. Ferguson (1896) 91, 110
political parties 3, 44–53, 59, 77; ambivalence towards 47; demise of second-party system and reasons 51–53; fear of promoting disunity by 44–45; and ideals of republicanism 45; reasons for formation of second party system 48–49; shared symbolism and ideological inspirations 46–47; view of by Washington 44
Ponca Affair 114–15
populism 104–5, 107
Populist Party 105, 108
Potter, David 66
poverty: and blacks 178; in New England 8
Pratt, Henry 117
presidential elections: as major stimulus to emergence of second party system 48
Pressly, Thomas 84
Preston, John S. 66
Progressive era 118, 133, 142, 143, 146
Prucha, Francis Paul 117, 120
Puerto Ricans 133, 139
Puritans 7, 8, 9

Quakers 9, 38
Quota Act (1921) 135

Rabinowitz, Howard 107
race 2, 24; role of in memory of Civil War 94–95, 96, 97, 98, 102
racial discrimination: in South during Reconstruction 89–90, 91–92
'racial nationalism' 1–2
racial profiling 197
racial segregation (South) 4, 103–11; blacks seen as threat to white

womanhood 108–9; exclusion of blacks from public accommodations 106; factors ensuring legal codification of Jim Crow 107–11; and *Plessy v. Ferguson* 91, 110; Woodward thesis and criticism of 104–7
Randall, James 54–55
Randolph, A. Phillip 156
Rauschenbusch, Walter 171
Readjusters 104, 105, 109
Reagan, Ronald 125, 176, 194
Reconstruction 3–4, 83–92, 152; black political activity 88; black religion 88–89; black schooling 89; black suffrage issue 90; and citizenship 86, 87; civil rights legislation 86–87, 90, 91; and civil rights movement 152; defining of liberty 86; 'Dunning school' of 84; political activism of black women during 144, 147; race relations 104; racial discrimination in South 89–90, 91–92; and revisionists 84, 87
religion: in colonies 9, 22; and early civil rights struggle 154–55; Reconstruction and black 88–89; and southern/Confederate nationalism 69–70
Republican Party 45, 46, 51, 53, 57, 59–60, 62, 66, 77, 87, 90–91
republicanism 44–45
revisionists: and American Civil War 55; and Reconstruction 84, 87
Rhett, Robert Barnwell 67, 68
Rhode Island 26, 30
Rice, Condoleezza 195
Rollin, Louisa 143
Roosevelt, Franklin D. 73, 156, 158, 185–86
Roosevelt, Theodore 134, 135
Rozbicki, Michal Jan 22
Rubin, Anne Sarah 69
Ruffin, Edmund 68
Russell, Richard 166

Schlesinger, Arthur M. 123
Sea Islands 79
second party system *see* political parties
Second World War 5, 157, 185–87, 194
Seddon, James 69

Vardaman, Governor James K. 109
Versailles, Treaty of 184
Vietnam war 5, 160, 168–69, 175,
  180, 187–88, 190, 195, 196
Virginia 9, 23, 27, 45; outlawing of
  slave trade (1778) 40; and slavery 10,
  13, 36, 40
Virginia Plan 28
vote *see* female suffrage
Voting Rights Act (1965) 152

Walker, Wyatt 173
Wallace, Governor George 176
'war on terror' 5, 190–99
Warren Court 82, 152
Washington, Booker T. 89, 153
Washington, George 19, 20, 27, 33,
  44, 132; farewell address 180; and
  slavery 35–39, 43, 55–56
Waters, Mary 138
Watson, Tom 105
Watts riots (Los Angeles) (1965) 168,
  175
West 4, 26, 122–31; African-
  Americans in 129–30; Asian-
  Americans in 130–31; as both
  process and place 126–27; and ethnic
  minorities 127, 128–31; frontier
  thesis 122–24, 125, 126, 127–28,
  131; and Indians 128–29; and
  Mexican culture 129; and New
  Western Historians 122, 124–25,
  126–27; racial prejudice in 130; as a
  region 126, 127; role of animals 124;
  stereotypes of 122; story of
  imperialism and conquest 124
Whigs 20, 48, 49, 50, 51, 52–53, 59
White, Richard 124
White, Walter 156
Wiencek, Henry 37
Wilentz, Sean 59
Willard, Frances 146

Williamsburg 37
Williamson, Joel 106
Willis, Charles 65
Wilmington Messenger 109
Wilmot Proviso 59
Wilson, Woodrow 101–2, 182–85,
  193–94
Wofford, Harris 161
Woman's Christian Temperance Union
  (WCTU) 146
women: anti-Chinese protests by 145;
  anti-suffrage campaign 147, 149; and
  Civil War memory 97–99; and
  Confederate nationalism 69; and
  domestication of politics 145, 147,
  150; and education 146; given vote
  in Nineteenth Amendment 145;
  involvement in voluntary associations
  and philanthropy 146–47; role in
  construction of public history of
  South 110–11; suffrage campaign 4,
  142–44, 148–49; and temperance
  movement 146; *see also* black women
Women's National Indian Association
  114
Women's Relief Corps (WRC) 98
Women's Trade Union League 149
Wood, Gordon 19, 20, 26, 31; *The
  Creation of the American Republic* 32
Woodward, C. Vann 92, 105; *The
  Strange Career of Jim Crow* 103–4,
  105–6
working class: political mobilisation of
  in colonies 8; women 148–49
Worster, Donald 124
Wythe, George 43

Yancey, William 68

Zangwill, Israel 134, 136
Zimmerman telegram 183
Zuckerman, Michael 6, 11